Masoud Kazemzadeh

The Iran National Front and the Struggle for Democracy

De Gruyter Contemporary Social Sciences

—

Volume 20

Masoud Kazemzadeh

The Iran National Front and the Struggle for Democracy

——

1949–Present

DE GRUYTER

ISBN 978-3-11-154065-8
e-ISBN (PDF) 978-3-11-078215-8
e-ISBN (EPUB) 978-3-11-078222-6
ISSN 2747-5689
e-ISSN 2747-5697

Library of Congress Control Number: 2022932021

Bibliographic information published by the Deutsche Nationalbibliothek
The Deutsche Nationalbibliothek lists this publication in the Deutsche
Nationalbibliografie; detailed bibliographic data are available on the internet at http://
dnb.dnb.de.

www.degruyter.com

I dedicate this book to all those who have struggled to establish freedom, democracy, human rights, and social justice in Iran.

Preface and Acknowledgments

This book deals with highly political and contentious subjects. This research contains segments that attempt to present factual descriptions of the activities of the Iran National Front (INF). This research also contains segments that engage in analysis of the policies of the INF and other political actors. The bulk of this book deals with description. In these segments, I have attempted, to the best of my abilities, to describe the activities and views of the INF objectively. These segments attempt to answer "what happened," "what the INF did," and "what the INF said." These segments have to be objective and factual. If there are any errors of fact, I would most appreciate if the readers and critics would point these out. Such corrections will add to our knowledge and would enhance our understanding of this major subject. If there are documents that my research has been ignorant of, I would be very happy to get access to them. Scholarship is a collective activity. By providing more documents, our knowledge will become more complete. Readers may send me such documents and corrections via my work e-mail. Updates and corrections will be made available through the website of the publisher: https://www.degruyter.com/document/isbn/9783110782 158/html.

This research also contains analytical segments. These segments attempt to answer "why the INF or other actors" did this or that action. There are only a few such segments in this book. All scholars may make errors of judgements or logical inconsistencies. Through criticism and debate, we can understand the shortcomings of our analyses. Consciously or unconsciously, scholars may cherry pick evidence to further a particular analysis. Through debate, we can learn and correct, or debunk such analyses.

Paradigmatic and theoretical frameworks also influence analyses. The primary goal of this book has been to provide an objective description; therefore, this work has avoided theoretical analysis. Those scholars who utilize particular paradigms or theories (e.g., feminism, Marxism) may ask questions or look for areas that my research has neglected. My book is not an all-encompassing work intended to answer all the questions pertaining to Iran. The primary contribution of this book is simply to provide a description of the activities of the INF. Other scholars who utilize various theoretical analyses enrich our understanding of Iranian politics and history.

A heartfelt thanks goes to Penny Watson, who read many drafts of this book and made many constructive suggestions and criticisms. This work owes a great debt to many members of the INF. I thank Kambiz Ghaemmagham and Dr. Homayoun Mehmaneche for their comments and suggestions on earlier drafts of

https://doi.org/10.1515/9783110782158-001

this book. I thank my friend Dr. Mohsen Ghaemmagham for the numerous discussions about the INF. I learned a great deal through e-mail exchanges with Dr. Hussein Moussavian and the late Abbas Amir-Entezam, as well as interviews with the late Khosrow Seif and Dr. Mehrdad Arfazadeh, and conversations with the late Dr. Saeed Fatemi, the late Hussein Razi, the late Abolqassem Lebaschi, and the late Hassan Lebaschi. I am solely responsible for any errors of fact or analysis.

The research for this book began when I was at Utah Valley University. I thank my former department chair and friend, Dr. Keith Snedegar, who provided class release so that I could conduct the basic research. I thank Dr. Jason Enia, my department chair, and Dr. Chien-pin Li, my Dean, for their support of a generous sabbatical leave, which allowed me to complete this book. I thank Faye Leerink, Michaela Göbels, and Gerhard Boomgaarden, my wonderful editors at De Gruyter, for their highly efficient work. It was a pleasure working with them on this project.

Contents

About the Author

Masoud Kazemzadeh is Associate Professor, Department of Political Science, Sam Houston State University, Huntsville, U.S.A. He received his B.A. in international relations from the University of Minnesota, U.S.A., and his M.A. and Ph.D. in political science from the University of Southern California, Los Angeles, U.S.A. He was a postdoctoral fellow at Harvard University's Center for Middle Eastern Studies. He is the author of *Iran's Foreign Policy: Elite Factionalism, Ideology, the Nuclear Weapons Program, and the United States* (London and New York: Routledge, 2020).

https://doi.org/10.1515/9783110782158-002

Chapter 1
Introduction

It is often said that Iran lacks strong (or even real) political parties.[1] Fakhreddin Azimi's seminal article on this subject reviews various political parties in Iran since 1906 and argues that with the exception of the Tudeh Party, Iran has not had a "real" political party.[2] Azimi further argues that the Tudeh Party became a real party due to the massive assistance provided to it by the Soviet Union.[3] Although briefly discussing the Iran National Front in three pages, Azimi believes that the Iran National Front disintegrated in August 1953.[4] In a pioneering study, Shahrough Akhavi discusses virtually all political parties in Iran since about 1900.[5] Akhavi devotes about one paragraph to the Iran National Front as well as a few pages to some other parties constituting the Iran National Front.[6]

Definition and Study of Political Parties

What is a political party? What distinguishes a "political party" from a "real political party"? Does Iran possess real political parties? Can one consider the Iran National Front a real political party? What is the relationship between real parties and democracy?

If one person creates a website and announces the establishment of a political party and adds a few pages of the entity's aims, should scholars use the term "political party" to refer to that entity? If a politician creates an organization for his electoral campaign and calls it a political party, should scholars use the term "political party" to refer to that entity? If one person in power or a group

---

1 BBC Persian, "*Ahzab Irani*" [Iranian Political Parties], (February 7, 2012), https://www.you tube.com/watch?v=v6JYeBkvwos.

2 Fakhreddin Azimi, "On Shaky Ground: Concerning the Absence or Weakness of Political Parties in Iran," *Iranian Studies*, Vol. 30, Nos. 1–2 (1997), pp. 53–75.

3 Ibid., pp. 60–62.

4 Azimi, ibid., pp. 63–65.

5 Shahrough Akhavi, "Iran," in Frank Tachau, ed. *Political Parties of the Middle East and North Africa*. (Westport, Connecticut: Greenwood Press, 1994), pp. 133–173.

6 Ibid., p. 163. Akhavi also briefly discusses the Iran Party (pp. 156–157), the Nation Party (p. 164), Third Force (p. 171), and the Liberation Movement of Iran (pp. 161–162). I discuss these parties in great detail in Chapter 3.

https://doi.org/10.1515/9783110782158-003

in power establish an entity to mobilize support and call it a political party, should scholars use the term "political party" to refer to that entity?

Since 1900, Iran has had hundreds of entities that have called themselves political parties.[7] What Iran has experienced is a dearth of what may be called "real political parties." Azimi uses the term "real political parties" to distinguish such entities from the hundreds of other entities that call themselves political parties. Azimi argues that real political parties are absent in Iran. John Aldrich, one of the foremost scholars of political parties, uses terms such as "durable" and "effective" to more or less refer to what Azimi considers "real" political parties.[8] Akhavi has a much lower threshold on what constitutes a real political party than those by Azimi and Aldrich. Akhavi considers ephemeral entities that have called themselves party as a party.

What do real political parties do? According to Norberto Bobbio, political parties would "perform the function of selecting, aggregating and transmitting demands originating in civil society... [which would] become objects of political decisions."[9] Joseph LaPalombara and Myron Weiner argue that political parties emerged in Europe and North America when political elites realized that it was no longer feasible for a few individuals to control leadership selection and policy making.[10] LaPalmbara and Weiner suggest that real political parties should have four characteristics:

(1) "continuity in organization," or longevity, so that the party "is not dependent on the life span of current leaders" or regimes;

(2) "manifest and presumably permanent organization at the local level" and an institutional relationship between the local and national levels;

(3) a conscious drive on the part of the leadership to seek governmental power, either alone or in coalition and "not simply to influence the exercise of power"; and

(4) "a concern on the part of the organization for seeking followers at the polls or in some manner striving for popular support."[11]

---

7 Akhavi, "Iran," op. cit.

8 John H. Aldrich, "Political Parties in and out of Legislatures," in Rhodes, R. A. W., Sarah A. Binder, and Bert A. Rockman, eds., *The Oxford Handbook of Political Institutions* (Oxford: Oxford University Press, 2006), pp. 555–576.

9 Norberto Bobbio, *Democracy and Dictatorship: Elements for a General Theory of* (Minneapolis, Minnesota: University of Minnesota Press, 1989), p. 25, cited in ibid., p. 75.

10 Joseph LaPalombara and Myron Weiner, eds. *Political Parties and Political Development.* (Princeton: Princeton University Press, 1966): p. 4, citied in Frank Tachau, "Introduction," in Frank Tachau, ed. *Political Parties of the Middle East and North Africa.* (Westport, Connecticut: Greenwood Press, 1994), p. xiii.

11 Tachau, "Introduction," op. cit., p. xiii.

Democracy and Political Parties

Clearly, there are parties that advocate democracy and parties that advocate dictatorship. Examples of parties that advocate dictatorships include Italy's Fascist Party, Germany's Nazi party, Communist Party of the Soviet Union, and the Chinese Communist Party. In Iran, both the Shah and Ayatollah Khomeini established parties that were anti-democratic. The Rastakhiz Party under the Shah and the Islamic Republican Party (IRP) under Khomeini were created with the purpose of consolidating the brutal dictatorships of their founders (see Chapters 2 and 5). The Shah ordered all Iranians to either join his party or go to jail or leave Iran. One of the main slogans of Khomeini's supporters was *"Hezb Faghat Hezbollah, Rahbar Faghat Ruhollah"* [The Sole Party is the Party of God, the Sole Leader is Ruhollah Khomeini]. The IRP was created with the primary mission to eliminate all non-fundamentalist parties and consolidate Khomeini's absolute rule (see Chapter 5).

There exists little scholarly works on the relationships between political parties and democracy. Aldrich summarizes this scholarship in the following words:

> It may not be true that parties are literally necessary condition for democracy to exist as Schattschneider (1942) famously wrote, but their ubiquity suggests that they are virtually, if not actually, a necessity for a democracy to be viable.
>
> ... Let me close with a fourth area which appears ripe for research breakthroughs. This chapter pointed towards a fully comparative political parties project. ... we are beginning to see more clearly that political parties are common to all democracies, and they are so because democracy is, indeed, unthinkable save through the agency of the party.[12]

As Aldrich argues, a democratic political party is not necessary for the establishment of democracy. If other pre-conditions for democracy are present, we have observed transitions to democracy. Recent examples may be transitions to democracy in Czechoslovakia (Czech Republic and Slovakia) and Hungry. One may also include the U.S. republic after its revolution. However, democratic parties soon emerged which assisted in democratic consolidation. What is analytically significant is that when there does not exist democratic opposition parties and the ruling authoritarian regime confronts highly dictatorial opposition parties or groups, then the lack of democratic opposition has actually retarded transition to democracy. We saw the most dramatic example of this in Algeria in 1991. When the mild secular authoritarian regime accepted free and fair elections, and when the opposition was dominated by Islamic Salvation Front (an extremely

---

12 Aldrich, op. cit., pp. 555, 572–573.

anti-democratic Islamic fundamentalist party), then there was a retreat to authoritarianism (with great support from both many domestic classes and strata as well as internationally). We have observed this phenomenon repeat itself in much of the Islamic world since the early 1980s.

In Chile and South Africa, there existed powerful pro-democracy parties, which increased the likelihood of incumbent authoritarian regime to accept free elections and accept a peaceful transition to democracy in 1989 and 1994 respectively. In Chile major opposition parties such as the Christian Democratic Party and the Socialist Party were advocates of parliamentary democracy. In South Africa, the African National Congress (ANC) was a powerful pro-democracy party (or to be more precise a coalition of parties). The existence of pro-democracy opposition parties created both domestic and international conditions conducive to democratic transitions.

In addition, weakness of pro-democracy parties may explain lack of democratic consolidation or democratic reversals in hybrid or illiberal regimes. Lack of strong pro-democracy parties have allowed charismatic authoritarian leaders, their supporters, and anti-democratic parties to undermine democratic gains. For example, democratic reversals in Turkey and Russia may be explained in some measures due to the fact that pro-democracy parties were weak which allowed authoritarian leaders such as Recep Tayyip Erdogan and his less extreme Islamic fundamentalist party (AKP) to undermine democracy in Turkey. In Russia, Vladimir Putin has been able to consolidate power in his own hands with the assistance of his supporters from the old security establishment.

In sum, there are several factors and pre-conditions that influence democratic transitions and democratic consolidations. The existence of pro-democracy party is one such factor. The existence of pro-democracy party is not absolutely necessary for transition to democracy, but its existence provides the population with a democratic alternative. If there are pro-democracy parties, that reality would increase the likelihood of democratic transition. The stronger the support for pro-democracy parties, the higher the likelihood for transition to democracy and democratic consolidation.

The Iran National Front and Democracy

In this book, I use definitions of political party that have been articulated by Aldrich, Bobbio, and LaPalombara and Weiner. I this study, I demonstrate that the Iran National Front [Jebhe Melli Iran] may be one of the few partial exceptions to the observation that Iran has lacked real political parties.

This book describes the activities of the Iran National Front (INF) from its founding in 1949 to October 2021. There are a number of excellent scholarly works on Dr. Mohammad Mossadegh and the August 1953 coup, which overthrew the INF government.[13] Other scholarly works on contemporary Iranian politics or the 1979 Revolution also briefly mention the activities of the INF.[14] There is, however, no major scholarly work on the activities of the INF since 1982.[15] This book attempts to fill that gap. Utilizing the INF's documents, other primary sources, and interviews, this study describes the activities, policies, platform, ideology, leadership, and strategies of the INF between 1979 and mid-2021, with primary emphasis on the INF's recent activities (i.e., 2015–2021). Before presenting the contemporary activities of the INF, it is necessary to provide the historical context. To do so, this book utilizes secondary sources to provide a brief history of the INF's activities between 1949 and 1979.

Iran has had many political parties. However, due to a variety of reasons, including harsh dictatorships, it has been hard to sustain political activities. Nevertheless, the INF and other parties have continued to exist. Moreover, this book shows that the INF continues to be Iran's main pro-democracy political party struggling to establish a system based on democracy, civil liberties, and human rights.

---

13 James A. Bill and Wm. Roger Louis, eds. *Musaddiq, Iranian Nationalism and Oil* (Austin: University of Texas Press, 1988); Richard Cottam, *Nationalism in Iran* (Pittsburgh: University of Pittsburgh Press, 1964); Farhad Diba, *Dr. Mohammad Mossadegh: A Political Biography* (London: Croom Helm, 1986); Mark Gasiorowski and Malcolm Byrne, eds. *Mohammad Mosaddeq and the 1953 Coup in Iran* (Syracuse: Syracuse University Press, 2005); Homa Katouzian, *Musaddiq and the Struggle for Power in Iran* (London: I. B. Tauris, 1990); Ali Rahnema, *Behind the 1953 Coup in Iran: Thugs, Turncoats, Soldiers, and Spooks* (Cambridge: Cambridge University Press, 2014); and Gregory Brew, "The Collapse Narrative: The United States, Mohammed Mossadegh, and the Coup Decision of 1953," *Texas National Security Review*, Vol. 2, Issue 4 (November 2019), https://tnsr.org/2019/11/the-collapse-narrative-the-united-states-mohammed-mossadegh-and-the-coup-decision-of-1953/.
14 Ervand Abrahamian, *Iran Between Two Revolutions* (Princeton: Princeton University Press, 1982); Homa Katouzian, *The Persians: Ancient, Mediaeval and Modern Iran* (New Haven: Yale University Press, 2009); Nikki R. Keddie, *Roots of Revolution: An Interpretive History of Modern Iran* (New Haven: Yale University Press, 1981); Sussan Siavoshi, *Liberal Nationalism in Iran: The Failure of a Movement* (Boulder, CO: Westview Press, 1990); and Misagh Parsa, *Democracy in Iran: Why It Failed and How It Might Succeed* (Cambridge, MA: Harvard University Press, 2016).
15 There are a handful of partial exceptions. See Afshin Shahi, "Iranian nationalism: A theoretical dilemma," e-international relations (January 26, 2009), https://www.e-ir.info/2009/01/26/iranian-nationalism-a-historical-overview/.

A Brief History of Democracy and Nationalism in Iran

Iran is the first country in the Middle East to have established a democracy. Modernist, constitutional, and democratic ideas that had been percolating since the late 18th century came to fruition in early years of the 19th century. The Constitutional Revolution of 1905 established a constitutional monarchy in Iran. The 1906 constitution was modelled after the Belgium constitution which itself was the written form of the British unwritten constitution. World War One badly undermined the constitutional system. The February 1921 coup brought Reza Khan Mirpang (later Reza Shah Pahlavi) into power as Head of the Armed Forces. By January 1926, Reza Shah destroyed the constitutional system and made himself the absolute dictator of Iran. However, demands for freedom and democracy did not die. By the removal of Reza Shah from power in August 1941, these demands resurfaced and formed the basis of support for Dr. Mossadegh and the INF.[16]

In his study of nationalism in Iran, Richard Cottam argues that as the process of modernization began in Iran, increasingly the masses became involved in politics. Mossadegh was a liberal nationalist who was both a reflection of the demands of increasing segments of the population for a liberal constitutional system and a leader who further popularized such demands.[17]

The classic study on the INF and Mossadegh is by Homa Katouzian. Katouzian argues that the term "*Nehzat Melli*" should be translated as "popular movement." He opposes the common translation as "nationalist movement." The word "*melli*" in Persian refers to both "popular" and "national." Katouzian does not like to use the terms "National Front" or "nationalist movement," and prefers to use "popular front" and "the popular movement." For Katouzian a powerful popular movement emerged in the 1940, which the INF became its organizational form and Mossadegh its leader. Katouzian's study stops at 1964.[18]

Misagh Parsa's study presents an excellent structuralist analysis on why the struggle for democracy has failed in Iran. He argues that the societal pre-conditions for democracy exist in Iran. His study stops at the revolutionary period 1979–1981.[19]

Azimi, Cottam, Katouzian, and Parsa agree with one major observation: the INF being the main and the largest democratic political entity in Iran. None of

---

16 Fakhreddin Azimi, *The Quest for Democracy in Iran: A Century of Struggle Against Authoritarian Rule* (Cambridge, MA: Harvard University Press, 2010).

17 Cottam, *Nationalism in Iran*, op. cit.

18 Katouzian, *Musaddiq and the Struggle for Power in Iran*, op. cit.

19 Parsa, *Democracy in Iran*, op. cit.

these studies discuss the role of the INF since 1981. In this book, I hope to fill that gap.

This book demonstrates that the INF has been both a political party as well as a coalition of political parties and civil society organizations. The INF was formed by political parties, but about 90% of the INF members are members only of the INF and not of any of its constituting parties or organizations. When it was formed in 1949, it was the beneficiary of the struggles of constitutionalist and democratic forces that have been struggling since the constitutional movement. Mossadegh was elected to the First Majles in 1906 but could not become a member because he was too young (he was 25 years-old and the minimum age of membership was 30). Mossadegh had served in the Majles, the cabinet (Minister of Treasury, Minister of Foreign Affairs), and governor of major provinces (Azerbaijan and Fars) before the establishment of the Pahlavi dictatorship in January 1926. For many Iranians, the term *"Jebhe Melli Iran"* [Iran National Front], has come to connote (and has become coterminous with) the movement for democracy. Many pro-democracy activists have throughout years have argued that the INF should become a broad-based coalition of all pro-democracy parties and groups.

For good or ill, the actual historical and political facts have been that there are pro-democracy parties and groups that have not been part of the actually existing INF. "What ought to be" and "what is" are not always the same. In this book, I treat the INF as what it actually is: its formal organization, leaders, platform, and the like.

This book will demonstrate that the INF has been a "real political party." Moreover, it argues that throughout its history of over 73 years of struggles, it has been Iran's main and largest pro-democracy political party. This book will conclude that if there is going to be a transition to democracy in Iran, the INF will be one of the main vehicles for that transition.

Chapter 2
The Struggle for Independence, Democracy, and Freedom: 1949 – 1977

The Founding

The INF was established in October 1949 by Mossadegh. In a brief statement, Mossadegh invited the people to join him in a rally supporting free elections on Friday October 14, 1949 at 10:00 a.m. The protests began in front of Mossadegh's house. Mossadegh gave a brief speech. Then Mossadegh, several dozen political leaders, and about 10,000 supporters marched to the Shah's palace a few blocks away.[20] In a meeting in Mossadegh's house on Sunday October 23, 1949, the group declared the founding of the INF. The initial group was very heterogeneous and soon many left. The INF that we know today has been consistent since late 1952 in terms of its leaders, principles, politics, and methods of struggle.

The INF had two primary objectives: (1) to force Mohammad Reza Shah Pahlavi to respect the 1906 constitution and allow free elections for the Majles [parliament]; and (2) to nationalize Iran's oil which had been under the control of the British.[21] The British were using their control of Iran's oil to control Iranian politics. The British policy was to support the Shah to concentrate power in his own hands in a dictatorial manner so that he would protect Britain's economic and political interests in Iran.[22] The INF was nationalist in the sense that it struggled to achieve Iran's *de facto* independence from British control. The INF was a mod-

---

20 Hussein Moussavian, "Interview with Radio Asr Jadid, Part 1," (October 21, 2018), https://melliun.org/iran/184415; Katouzian, *Musaddiq and the Struggle for Power*, pp. 73–77; and Amir Shahab Razavian, "*18 Ask Montasher Nashodeh Az Rahpeymaee Mossadegh Va Hamrahaneshan Beh Kakh Marmar*" [18 Unpublished Photos of the March of Mossadegh and Those Who Were With Him to Marmar Palace], Gooya News, (October 21, 2010), https://news.gooya.com/politics/archives/2010/10/112337.php.
21 Mohammad Musaddiq, *Musaddiq's Memoirs*, trans S. H. Amin and H. Katouzian (London: Jebhe National Movement of Iran, 1988), p. 315; and Jebhe Melli Iran, "*Haftad Saal*" [Seventy Years], *Payam Jebhe Melli Iran*, No. 199 (December 5, 2019), p. 1, https://melliun.org/v/wp-content/uploads/2019/12/payam-jebhe-melli-iran-199.pdf.
22 Habib Ladjevardi, "The Origins of U.S. Support for an Autocratic Iran," *International Journal of Middle East Studies* Vol. 15, No. 2 (May 1983), pp. 225–239; and Wm. Roger Louis, "Musaddiq and the Dilemmas of British Imperialism," in Bill and Louis, eds. *Musaddiq, Iranian Nationalism and Oil*, pp. 228–260.

https://doi.org/10.1515/9783110782158-004

erate liberal democratic organization that pursued political and non-violent methods of struggle to establish democracy in Iran. The INF wanted the Shah to reign but not rule, respect the 1906 constitution, and allow free democratic elections for the parliament (which would then choose the prime minister and cabinet).[23]

Initially, the INF succeeded. The Shah retreated and acquiesced to free elections. Mossadegh won the highest number of votes for the parliament. In addition to Mossadegh, six INF members won seats. Ayatollah Abolqassem Kashani, who was also on the INF list, won a seat.[24] Mossadegh became prime minister on April 29, 1951. Mossadegh had been offered the post of prime minister on several occasions before, but he had refused to accept. In March 1951, the situation was different. Prime Minister Gen. Haj-Ali Razmara was assassinated. Although the person arrested was a member of the Fadaian Islam, the evidence discovered later indicates that the Shah and his top adviser Amir Asadollah Alam (later Minister of the Court and Prime Minister) had orchestrated the assassination.[25] Recent declassified CIA documents also indicate that the Shah not only had a major role in Gen. Razmara's assassination in March 1951 but also had a role in the 1953 assassination of Gen. Mahmoud Afshartus, the pro-Mossadegh Commander-in-Chief of the National Police. According to the CIA document:

> In 1956, the then minister of court in a conversation with a US Embassy officer "clearly implied" that former prime minister Razmara had been murdered "with the full knowledge of the Shah, if not on his direct Order." The minister of court also stated that he had acted as

---

23 The 1906 constitution was primarily based on the Belgian constitution of 1831 and the British (unwritten) constitutional principles. A number of amendments were added the following year. The monarch was to be primarily a symbolic figure with free elections for a parliament (Majles), which would choose the prime minister. Government power and responsibility were to be in the hands of the prime minister and the cabinet. Using violence and anti-democratic means, the Pahlavi kings imposed highly anti-democratic amendments, which drastically increased the powers of the king. Both Pahlavi kings ignored the constitution (even the one with their own amendments) and ruled in absolutist manner.

24 Katouzian, *The Persians*, p. 244.

25 Katouzian, *Musaddiq and the Struggle for Power*, pp. 83–84. In 1951, Princess Ashraf, the Shah's twin sister, had begun spreading rumors that Mossadegh was behind the assassination of Gen. Razmara. After the revolution, fundamentalists have tried to hide the fact of the cooperation between Fadaian Islam and the Shah and Seyyed Zia Aldin Tabatabai both on Razmara's assassination and on the 1953 coup.

intermediary between "the court" and the murderers of Mossadeq's police chief, General Afshartus.[26]

In March 1951, three individuals were the most powerful players in Iran: Gen. Razmara, the Shah, and Mossadegh. The Shah feared Razmara the most and wanted to use Mossadegh to get rid of Razmara. Mossadegh had refused to co-operate with the Shah. Razmara had developed good relations with the U.S., the U.K., and the Soviet Union, a surprising feat.[27] Razmara had also developed good relations with the Tudeh Party and was using it to undermine the INF.[28] After killing Razmara, the Shah wanted to make Seyyed Zia Aldin Tabatabai prime minister. Zia was fully subservient to the British and highly authoritarian. Mossadegh believed that Zia's premiership would put an end to the lukewarm democracy Iran had enjoyed since Reza Shah's abdication in 1941. Therefore, Mossadegh accepted to become prime minister in order to defeat the Shah's plan to destroy Iran's constitutional system.[29] Mossadegh surprised the Shah by accepting to become prime minister. He told members of the parliament that he would do so if the parliament would vote for the nationalization of oil.

The 1953 Coup

In August 1953, the CIA and the British intelligence along with their Iranian collaborators overthrew Mossadegh.[30] From 1953 until the late 1990s, the U.S. de-

---

26 The 1972 intelligence report has been published by the U.S. State Department's Office of the Historian, Foreign Relations of the United States, https://history.state.gov/historicaldocuments/frus1969-76ve04/d180.

27 Katouzian, *Musaddiq and the Struggle for Power*, op. cit.

28 Abrahamian, *Iran Between Two Revolutions*, op. cit.

29 Musaddiq, *Musaddiq's Memoirs*, pp. 264 – 257.

30 Gasiorowski and Byrne, *Mohammad Mosaddeq and the 1953 Coup in Iran*. For an excellent documentary produced by a British documentary television producer see Granada Television, "End of Empire, Chapter 7, Iran," (1985), You Tube, (2014), https://www.youtube.com/watch?v=xhCgJElpQEQ. This documentary includes interviews with MI6 and CIA officials involved in the coup as well as other British and American officials. For an excellent collection of U.S. government archives see https://nsarchive.gwu.edu/project/iran-us-relations. For excellent brief reports see James Risen, "Secrets of History: The CIA in Iran," *The New York Times*, (April 16, 2000), https://archive.nytimes.com/www.nytimes.com/library/world/mideast/041600iran-cia-index.html; and James Risen, "Secrets of History: The C.I.A. In Iran – A Special Report; How a Plot Convulsed Iran in '53 (and in '79)," *The New York Times*, (April 16, 2000), https://www.nytimes.com/2000/04/16/world/secrets-history-cia-iran-special-report-plot-convulsed-iran-53-79.html?.

nied its role in the coup. The reason was provided by President Dwight Eisenhower for keeping American orchestration of the coup secret. Eisenhower wrote in his diary in 1953 that if the knowledge of the coup became public, "We would not only be embarrassed in that region, but our chances to do anything of like nature in the future would almost totally disappear."[31] The U.S. government and the CIA have acknowledged their role and have released substantial amounts of previously classified documents.[32] Declassified U.S. government documents show that the British government had been lobbying the U.S. to organize a coup against Mossadegh.[33] As of March 2021 the British government has not publicly acknowledged its role although top MI6 officials responsible for the coup have done so.[34]

Within days after Mossadegh became prime minister, MI6's top Persian-speaking officer and Iran expert, Norman Darbyshire, was ordered to go back to Tehran and organize Mossadegh's dismissal through legal or other means.[35] The MI6 believed that it would be able to do so within two months by bribing members of the Majles.[36] When that failed, the MI6 began planning for a coup

---

31 VOA, "US Publishes Report on Its Role in 1953 Iran Coup," (June 29, 2017), https://www. voanews.com/middle-east/us-publishes-report-its-role-1953-iran-coup.

32 U.S. Government, Department of State, Office of the Historian, *Foreign Relations of the United States, 1952–1954, Iran, 1951–1954* (Washington, DC: U.S. Government, 2017), https://history. state.gov/historicaldocuments/frus1951-54Iran; and U.S. Government, CIA Clandestine Service History, "Overthrow of Premier Mossadeq of Iran, November 1952-August 1953," March 1954, by Dr. Donald Wilber, https://nsarchive2.gwu.edu/NSAEBB/NSAEBB28/.

33 U.S. Government, Department of State, "Memorandum of Conversation: Byroade to Matthews, Proposal to Organize a Coup d'etat in Iran," (December 3, 1952), https://nsarchive.gwu. edu/dc.html?doc=3914380-02-State-Department-Memorandum-of-Conversation; and U.S. Government, Department of State, "Memorandum of Conversation: British Proposal to Organize a Coup d'etat in Iran," (November 26, 1952), https://nsarchive.gwu.edu/dc.html?doc=3914379-01-State-Department-Memorandum-of-Conversation.

34 Julian Borger, "British spy's account sheds light on role in 1953 Iranian coup," *The Guardian* (August 17, 2020), https://www.theguardian.com/world/2020/aug/17/british-spys-account-sheds-light-on-role-in-1953-iranian-coup; Norman Darbyshire, "Transcript of Interview with Norman Darbyshire for End of Empire," 1985, National Security Archives, https://nsarchive.gwu.edu/ dc.html?doc=7033886-National-Security-Archive; Vanessa Thorpe, "MI6, the coup in Iran that changed the Middle East, and the cover-up," *The Observer* (August 2, 2020), https://www.the guardian.com/world/2020/aug/02/mi6-the-coup-in-iran-that-changed-the-middle-east-and-the-cover-up; and Owen Bowcott, "Secret CIA study reveals British role in Iran coup," *The Guardian* (April 16, 2000), https://www.theguardian.com/world/2000/apr/17/iran.

35 Darbyshire, "Transcript of Interview," op. cit.

36 Ibid.

with the code name "Boot."[37] The British government took Iran to the World Court and the UN Security Council. Mossadegh prevailed at both venues. The British were not able to convince the Truman administration to support their efforts. The British, however, succeeded in convincing the Eisenhower administration to carry out a coup against Mossadegh.[38] Beginning from January 1953, the CIA and MI6 began the joint effort to overthrow Mossadegh in a coup. The CIA chose the code name "Ajax" for its operations.[39]

Gen. Mahmoud Afshartus was Mossadegh's highly competent Chief of National Police. Earlier in his career, he was a supporter of Reza Shah.[40] However, with the emergence of the nationalist movement in 1951, he became a supporter of Mossadegh. During the conspiracy to murder Mossadegh on February 28, 1953, Afshartus personally saved Mossadegh's life and arrested Shaaban "*Bimokh*" [Brainless] Jafaari, one of the conspirators who had attacked Mossadegh's house.[41] The events on February 28 were a turning point. The Shah had asked Mossadegh to go to his palace to discuss his plan to leave the country. When Mossadegh arrived at the palace, a large crowd was there. They had plans to murder him when he was leaving the palace. Mossadegh left the palace from a different gate and went to his house not far from the palace. The crowd followed him, smashed his house's gates and attacked the house. The mob was under the leadership of Shaaban and organized by Ayatollah Kashani, Ayatollah Behbahani, Ayatollah Nouri, and Baghaei. Mossadegh believed that the con-

---

37 Ibid. The original plan for the coup was drawn by MI6 official C. M. Woodhouse. See Woodhouse, *Something Ventured* (London: Granada, 1982).

38 U.S. Government, Department of State, "Memorandum of Conversation: Byroade to Matthews, Proposal to Organize a Coup d'etat in Iran," (December 3, 1952), https://nsarchive.gwu.edu/dc.html?doc=3914380-02-State-Department-Memorandum-of-Conversation; and U.S. Government, Department of State, "Memorandum of Conversation: British Proposal to Organize a Coup d'etat in Iran," (November 26, 1952), https://nsarchive.gwu.edu/dc.html?doc=3914379-01-State-Department-Memorandum-of-Conversation.

39 The CIA already had clandestine operations in Iran countering the Tudeh Party, the Soviet Union, and the KGB. Their code names were BADMAN and "TPAJAX." TP stood for Tudeh Party and Ajax was a famous cleaning agent. From January 1953, that operation (with all its network and agents) changed its main objective to overthrowing Mossadegh. The British intelligence had very extensive network in Iran, which was put under the CIA control after January 1953.

40 Hamid-Reza Mosaiebian, *Sarlashkar Mahmoud Afshartus* [General Mahmoud Afshartus] (Kermanshah, Iran: 2016), https://melliun.org/v/wp-content/uploads/2016/01/12-Afshartus_Mahmood_950807_146.pdf.

41 Ibid.

spiracy was planned by the Shah.[42] Mossadegh knew that the Shah was behind Razmara's assassination and thought that he was going to kill him as well.[43]

In the preparations for the coup, Darbyshire organized the kidnapping of Gen. Afshartus. Darbyshire says that the murder of Gen. Afshartus was not his intension and that things got out of control.[44] Darbyshire ordered the Rashidian brothers (well-known British agents that operated as go-betweens) to organize several monarchist military officers to kidnap Gen. Afshartus in April 1953.[45] The operation was carried out by associates of Gen. Fazlollah Zahedi and Mozaffar Baghaie-Kermani (and Baghaie's close associate Hussein Khatibi).[46] Soon, police investigations revealed the role of Zahedi and Baghaie. Ayatollah Kashani, who was Speaker of the Majles then provided support and immunity to Zahedi and Baghaie from arrest and prosecution. Baghaie was a member of the Majles and had parliamentary immunity. Mossadegh asked the Majles to strip Baghaie from the parliamentary immunity, but under Ayatollah Kashani's orders and support Majles members refused to do so. Baghaei was arrested on August 17 after the coup attempt of august 16 and after the Majles was dissolved. Gen. Zahedi also went to Majles and took *"bast"* (sanctuary) with support from Ayatollah Kashani. Mossadegh respected the rule of law and did not send police to arrest them.[47] Baghaie claims that he was not involved in the kidnapping and murder of Gen. Afshartus.[48] However, there exits substantial evidence that he was. For example, on October 20, 1953, Henderson, the U.S. ambassador to Tehran, sent the following report to the State Department:

---

42 For details of the events see Katouzian, *Musaddiq and the Struggle*, pp. 178–183.

43 Ibid.

44 Darbyshire, "Transcript of Interview," op. cit.

45 Wm. Roger Louis, "Britain and the Overthrow of the Mosaddeq Government," in Gasiorowski, Mark J., and Malcolm Byrne, eds. *Mohammad Mosaddeq and the 1953 Coup in Iran* (Syracuse: Syracuse University Press, 2005), pp. 314–315, endnote 170.

46 Homa Katouzian, "Mosaddeq's Government in Iranian History: Arbitrary Rule, Democracy, and the 1953 Coup," in Mark J. Gasiorowski and Malcolm Byrne, eds. *Mohammad Mosaddeq and the 1953 Coup in Iran* (Syracuse: Syracuse University Press, 2005), pp. 15, 19.

47 Fakhreddin Azimi, "Unseating Mosaddeq: The Configuration and Role of Domestic Forces," in Mark J. Gasiorowski and Malcolm Byrne, eds. *Mohammad Mosaddeq and the 1953 Coup in Iran* (Syracuse: Syracuse University Press, 2005), p. 64.

48 Mozaffar Baghaie-Kermani, "Interview," Harvard University, Iranian Oral History Project, Franklin Lake, New Jersey, U.S., (April 11, 1986), https://curiosity.lib.harvard.edu/iranian-oral-history-project/catalog?f%5Binterviewee_ssim%5D%5B%5D=Baghaie-Kermani%2C+Mozaffar; audio available at https://www.youtube.com/watch?v=oUJy80mMap0&list=PL-PRP1hqq8eK6WhFOLGa3MQyO9fL5v70q.

Dr. Baqai's political future can quickly be ended by the prosecution of the Afshartus affair. The Military Governor of Tehran, Maj. Gen. Dadsetan, stated on October 18th that he had proof certain that Dr. Baqai was directly implicated in the murder of the former Police Chief. That fact means that in order to be safe, Dr. Baqai and his men must control the General Staff, the Police Department, and the Office of the Military Governor. During the last two weeks Dr. Baqai's men have been attempting to capture those positions or to neutralize them. Gen. Zahedi's hands are momentarily tied in this matter because he has decided to free all of the military officers who plotted against the life of Afshartus and who executed him. At the moment, therefore, Dr. Baqai may with impunity criticize the Zahedi administration. As an insurance measure, however, his men continue to attempt to capture the posts mentioned above.[49]

According to the CIA document mentioned earlier, Alam told the CIA that the Shah was aware and supportive of the kidnapping and murder of Gen. Afshartus.[50]

The kidnapping of Gen. Afshartus was part of a larger plan. The main persons were Baghaie and Gen. Fazlollah Zahedi. Gen. Zahedi had his nephew Gen. Nasrollah Zahedi, who was a close friend and military academy classmate of Gen. Afshartus to talk with Afshartus. The Shah called Gen. Afshartus and told him that a number of officers wanted to talk with him and asked him to talk with Gen. Nasrollah Zahedi to organize the meeting. Gen. Afshartus called his old friend Gen. Nasrollah Zahedi, who told him to meet him at the home of Hussein Khatibi (Baghaie's close associate). When Afshartus arrived at Khatibi's house, he was ambushed. He was then taken to a cave outside Tehran. He was severely tortured and suffocated to death.[51]

Several monarchist officers including four generals, two colonels, and one captain were implicated in the kidnapping and murder. In addition to the two Zahedis, they were Gen. Nosratollah Bayandor, Gen. Ali Asghar Mazini, and Gen. Ali Akbar Manzeh. In his confessions, captain Baluch said: "They took Gen. Afshartus in order to create chaos in the country, so that the cabinet would be overthrown.

---

49 U.S. Government, Department of State, Letter From the Ambassador to Iran (Henderson) to the Director of the Office of Greek, Turkish, and Iranian Affairs, Bureau of Near Eastern, South Asian, and African Affairs (Richards), Tehran, (October 20, 1953), https://history.state.gov/his toricaldocuments/frus1951-54Iran/d335.

50 The 1972 intelligence report has been published by the U.S. State Department's Office of the Historian, Foreign Relations of the United States, https://history.state.gov/historicaldocuments/ frus1969-76ve04/d180.

51 Tarikh Irani, "*Jasad Afshartus Peyda Shod*" [The Body of Afsharus Was Found], (April 26, 1953), http://tarikhirani.ir/fa/calendar/151; and Jamal Safari, "*Sarlashkar Mahmoud Afshartus*" [Gen. Mahmoud Afshartus], Enghelab Eslami, (June 25, 2014), https://www.enghelabe-eslami. com/component/content/article/35-didgagha/nevisandegane-ma/9422-20140625-js-1.html.

The plan was that after killing Afshartus to kidnap Dr. Fatemi, Gen. Riahi, Dr. Moazemi, Dr. Shaeygan, Zirakzadeh, and Gen. Mahna."[52] As soon as Afshartus was kidnapped, Mossadegh ordered an extensive investigation to find the perpetrators. The investigation soon found out the identity of the perpetrators. After coup, the Shah freed all those involved in the kidnapping, torture, and murder of Gen. Afshartus.

On August 16, 1953, around 11:45 p.m., armed military personnel went to the homes of several cabinet ministers and arrested them and took them (while wearing their pajamas) to the garrison at the Shah's Saadabad Palace. Among these were Dr. Hussein Fatemi (Foreign Minister and Deputy Prime Minister), Ahmad Zirakzadeh (one of the founders of the Iran Party, Member of Parliament, and adviser to Mossadegh), and Jahangir Haghshenas (Minister of Roads).[53] The coup plotters also wanted to arrest Gen. Taghi Riahi (Chairman of the Chiefs of Staff), but he had gone to his office at the military headquarters.[54] Over 60 military personnel had gone to the home of Dr. Fatemi and arrested him around mid-night.[55] Apparently, the plan was to arrest all the cabinet ministers but the coup failed before that. Col. Nemattollah Nasiri (of Imperial Guards, the branch staffed with extreme monarchists) arrived at Mossadegh's home around 1:00 a.m. with large numbers of armed soldiers in four armored vehicles. Mossadegh, who had been told about the coup, had his military guards arrest Col. Nasiri.[56] By the morning, outraged and jubilant crowds in Tehran and provinces went to the streets shouting support for Mossadegh, and bringing down statues of Mohammad Reza Shah and Reza Shah. Kermit Roosevelt re-organized his forces and made a second coup attempt on August 19, which succeeded in overthrowing Mossadegh.[57]

---

52 Safari, "*Sarlashkar Mahmoud Afshartus*" [Gen. Mahmoud Afshartus], ibid. Fatemi was Foreign Minister, Gen. Riahi was the Chairman of the Chiefs of Staff, Moazemi, Shaeygan and Zirakzadeh were members of cabinet, Majles and top leaders of the INF, and Gen. Mahna was Deputy Chairman of the Chiefs of Staff.

53 Ahmad Zirakzadeh, "Interview," Harvard University, Iranian Oral History Project, Arlington, Virginia, U.S., (May 1986), https://curiosity.lib.harvard.edu/iranian-oral-history-project/catalog/32-zirakzadeh__ahmad01, audio available at https://www.youtube.com/watch?v=T_uZhbPEX28; and https://www.youtube.com/watch?v=6vkJhWC7GlU.

54 Ibid.

55 Hussein Fatemi, *Neveshteh-hay Makhfigah Va Zendan: 28 Mordad 1332 – 19 Aban 1333* [Writings from the Hideout and Prison: 19 August 1953 – 10 November 1954], (London: Daftar-hay Azadi, 2004), https://melliun.org/v/wp-content/uploads/2017/06/yaddasht-haye-dr.-Fatemi.pdf.

56 Ibid.

57 For an account of the events from the perspective of Dr. Gholam-Hussein Sadighi, who was the Ministry of Interior then, see Gholam-Hussein Sadighi, "*Kodeta-e 28 Mordad Beh Ravayat*

CIA, Shia Clerics, Islamic Fundamentalists, and the Coup

Islamic groups and clerics collaborated with the CIA, MI6, and the monarchists in the coup that overthrew Mossadegh.[58] Ayatollah Mahmoud Kashani, Ayatollah Mohammad Behbahani, and Ayatollah Mohammad Taqi Falsafi played major roles during the coup as did the fundamentalist group "Fadaian Islam."[59] On June 15, 1981, Ayatollah Ruhollah Khomeini condemned both Mossadegh and the INF as apostate. Khomeini said:

> He [Mossadegh] was not a Muslim. On that day, I was in the home of one of the clerics [Aya-tollah Behbahani] in Tehran when I heard the news that they had put glasses on a dog and called it 'Ayatollah' and walked the dog around Tehran. I told the said cleric that this is not only an opposition to one person. He [Mossadegh] will be slapped in the face. Shortly after-ward, that he [Mossadegh] was slapped. And if he [Mossadegh] remained, he would have slapped Islam.[60]

The INF had called a rally on June 15, 1981 to oppose five bills under discussion by the Majles, including the "Bill of Retribution" (see Chapter 4). Khomeini not only declared the INF apostate, which would mean that their members should be killed, but that he went so far as to condemn Mossadegh, who had passed away in 1967, as apostate as well. Moreover, Khomeini provided legitimacy to the coup against Mossadegh by saying that Mossadegh was harming Islam. The word "slap" in Persian has the connotation of being hostile and taking actions that harm the target.

Ayatollah Kashani began opposing Mossadegh beginning in late 1952 and early 1953. There were a number of issues that divided them. According to Abra-hamian, Kashani opposed Mossadegh because Mossadegh "drafted an electoral bill enfranchising women, tended to favor state enterprises over the bazaar, re-fused to ban alcohol, and declined amnesty to assassins from the Fedayan-e Islam. Moreover, mundane matters, such as awarding of government contracts,

---

Gholam-Hussein Sadighi" [The 1953 Coup According to Gholam-Hussein Sadighi], Tarikh Irani, (August 23, 2011), http://tarikhirani.ir/fa/news/1190/.

58 For recent declassified U.S. and British documents see https://nsarchive.gwu.edu/briefing-book/iran/2018-03-07/new-findings-clerical-involvement-1953-coup-iran.

59 Katouzian, *Musaddiq and the Struggle for Power*, pp. 156 – 176; Masoud Kazemzadeh, "The CIA Coup in Iran," *Middle East Policy*, Vol. 11, No. 4 (2004), pp. 122 – 129; Shahrough Akhavi, "The Role of the Clergy in Iranian Politics, 1949 – 1954," in Bill and Louis, eds. *Musaddiq, Iranian Nationalism and Oil*, pp. 91 – 117; and Eravand Abrahamian, *Khomeinism: Essays on the Islamic Republic* (Berkeley and Los Angeles: University of California Press, 1993), pp. 105 – 110.

60 Ayatollah Ruhollah Khomeini, *Sahifeh Noor*, Vol. 14, June 15, 1981, https://emam.com/posts/view/2645/.

also played a role."[61] Ayatollah Kashani began asking the British and Americans to assist him.[62] Recent declassified American documents show the close cooperation between Ayatollah Kashani and the CIA.[63] These documents show close collaboration between Kashani and the CIA and that Ayatollah Behbahani received money from the CIA in the operations against Mossadegh.[64] In a document provided to Stanford University by Ardeshir Zahedi, a hand-written bill of the funds that were provided to various individuals and groups to support Gen. Zahedi (during the coup and days after the coup) exists. According to this document, Gen. Zahedi distributed the CIA funds to the following: Ayatollah Kashani 800,000 rials; Ayatollah Behbahani 800,000 rials; other Shia clerics 500,000 rials; Shaaban Jafaari 200,000 rials; as well as SUMKA (Iran's official Nazi Party) and Arya Party (a far-right party) 200,000 rials.[65] Ayatollah Kashani also began closely working with the Shah, Gen. Zahedi, and Mozaffar Baghaei preparing for the coup.[66]

Moreover, after the revolution, many leaders of the INF were persecuted, jailed, executed or assassinated by the fundamentalist regime. Many others were badly tortured by the fundamentalist regime.[67] In large measures due to extreme repression and censorship under the Shah, many Iranians in 1978–79, were unaware of the role of the fundamentalists in the coup against Mossadegh. Khomeini had hidden his antagonistic views on Mossadegh, the INF, the Constitutional Revolution of 1905–1911, as well as his admiration of Sheikh Fazlollah

---

61 Abrahamian, *Khomeinism*, p. 108.

62 Ibid., p. 109.

63 Kambiz Fattahi, "*Kodetay 28 Mordad: Naghsh Kashani Beh Ravayat Asnad America*" [The August 19, 1953 Coup: The Role of Kashani According to the American Documents], BBC Persian, (July 22, 2017), https://www.bbc.com/persian/iran-features-40662792.

64 Kambiz Fattahi, "*Kodetay 28 Mordad: 'Sorat Hesab Majera'*" [The August 19, 1953 Coup: "The Bill for the Event"], BBC Persian, (August 20, 2018), https://www.bbc.com/persian/iran-45253663; and Kambiz Fattahi, "*Payam Makhfiyaneh Abolghassem Kashani Beh Eisenhower*" [Secret Message from Abolghassem Kashani to Eisenhower], BBC Persian, (February 14, 2018), https://www.bbc.com/persian/iran-features-43053577.

65 Kambiz Fattahi, "*Kodetay 28 Mordad: 'Sorat Hesab Majera'*" [The August 19, 1953 Coup: "The Bill for the Event"], BBC Persian, (August 20, 2018), https://www.bbc.com/persian/iran-45253663.

66 Kambiz Fattahi, "*Kodetay 28 Mordad: Farziyha Dar Mored Sanad Hazineh-ha*" [The August 19, 1953 Coup: Assumptions on the Document on the Costs], BBC Persian, (August 24, 2018), https://www.bbc.com/persian/iran-45300129.

67 I use the term "fundamentalist regime" for "*Nizam Velayat Faqih.*" The literal translation would be the "system of rule by a high-ranking Shia cleric." I use the term "fundamentalist oligarchy" to refer to those who supported Khomeini's interpretation of Islam and were officials in the post-June 1981 regime. Please see Chapter 5 for details.

Nouri (the highest-ranking cleric and an opponent of the Constitutional revolution), and support for the Fadaian Islam.[68] These facts gradually come out after 1979.

CIA, Iranian Nazis, and the Coup

In addition to the far-right Islamic forces, the CIA also mobilized *Hezb SUMKA* [Nationalist Socialist Workers Party of Iran], Iran's Nazi Party.[69] According to Abrahamian, "...the CIA worked through local Nazis, and had a direct role in kidnappings, assassinations, torture, and mass street killings."[70] The Leader of SUMKA was Davood Monshizadeh and the leader of its youth section was Dariush Homayoun.[71] Monshizadeh had attended university in Germany in the late 1930s and early 1940s. He had joined the Nazi Party of Germany and worked closely with the SS. Hitler was attempting to mobilize Iranians (as well as Arabs and Turks) against the United Kingdom. Nazi Germany invested greatly in gaining support from Iranians including establishing Radio Berlin with daily broadcasts in Persian. Germany assisted Reza Shah Pahlavi to build ammunition and armament factories, air force, railroad, and the like. In August 1941, the U.K. and the USSR invaded Iran and replaced Reza Shah (who was slowly moving away from the U.K. and establishing close relations with Nazi Germany) with his son Mohammad Reza Shah Pahlavi, after Reza Shah refused to heed the British ultimatum to expel (about 400) German military and intelligence officers and advisers from Iran.

The Germans had cultivated close connections with several high-ranking military officers including Gen. Fazlollah Zahedi. The British kidnapped Gen. Za-

---

68 Ali Asghar Haj Seyyed Javadi, "Interview," Harvard University, Iranian Oral History Project, Paris, (March 1, 1984), https://curiosity.lib.harvard.edu/iranian-oral-history-project/catalog/32-hajiseyd-djavadi__ali-asghar01; and Ali Asghar Haj Seyyed Javadi, *"Beh Dalil Sansoor, Mardom Va Roshanfekran Ma Az Tarh Ayatollah Khomeni Baray Ijad Velayat Faghgih Agahi Nadashtand"* [Because of Censorship, Our People and Intellectuals Did Not Know About Ayatollah Khomeini's Plan for Rule of the Clerics], Radio France International, (September 19, 2017), see the bibliography for the hyperlink.

69 Abrahamian, "The 1953 Coup in Iran," *Science & Society*, Vol. 65, No. 2 (Summer 2001), pp. 184, 206.

70 Ibid., p. 184.

71 Gooya News, "Pictures of the Nazi Junta of Homeland," (June 7, 2021), http://onenewsbox.com/2021/06/06/pictures-of-the-nazi-junta-of-homeland/; and http://onenewsbox.com/2021/06/06/pictures-of-the-nazi-junta-of-homeland/2/.

hedi and took him to their military prison in mandatory Palestine. Stephen Kinzer writes:

> Zahedi shared Reza Shah's view of what Iran needed. Both men were soldiers at heart, strong, harsh and ambitious. When World War II broke out, both sought to help the Germans. After the British deposed Reza Shah and forced him into exile, they focused on Zahedi. They identified him as a profiteer who was making huge sums from grain hoarding, but would have left him to his devices had it not been for his close connections to Nazi agents. When they discovered that he was organizing a tribal uprising to coincide with a possible German thrust into Iran, they decided to act... In 1942, the British kidnapped Zahedi from Isfahan and interned him in a British prison in Palestine.[72]

After WWII, Gen. Zahedi developed close ties with the British. The SUMKA Party was established in 1952 and had close connections with Gen. Zahedi. SUMKA was a monarchist party. It organized its storm troopers *"Grohhe Hamleh"* [Attack Group], which violently attacked members of the INF and the Tudeh Party.[73] Monshizadeh and Homayoun were put on trial, during Mossadegh's government, for their violent assaults on non-violent political activists. It is widely believed that between 1952 and 1958, the Shah had secretly provided funds for the SUMKA.[74]

Gen. Zahedi became prime minister after the coup. Dariush Homayoun was given several top positions by the Shah including Minister of Information and Tourism, editor-in-chief of *Ayandegan* daily (third largest newspaper before the revolution), and Deputy Secretary General of the Rastakhiz Party. After the revolution, Homayoun established the *Hezb Mashrooteh Iran* [Constitutional Party of Iran].[75]

A famous and influential Iranian Nazi was Shah Bahram Shahrokh.[76] He was the famous Berlin Radio's Farsi program announcer during the Nazi rule. His programs were approved by Joseph Goebbels. After WWII, he became close to the British and was put on British payroll. Shahrokh became Director of the Office of Propaganda in Iran after WWII. He was an active participant of the 1953

---

72 Stephen Kinzer, *All the Shah's Men: An American Coup and the Roots of Middle East Terror* (Hoboken, New Jersey: Wiley, 2003), pp. 142, 143 – 144.
73 Ibid, also see http://onenewsbox.com/2021/06/06/pictures-of-the-nazi-junta-of-homeland/5/.
74 Ibid, also see http://onenewsbox.com/2021/06/06/pictures-of-the-nazi-junta-of-homeland/6/.
75 Dariush Homayoun, "Interview," Harvard University, Iranian Oral History Project, Washington, DC, (1983), audio available at https://www.youtube.com/watch?v=CDsAu4tGVwA; and https://www.youtube.com/watch?v=pJZMu9nnDwo. Homayoun married Gen. Zahedi's daughter, Homa.
76 Fatemeh Mozi, "Shah Bahram Shahrokh," Institute for Iranian Contemporary History, (no date), http://www.iichs.ir/s/1102.

coup against Mossadegh. As reward, Gen. Zahedi made him the Director-General of the Hamedan dam after the coup.[77]

Jafaar Sharif-Imami, was arrested and jailed by the Allies in September 1941 for his pro-Nazi activities in the 1940s. The Shah gave Sharif-Imami several positions after the 1953 coup, including Secretary General of the Oil Industry, President of the Senate for 15 years, President of the Pahlavi Foundation, and Prime Minister (twice).[78]

Iran After the Coup

With the coup, the Shah was restored to an absolutist dictator and Iran's oil was given to a consortium of oil companies with 40% for the British Petroleum, 14% for the Royal Dutch Shell (co-owned by Britain and the Netherlands), 40% for American companies (five largest American oil companies each getting 8%), and the remaining 6% went to French oil company (Total).[79] These eight oil companies constituted the so-called "Seven Sisters" (seven largest oil companies in the world) plus Total. Today these companies are referred to as "Supermajors" and "Big Oil." In this deal, *de facto* control of Iran's oil was given to the consortium and the profits were to be shared 50 – 50, but Iran was not allowed access to records (e.g., production, sales). The agreement was for 25 years (1954 – 1979) and gave exclusive rights to Iran's oil to the consortium.[80] In 1973, the Shah signed another agreement with the consortium. The 1973 agreement was for 20 years (1973 – 1993) and the number of oil companies was increased. The Shah's official propaganda declared this agreement to have finally achieved *de facto* nationalization of Iran's oil.[81] The substantial increase in Iran's oil income in 1974 was not due to this agreement but rather due to the Arab oil boycott which resulted in the four-fold increase in the price of oil as well as the fact that while Arab oil

---

77 Ibid.
78 Sharif-Imami, Jafaar. "Interview," Harvard University, Iranian Oral History Project, Washington, D.C., (1982–1983), audio available at https://www.youtube.com/watch?v=tY_Zwn2m4YY; https://www.youtube.com/watch?v=r5dOUss8UmY; and https://www.youtube.com/watch?v=v4F_Awza_80.
79 Mary Ann Heiss, "The United States, Great Britain, and the Creation of the Iranian Oil Consortium, 1953–1954," *The International History Review*, Vol. 16, No. 3 (August 1994), pp. 511–535; and Keyvan Husseini, "*Sarnevesht Naft Iran Baad Az Kodetay 28 Mordad Cheh Shod?*" [What Happened to the Iranian Oil After the 1953 Coup?], Radio Farda, (August 12, 2014), https://www.radiofarda.com/a/fk_downfall_e41/25429849.html.
80 Keyvan Husseini, [What Happened to the Iranian Oil], ibid.
81 Ibid.

producers were boycotting oil exports, the Shah continued to export oil to the West.[82] According to Ervand Abrahamian, these agreements were *de facto* abolition of the 1951 oil nationalization. Abrahamian argues that Iran's oil was under the control of the consortium until 1979, when the provisional government abolished the Shah's agreements with the consortium.[83] The companies constituting the consortium sued Iran at the World Court, and the World Court ruled in favor of Iran and against the companies in November-December 1990.[84]

INF Government's Achievements and Failures

Although the coup defeated the INF, one may mention major achievements of the INF. Mossadegh was prime minister for about two years and four months between April 1951 and August 19, 1953, with the exception of five days in July 1952 when Mossadegh resigned when the Shah did not agree to allow him to choose the Minister of Defense as stipulated by the Constitution (the Shah was choosing the Minister of Defense in violation of the Constitution). The Mossadegh period witnessed the freest period for the press in Iran's history. This is the only period that not a single political critic was executed, a stark contrast with both the Islamic Republic and the Shah's regime that were responsible for killings of opponents. The INF government is the only period that the government respected the basic rights of all political parties from the far-right (e.g., monarchists, Nazi SUMKA Party, and Fadaian Islam) to the far-left (e.g., Communist Tudeh Party).

The very first land reform was carried out by the INF cabinet. During the INF government, Iran's state universities were given autonomy and independence from the government in their leadership. Faculty members would choose college deans, and then college deans would choose university presidents.[85] Under the monarchy, the Shah would choose the university president, and under the Islamic Republic, the president does so. During the INF government, *Kanon-e Vokala-e Dadgostari* (Lawyers Association) was established as an independent professional association and its rights were fully respected.[86] For the first time in Iran,

---

82 Ibid.
83 Ibid.
84 Ibid.
85 Hussein Moussavian, "Interview with Radio Asr Jadid, Part 5," (December 29, 2018), https://melliun.org/iran/192128.
86 Ibid.

Mossadegh's government established the Social Security Organization in order to provide health insurance and retirement programs for the workers.[87] Mossadegh's cabinet also drafted a bill enfranchising women, the first time that a cabinet had done so in Iran. Mossadegh had to postpone submitting it to the Majles due to vociferous opposition by Ayatollah Behbahani and Grand Ayatollah Brujerdi.[88]

On the Nature of the Shah's Regime

The Iranian people, by and large, considered the Shah to be a puppet of the U.S. and the British. This was also the view of the INF and virtually all the opposition parties and groups. Declassified British and U.S. government documents vindicate the view of the Shah as being subservient to the interests of the British and the United States.[89] For example, a British Foreign Office document from May 1953 discussing a report sent to them by the U.S. State Department on the Shah and the situation in Iran contains the following message from the Shah:

> The State Department informed us today on a number of occasions associates of the shah have told Henderson that His Majesty is uncertain about the British attitude towards himself. He is reported to be harping on the theme that the British had thrown out the Qajar Dynasty, had brought in his father and had thrown his father out. Now they could keep him in power or remove him in turn as they saw fit. If they desired that he should stay and that the Crown should retain the powers given to it by the Constitution, he should be informed. If on the other hand they wished him to go, he should be told immediately so that he could leave quietly....
>
> On May 17 the Shah sent an emissary to Henderson to say that it would do much to clarify the situation if the ambassador could ascertain secretly and unequivocally the British attitude towards him.[90]

---

87 Hussein Moussavian, *"Goftego Ba Rooznameh Kar Va Kargar"* [Talking With Labor and Laborers Newspaper], *Kar Va Kargar* (August 16, 2020), http://jebhemeliiran.org/?p=2169; and Katouzian, *Musaddiq and the Struggle*, pp. 128 – 129.

88 Katouzian, ibid., pp. 129 – 130.

89 Mark J. Gasiorowski, *U.S. Foreign Policy and the Shah: Building a Client State in Iran* (Cornell: Cornell University Press, 1991); Kazemzadeh, "The CIA Coup in Iran"; and Ladjevardi, "The Origins of U.S. Support for an Autocratic Iran."

90 For the copy of the document see: Karim Sanjabi, *Omid-ha Va Naomidi-ha: Khaterat Siasi Doktor Karim Sanjabi* [Hopes and Disappointments: Political Memoirs of Dr. Karim Sanjabi], (London: Jebhe National Movement of Iran, 1989), http://jebhemeliiran.org/wp-content/up loads/2015/09/Ebook-Sanjabi.pdf, p. 449. Henderson is the name of the U.S. ambassador to Iran. The date of the document is May 1953.

Upon the election of Jimmy Carter to the U.S. presidency, the Shah is reported to have said to one of his confidants, "It looks like we are not going to be around much longer."[91] In the Shah's view, he had to do what the U.S. wanted him to do. The Shah believed that the revolution was orchestrated by the U.S. and or Britain although he had been loyal to both the United States and Britain. When in 1979 the Shah was at a New York hospital for treatment of his cancer, Richard Helms the former Director of the CIA (1966–1973) and ambassador to Iran (1973–1977), paid him a visit. Helms writes in his memoirs: "His [the Shah's] bitterness was apparent. He could not understand why the United States had abandoned him… the ashen Shah asked, 'Why did you do this to us?'"[92]

Interviews with the Shah's top officials show that the Shah was subservient to the interests of the U.S. and the British.[93] According to Dr. Nahavandi, one of the Shah's top advisers in 1978, the U.S. wanted the Shah to leave. Nahavandi says that the Shah took what the American and British ambassadors said over what his own top advisers and officials recommended to him.[94] The Shah had a history of doing what the American officials told him to do. This was the case in 1953 coup as well as during 1978–1979 revolutionary period. As soon as the CIA orchestrated coup failed on August 16, 1953, the Shah left for Baghdad. In Baghdad he asked to meet the U.S. Ambassador. In a top secret telegram that he sends to Washington, American ambassador describes his conversation with the Shah.

---

91 Ahmad Ashraf and Ali Banuazizi, "The State, Classes and Modes of Mobilization in the Iranian Revolution," in *State, Culture and Society*, Vol. 1, No. 3 (1985), p. 4.
92 Richard Helms and William Hood, *A Look Over My Shoulder: A Life in the Central Intelligence Agency* (New York: Random House, 2003), https://books.google.com/books?id=TWDDd58cd TIC&pg=PT595&lpg=PT595&dq=His+bitterness+was+apparent.+He+could+not+understand +why+the+United+States+had+abandoned+him%E2%80%A6+the+ashen+Shah+asked,+%E2% 80%98Why+did+you+do+this+to+us+Richard+Helms&source=bl&ots=JurvpePEJH&sig=AC fU3U0KSPj_jXCCaum6tqarlP5hNXoD8g&hl=en&sa=X&ved=2ahUKEwjIz_qCOuX uAhVEXK0KHZ0vAKQQ6AEwAHoECAgQAg#v=onepage&q=His%20bitterness%20was%20appa rent.%20He%20could%20not%20understand%20why%20the%20United%20States%20had% 20abandoned%20him%E2%80%A6%20the%20ashen%20Shah%20asked%2C%20%E2%80% 98Why%20did%20you%20do%20this%20to%20us%20Richard%20Helms&f=false.
93 See the views of Houshang Nahavandi in "*Goftogo Ba Houshang Nahavandi*," BBC Persian, (February 2, 2012), http://www.bbc.com/persian/tvandradio/2012/02/120126_hardtalk_housh ang_nahavandi. Nahavandi was a senior adviser to the Shah and the Chief of the Office of Empress Farah Diba Pahlavi. See the views of Parviz Raji in Parviz Raji, "BBC Interview," BBC Persian, via You Tube, (February 23, 2010), https://www.youtube.com/watch?v= 1GSN8wrXn7U. Raji was Iran's ambassador to the U.K. under the Shah.
94 See the views of Nahavandi in ibid.

The Shah said that he is utterly at loss to understand why the plan failed. Trusted Palace officials were completely sure of its succeeding. The American friend was absolutely confident of its success. When he had said to the American if it should fail what should he do, the American scouted the possibility of failure adding when pressed, that the Shah should go to Baghdad. The Shah said that is why he came to Baghdad when the plan miscarried. Now he needs information and advice upon his next move.[95]

The INF and Mossadegh After the Coup

The Shah wanted to humiliate, discredit, and destroy Mossadegh after the coup. So, he decided to put Mossadegh on a public show trial with charges of treason and apostasy with punishment of execution. The Shah had badly miscalculated Mossadegh's character. Mossadegh turned the situation around and put the Shah and the coup plotters on trial.[96] Mossadegh was Iran's leading constitutional lawyer, a great orator, and had a superb sense of humor. Moreover, Mossadegh was truly brave, a personality character that he had demonstrated throughout his life. For example, Mossadegh had spoken out against Reza Shah and publicly opposed his becoming king in 1925, for which he was threatened with death and spent many years in jail. During the military trial, Mossadegh systematically attacked the Shah and the British colonialist policies in Iran. Mossadegh defended the legitimacy of the pro-democracy struggle for Iran's independence.[97] The presiding judge was a general with little knowledge of the law and very poor public speaking abilities. The military prosecutor was not much better than the judge. Mossadegh mocked and admonished the judge and the prosecutor. Colonel Bozorgmehr was Mossadegh's court-appointed military lawyer. Bozorgmehr did a highly effective job in defending Mossadegh, so much so that Mossadegh chose him to represent him at the appeals trial. Bozorgmehr was forced

---

95 U.S. government, Department of State, "Report from U.S. Ambassador in Baghdad to Department of State," (August 17, 1953), https://enghelabe-eslami.com/component/content/article/21-didgagha/tarikhi/34507-2019-08-15-17-19-41.html. The American friend that the U.S. ambassador refers to appears to be Kermit Roosevelt, the CIA Middle East station chief, who had gone to Tehran to convince the Shah to go along with the coup.

96 Colonel Jalil Bozorgmehr, *Mossadegh Dar Mahkameh Nezami* [Mossadegh at the Military Trial], Vol. 1, (Entesharat Nehzat Moghavemat Melli Iran, no date), http://jebhemeliiran.org/wp-content/uploads/2015/09/Mosadegh_Dar_Mahkameh_1.pdf; and Jalil Bozorgmehr, *Mossadegh Dar Mahkameh Nezami* [Mossadegh at the Military Trial], Vol. 2, (Entesharat Nehzat Moghavemat Melli Iran, no date), http://jebhemeliiran.org/wp-content/uploads/2015/09/Mosadegh_Dar_Mahkameh_2.pdf.

97 Ibid.

into retirement right after the appeals trial. He kept the trial documents for many years and then published them in three books.[98] His books on the trials have become classics of modern Iranian history and politics.

Mossadegh's trial cemented his status as the statesman valiantly struggling for Iran's rights and the Shah as an illegitimate puppet of foreign powers for vast segments of the population. Ever since the trial, excerpts of Mossadegh's defense have been repeatedly re-published as inspiration for and by the pro-democracy activists in Iran. Mossadegh was sent to prison for three years and placed under house arrest for the rest of his life.

According to Kermit Roosevelt, the Shah wanted to try, condemn to death and then either execute Mossadegh or murder him. In a secret message he sent to Washington, Roosevelt wrote:

1. The Shah has decided that former Prime Minister Mossadeq must be tried and condemned to death, but he has not decided whether Mossadeq should then be pardoned by royal decree and immediately banished from Iran or executed.

2. The Shah believes that any delay in disposing of Mossadeq, following the trial, would invite Tudeh (and pro-Mossadeq) counter-attack under a slogan such as "Save Mossadeq's Life".

3. In the event of a Tudeh move (see paragraph 2 above) prior to sentencing Mossadeq the Shah has ordered that Mossadeq be killed immediately by his guards.[99]

Dr. Hussein Fatemi, foreign minister in Mossadegh's cabinet, was number two in the INF after Mossadegh. He was a prolific writer, bright, and courageous.[100] He was the youngest foreign minister Iran has ever had. Fatemi was executed by the Shah.[101] Before being executed, Fatemi was knifed by Shaaban "*Bi-Mokh*" Ja-

---

98 Hamid-Reza Mosaiebian, *Sarhang Jalil Bozorgmehr* [Colonel Jalil Bozorgmehr], (Kermanshah, Iran: 2016), https://melliun.org/yaranmos/y06/08/12bozorgmehr.htm.
99 U.S. Government, Kermit Roosevelt, (October 2, 1953), https://enghelabe-eslami.com/component/content/article/21-didgagha/tarikhi/39146-2020-08-15-17-17-06.html. The information on to whom the telegram was sent to is redacted after declassification. It was probably sent to the CIA, the National Security Council, or the White House.
100 Hussein Fatemi, *Neveshteh-hay Makhfigah Va Zendan: 28 Mordad 1332 – 19 Aban 1333* [Writings from the Hideout and Prison: 19 August 1953 – 10 November 1954], (London: Daftar-hay Azadi, 2004), https://melliun.org/v/wp-content/uploads/2017/06/yaddasht-haye-dr.-Fatemi.pdf; and Hussein Fatemi, *Khaterat Va Mobarezat Doktor Hussein Fatemi* [Memoirs and Struggles of Dr. Hussein Fatemi], collected by Bahram Afrasiabi, (Tehran: Entesharat Sokhan, 1987).
101 Hamid-Reza Mosaiebian, *Dr. Hussein Fatemi* (Kermanshah, Iran: 2015), https://melliun.org/v/wp-content/uploads/2015/11/Fatemi_Dr-Hosein_940819_96.pdf.

faari in an apparent attempt to murder him, but his sister throwing herself between Fatemi and Shaaban saved his life.[102]

Amir Mokhtar Karimpour-Shirazi, the famous pro-Mossadegh journalist (who had published scathing criticisms of the Shah's dictatorship and Pahlavi family corruption) was arrested, severely tortured, and was set ablaze by pouring kerosene on him and burned alive.[103] Captain Mahmoud Sakhaee, a pro-Mossadegh officer and chief of police of Kerman, was beaten to death by the monarchists after the coup because he refused to condemn Mossadegh.[104] Abdol-Ali Lotfi, Minister of Justice, was murdered by monarchists.[105]

Mossadegh's government as well as the actions and words of Mossadegh, Fatemi, Karimpour-Shirazi, Sakhaee, and other INF members after the coup established massive political capital for the INF. Until the preset day, the INF enjoys a status that no other political party enjoys in Iran.

After the coup, there were no freedoms of expression, press, political parties, or elections. The Shah's secret police, SAVAK, arrested and severely tortured dissidents. Opponents were executed and assassinated by the Shah's regime. The Shah and his family were corrupt. The Pahlavi kings stole private properties of the people and from the state treasury.[106]

The resistance to the coup began the day after the coup.[107] The four political parties constituting the INF along with many individual supporters created the

---

102 Ibid.

103 Hamid-Reza Mosaiebian, *Amir Mokhtar Karimpour Shirazi* (Kermanshah, Iran: 2016), https:// melliun.org/v/wp-content/uploads/2016/12/karimpour-shirazi.pdf; Fariba Marzban, *"Chengonegi Koshteshodan Roozname-negar Tarafdar Nehzat Melli, Amir Mokhtar Karimpour Karimpour Shirazi"* [How Was Amir Mokhtar Karimpour Shirazi, the Pro-Nationalist Journalist, Killed], Melliun, (February 2012), https://melliun.org/iran/80940. Karimpour Shirazi was the publisher of *Shuresh*. This newspaper is archived at: https://luna.manchester.ac.uk/luna/servlet/view/search?q=shurish&search= SUBMIT&QuickSearchA=QuickSearchA&sort=title%2Cmediafilename%2Cidentifier&pgs=50&res= 1&cic=Manchester%7E18%7E18.

104 Hamid-Reza Mosaiebian, *Sargord Mahmoud Sakhaei* [Captain Mahmoud Sakhaei] (Kermanshah, Iran: 2016), https://melliun.org/v/wp-content/uploads/2016/08/sargord-sakhaei.pdf; Sheyda Mosadegh, *"Shahid Rah Azadi, Sargord Seyyed Mahmoud Sakhaee"* [Martyr on the Path of Freedom, Captain Seyyed Mahmoud Sakhaee], (June 29, 2013), http://www.drmosa degh.blogsky.com/1392/04/08/post-15/; and Parviz Davarpanah, *"Takhrib Maghbareh Sargord Mahmoud Sakhaee Afsar Shaheed Jebhe Melli Iran"* [Destruction of the Tomb of Captain Mahmoud Sakhaee the Martyred Officer of the Iran National Front], Iran Liberal, (October 5, 2008), http://www.iranliberal.com/Maghaleh-ha/EXtra/Davar_Sakhaie.htm.

105 Abrahamian, *Iran Between Two Revolutions*, p. 280.

106 Keddie, *Roots of Revolution*, pp. 149, 172, 178, and 180.

107 Khosrow Seif, *"Chegoonegi Tashkil Nehzat Moghavemat Melli Va Nameh 3 Emzae"* [How the National Resistance Movement Was Established and About the Letter Signed by 3], Melliun,

underground organization the *"Nehzat Moghavemat Melli"* (National Resistance Movement). The organization declared its three principles and published an underground paper called *Rah-e Mossadegh* (Mossadegh's Path). It's three principles were: (1) continuation of the nationalist movement, restoration of Iran's independence, and establishment of popular sovereignty; (2) struggle against any form of foreign imperialism; and (3) struggle against all governments [in Iran] that are puppets of foreign countries.[108]

The INF 1961–1964

The popularity of the INF was on display as soon as the Shah reduced repression briefly between 1961 and 1963. Under pressure from the Kennedy administration, the Shah appointed Dr. Ali Amini prime minister. Amini asked the INF for support and offered several cabinet posts. The INF refused the cabinet offer and instead demanded free elections for the parliament. The INF called its supporters to attend a rally on May 18, 1961 at Jalalieh Field (currently called Park-e Laleh) in Tehran. According to reliable sources somewhere between 80,000 and 120,000 people attended the INF rally.[109]

The INF leaders reorganized the organization, which became known as "the Second National Front." Between 1960 and 1964, more than 20,000 individual filled INF membership forms and officially became members throughout Iran. In December 1962, the INF held its first Congress. The INF members throughout Iran elected their delegates to the INF Congress held in Tehranpars section of Tehran. The Congress was formed by the 170 elected members. It met for seven day from December 25, 1962 to January 1, 1963. The delegates in the congress then elected INF leaders (members of the Central Committee and Executive Committee). Among those elected to the central committee were two females: Parvaneh Eskandari-Forouhar and Dr. Homa Darabi.[110] This is the

---

(November 2020), https://melliun.org/v/wp-content/uploads/2020/11/chegunegi-tashkil-nehzat-moghavemat-melli.pdf.

108 Ibid.

109 Abdol Hussein Azarang, *"Jebhe Melli Iran, Bozorgtarain Eatelaf Nirohayeh Siasi Iran Dat Tarikh Moaser Iran Ta Pish Az Enghelab Islami 1357"* [Iran National Front, the Largest Coalition of Political Forces in Iran's Contemporary History Until the Islamic Revolution of 1979], Encyclopedia Islamica (no date), https://web.archive.org/web/20150318064343/http:/www.encyclopaediaislamica.com/madkhal2.php?sid=4503.

110 Parvaneh Eskandari-Forouhar was murdered by the agents of the Ministry of Intelligence in November 1998. Dr. Homa Darabi self-immolated in a public thoroughfare in 1990 in protest against compulsory hejab. Dr. Darabi received her M.D. from the University of Tehran Medical

first time in Iranian history that a political party had chosen females in its leadership. Several conservative delegates objected and considered it un-Islamic to have females in leadership. They threatened to walk out. Those who had been elected as leaders unanimously said that these are the elected members by the Congress. About three delegates walked out. Ayatollah Reza Zanjani, a delegate, did not support the three, and remained a delegate at the Congress. Among the members of the INF Congress were many future leaders: Dr. Shapour Bakhtiar, the last prime minister under monarchy; Mehdi Bazargan, the first prime minister after the overthrow of the monarchy; and Dr. Abol-Hassan Bani Sadr, the first elected President of Iran.[111] The Congress passed resolutions demanding return to constitutional rule, free democratic elections for the parliament, land reform, female franchise, and a literacy campaign to drastically increase literacy among the population.

Soon after securing the support of the U.S., the Shah dismissed Amini and appointed Assadollah Alam as his prime minister. Alam entered into negotiations with the INF and offered it several cabinet posts and the power to administer the elections for the parliament in Tehran, Tabriz, Isfehan, Mashhad, and Yazd. The INF refused the offer and made three demands: (1) the Shah respect and abide by the constitution; (2) allow free elections for parliament all over Iran; and (3) the Shah should not interfere in those areas that the constitution states that he does not have the authority to engage in.[112]

The INF policy was to support the substance of reforms while opposing the Shah's dictatorship. The reforms that had been imposed on the Shah by the Kennedy administration included land reform, female franchise, and changing of the oath for taking high office from the Koran to a holy book (which would have allowed Zoroastrians, Jews, Christians, and Baha'is to also assume high offices).[113] The turning point came in January 1963. The Shah was holding a refer-

---

School and her psychiatry from the U.S. She was a professor of psychiatry at the University of Tehran. She was a member of the Iran Nation Party. She was fired from her position at the university under the pretext that she was not fully observing the rule on compulsory hijab. Moreover, she was constantly harassed by the fundamentalist regime. See https://ir.voanews.com/persiannewsiran/iran-human-rights-hijab-homa-darabi; and https://www.radiozamaneh.com/258707.

111 Bani Sadr was a student member of the INF between 1960 and 1964. He was one of the student leaders who had organized university students and was elected by them to the Congress. Moussavian, Hussein. "Interview," Radio Farda, (October 9, 2021), https://www.radiofarda.com/a/31501122.html.

112 Ibid.

113 Willem Floor, "The Revolutionary Character of Iranian Ulama: Wishful Thinking or Reality?" *International Journal of Middle East Studies*, Vol. 12, No. 1 (December 1980), pp. 501 – 524.

endum on January 26, 1963 on the reforms. On January 23, the INF released a short statement that became known as "Reforms Yes, Dictatorship No" statement.[114] This became the INF slogan on the Shah's referendum. On January 26, the INF released an analytical statement (about five pages).[115] It harshly criticized the Shah's dictatorship and his subservience to colonial powers. It re-stated the INF's long-standing demand for land reform.[116] The Shah responded by unleashing the SAVAK on the INF. More than 150 top leaders and members of the INF were arrested. Many were in jail for months without any court verdict.[117] From 1963 until 1978, harsh and brutal repression became the Shah's policy.

Khomeini who had been a supporter of the system of monarchy and the Shah, opposed these reforms.[118] Khomeini issued fatwas declaring female franchise and land reform to be against Sharia law.[119] In June 1963, after a fiery speech by Khomeini, many angry conservative religious supporters protested in many cities. The Shah put down the protests with violence killing several dozen. Many right-wing Islamic groups that had supported the Shah and the coup in 1953 sided with Khomeini in June 1963, among them Ayatollah Mohammad Taghi Falsafi.[120] The INF did not support Khomeini's uprising.

---

114 Jebhe Melli Iran, *"Bayanieh Jebhe Melli Iran Dar Bareh Enqelab Sefid Va Hameh-Porsi Enqelab Sefid 6 Bahman 1341"* [Statement of the Iran National Front on the White Revolution and the Referendum on January 26, 1963], (January 23, 1963), https://melliun.org/iran/195488. My translation of the full text is available in Part II of this book.

115 Jebhe Melli Iran, *"Bayanieh Jebhe Melli Iran Dar Bareh Enqelab Sefid Va Hameh-Porsi Enqelab Sefid 6 Bahman 1341"* [Statement of the Iran National Front on the White Revolution and the Referendum on January 26, 1963], (January 26, 1963), https://melliun.org/iran/195488.

116 See my translation of excerpts of the statement in Part II of this book.

117 Jebhe Melli Iran, *"Bayanieh Tarikhi Jebhe Melli Iran Dar Bareh Enqelab Sefid Va Hameh-Porsi Enqelab Sefid 6 Bahman 1341"* [The Historical Statement of the Iran National Front on the White Revolution and the Referendum on January 26, 1963], (January 26, 2019), https://melliun.org/iran/195488.

118 Floor, "The Revolutionary Character of"; and Abrahamian, *Khomeinism*, pp. 8–11.

119 Floor, "The Revolutionary Character of." The text of Khomeini's fatwa and telegram against female franchise are available at Jamshid Barzegar, *"Hagh Ray Zanan: Az Fohasha ta Hefz Islam"* [Female Franchise: From Prostitution to Protection of Islam], BBC Persian, (July 15, 2014), https://www.bbc.com/persian/iran/2014/07/140715_l10_jb_women_vote.

120 Ayatollah Mohammad Taghi Falsafi, *"Khaterat Ayatollah Mohammad Taghi Falsafi"* [Memoirs of Ayatollah Mohammad Taghi Falsafi], Tarikh Shafai Iran, Markaz Asnad Enghelab Islami, https://www.youtube.com/watch?v=GeVYbNqNIIA (posted on You Tube November 11, 2019).

Chapter 3
INF Parties

The INF has been and is a coalition of parties, civil society organizations, and individuals. University student groups, labor unions, and professional associations have joined it. It acts both as a single party and as a coalition of parties. Some of the parties that are or have been part of the INF include: Iran Party, Third Force Party, Socialist Party of Iran, Iran Nation Party, Iran People Party, and Iran Liberation Movement.

Iran Party

The main pillar of the INF has been the *Hezb Iran* (Iran Party). The Iran Party is Iran's oldest pro-democracy party. The Iran Party was officially established in 1944, but its roots go back to 1941. Among its founders were Dr. Karim Sanjabi, Ahmad Zirakzadeh, and Nezamoldin Movahed.[121] Several small social democratic parties coalesced in the early 1940s and created the Iran Party. One of them was the *Hezb Mihan* (Country Party) under the leadership of Dr. Karim Sanjabi. Most of Iran Party leaders may be described as social democrats or liberal democrats.[122] For the 14th Majles elections (1943–1944), five members of the Iran Party were elected to the parliament.[123] In addition, the party was the major supporter of Mossadegh, who also got elected to the parliament. Among its leaders have been Dr. Allahyar Saleh, Dr. Shapour Bakhtiar, Dr. Karim Sanjabi, Nezamoldin Movahed, and Ahmad Zirakzadeh.[124]

---

121 Iran Party, *"Zendegi-nameh Siasi Ahmad Zirakzadeh"* [Political Biography of Ahmad Zirakzadeh], (no date), https://hezbeiran.com/?p=111; and Iran Party, *"Zendegi-nameh Siasi Nezamaldin Movahed"* [Political Biography of Nezamaldin Movahed], (no date), https://hezbeiran.com/?p=125.

122 Sanjabi, *Omid-ha Va Naomidi-ha*, pp. 63–72.

123 Abrahamian, *Iran Between Two Revolutions*, p. 190.

124 Ahmad Zirakzadeh, "Interview," Harvard University, Iranian Oral History Project, Arlington, Virginia, U.S., (May 1986), https://curiosity.lib.harvard.edu/iranian-oral-history-project/catalog/32-zirakzadeh__ahmad01; Iran Party, *"Zendegi Siasi Ahmad Zirakzadeh"* [Political Life of Ahmad Zirakzadeh], (no date), https://hezbeiran.com/?p=111; Seyyed Morteza Moshir, *Khaterat Allahyar Saleh* [Memories of Allahyar Saleh], (Tehran: Vahid Publishers, 1985), https://hezbeiran.com/wp-content/uploads/2020/09/%D8%AE%D8%A7%D8%B7%D8%B1%D8%A7%D8%AA-%D8%A7%D9%84%D9%87%DB%8C%D8%A7%D8%B1-%D8%B5%D8%A7%D9%84%D8%AD.pdf; Iran Party, *"Zendegi-nameh Siasi Allahyar Saleh"* [Political Biography of Allahyar Saleh], (no

https://doi.org/10.1515/9783110782158-005

The Iran Party has a website.[125] Its main slogan has been *"Kaar, Dad, Azadi"* [Work, Justice, Liberty]. Since the passing of Nezamoldin Movahed, its last Secretary-General, in 2006, the Iran Party has not chosen a Secretary-General. Since then, its leadership has been collective and it will continue to be so until there would exist a minimum of freedom to hold a congress or plenum to elect one.[126]

The Iran Party commemorated the 77th anniversary of its founding on May 20, 2021.[127] The program was conducted online due to Covid-19 pandemic. Members of the Iran Party and the INF participated in that event and gave speeches about the Iran Party's current policies. Ms. Firouzeh Soghian criticized the *de jure* and *de facto* discriminations against women under the fundamentalist regime. Another member, Masoud Salehi, criticized foreign policy of the fundamentalist regime as undermining the national interests of Iran. Another member, Mohammad Asadi, criticized *de jure* and *de facto* discriminations against various ethnic and religious minorities by the fundamentalist regime and called for juridical equality of all Iranians.[128]

Third Force Party and the Socialist Party of Iran

The *Hezb Niroyeh Sevvom* (Third Force Party) was a major component of the INF. The Third Force Party was a Marxian democratic socialist group, and its leader was Khalil Maleki. Many of Iran's preeminent intellectuals have been members of this group. They include Ali Asghar Haj Seyyed Javadi, Dr. Mansour Farhang, Dariush Ashoori, Dr. Mohammad Ali Homayoun Katouzian, and Dr. Amir Pishdad.[129] Dr. Mohammad Maleki and Abbas Amir-Entezam were also members of the Third Force Party.[130]

---

date), https://hezbeiran.com/?p=120; and Iran Party, *"Zendegi-nameh Siasi Nezamaldin Movahed"* [Political Biography of Nezamaldin Movahed], (no date), https://hezbeiran.com/?p=125.

125 See https://hezbeiran.com/.

126 See the Iran Party's statement at https://hezbeiran.com/?p=170.

127 Iran Party, *"Marasem 77 Salgard Taasis Hezb Iran Beh Sorat Majazi Bargozar Shod"* [The Commemoration of the 77th Anniversary of the Founding of the Iran Party Was Conducted Online], (May 20, 2021), https://hezbeiran.com/?p=441.

128 Ibid.

129 Dariush Ashoori, "Interview," with Ali Limonadi, IRTV, (June 25, 2021), https://www.youtube.com/watch?v=UeXIOEqFyLU; Amir Pichdad, "Interview," Harvard University, Iranian Oral History Project, Le Chesnay, France, (March 3, 1983), https://curiosity.lib.harvard.edu/iranian-oral-history-project/catalog/32-pichdad__amir01, audio available at https://www.youtube.com/watch?v=XbjDOKtUdJk; https://www.youtube.com/watch?v=jAzCjtl5NeQ; and https://www.youtube.com/watch?v=LJF57jSDtGw.

Several days before the 1953 coup, the Third Force Party split into two groups.[131] A smaller group remained with Khalil Maleki and chose the name *"Jameeh Socialistha"* [Society of Socialists].[132] They continued to consider themselves Marxist and were highly critical of Stalinism and the Soviet Union.[133] A larger group under the leadership of Dr. Mohammad Ali Khonji and Dr. Masoud Hejazi chose the name *"Hezb Socialist Iran"* [Socialist Party of Iran].[134] They considered themselves social democrats. In 1961, the Socialist Party of Iran dissolved itself and told its members to join the INF as individual members and make the INF a strong party. Khonji and Hejazi served as members of INF Central Committee and Executive Committee.

Iran Nation Party (INP)

A right-of-center nationalist group called *Hezb Mellat Iran* (Iran Nation Party) under the charismatic leadership of Dariush Forouhar joined the INF in 1949.[135] According to Khosrow Seif, the INP began as a nationalist party and had little knowledge of political systems and ideologies. However, under the influence of Mossadegh's teachings and policies, the INP embraced democracy and

---

130 Dr. Mohammad Maleki became the first president of Tehran University after the revolution. He bravely opposed the repressive policies of the fundamentalists and spent many years as a political prisoner in Evin prison. His dictum was *"Ze gahvareh ta goor, azadi bejooy"* [From cradle to grave, seek liberty]. His actions matched his words. He endured great abuse and mistreatment at the hands of the fundamentalist security forces for his support of political prisoners and human rights lawyers. He passed away on December 1, 2020. On Amir-Entezam, see Chapter 8.
131 The official publications of the Third Force Party are available at https://luna.manchester. ac.uk/luna/servlet/view/search;JSESSIONID=be513680-fea9-4647-9d63-ebab86b2ebdd?q=title% 3Dniru%20AND%20%3D%D8%A7%D8%B1%DA%AF%D8%A7%D9%86%20OR%20%D8%AD %D8%B2%D8%A8%20OR%20%D8%B2%D8%AD%D9%85%D8%AA%DA%A9%D8%B4%D8% A7%D9%86%20OR%20%D9%85%D9%84%D8%AA%20OR%20%D8%A7%D9%8A%D8%B1% D8%A7%D9%86%20LIMIT%3AManchester%7E18%7E18&sort=title%2CmediafileName%2Ci dentifier&pgs=50&res=1&cic=Manchester%7E18%7E18.
132 Khalil Maleki, *Khaterat Siasi, Ba Moghademe Mohammad Ali Homayoun Katouzian* [Political Memoirs, with introduction by Mohammad Ali Homayoun Katouzian], (Hannover, West Germany: 1981); and Homa Katouzian, *Khalil Maleki: The Human Face of Iranian Socialism* (London: Oneworld Academic, 2018).
133 Ibid. and Pichdad, "Interview," op. cit.
134 Masoud Hejazi, *Roydadha Va Davari, 1329–1339: Khaterat Masoud Hejazi* [Movements and Judgment, 1950–1960: Memoirs of Masoud Hejazi], (Tehran: Niloufar, 1997).
135 For a large number of primary documents on Darisuh Forouhar, Parvaneh Eskandari-Forouhar, and the INP, see https://www.forouharha.net/.

freedom.[136] Although in 1979, the INP split from the INF, the two parties neverthe-less cooperate very closely, attending each other's rallies, conferences, funerals, and programs. The top two leaders of the INP, Dariush Forouhar and his wife Parvaneh Eskandari-Forouhar, were murdered by the Ministry of Intelligence agents in 1998 in their home in Tehran. In the largest protest since June 1981, large crowds participated in their public funeral. The estimate of the protesters is somewhere between 50,000 and 100,000. In response to the outrage, the re-gime arrested Deputy Minister of Intelligence, Saeed Imami (aka Saeed Islami) for organizing the murders. It is believed that the murders were ordered by the Supreme Leader Khamenei and authorized by the Minister of Intelligence Dorri Najafabadi. The regime claims that Imami committed suicide in prison. It is be-lieved that he was murdered in order to silence him because he had begun talk-ing and revealing a large number of assassinations and explosions that the Min-istry of Intelligence had carried out.

The secretary-general of the INP is Khosrow Seif. Before he was murdered, Dariush Forouhar and the INF were engaged in negotiations for the INP to rejoin the INF. The two INF officials responsible for the negotiations were Dr. Hussein Moussavian and Hassan Lebaschi.[137]

Iran People Party

A group that attempted to combine Islam and socialism also joined the INF. This group included thinkers such as Mohammad Nakhshab, Dr. Ali Shariati, and Hussein Razi. The current name of the group is *Hezb Mardom Iran* (Iran Peo-ple Party) and is a member of the INF.[138] In the early 1950s, the party was called "*Khoda-parastan Socialist*" (God-worshiping Socialists), and published a paper called *Mardom Iran* (The People of Iran).[139]

---

136 Personal interview with Khosrow Seif, Los Angeles, 2004.

137 Hussein Moussavian, "Interview with Radio Asr Jadid, Part 4," (November 25, 2018), https://melliun.org/iran/188055.

138 Personal interview with Hussein Razi, San Jose, California, 2002.

139 The papers are available at https://luna.manchester.ac.uk/luna/servlet/view/search?q= Mardum-i+Ir%C4%81n&search=SUBMIT&QuickSearchA=QuickSearchA&sort=title%2Cmediafile Name%2Cidentifier&pgs=50&res=1&cic=Manchester%7E18%7E18.

Iran Liberation Movement (ILM)

Mehdi Bazargan who had been a member of the INF, established the *Nehzat Azadi Iran* (Iran Liberation Movement) in 1961. The ILM was briefly part of the INF, but soon split from it in 1961.[140] Another founder of the ILM was Ayatollah Mahmoud Taleghani. Members of the ILM attempted to articulate a modernist and liberal interpretation of Islam. They did politicize Islam but were not clear exactly what their goals were. Bazargan primarily wanted to show that Islam was compatible with science and democracy. However, it was never clear did Bazargan or the ILM want a secular political system and the ILM similar to Christian Democratic parties in Western Europe or did they want an Islamic political system.

In June 1963, ILM supported Khomeini's uprising against the Shah's reforms in contrast to the INF, which did not support Khomeini's position. During the revolution (1977–1981), the ILM was a close ally of the INF. There were also several top members of the ILM who although practicing Muslims, wanted a secular political system. These included Abbas Amir-Entezam and Hassan Nazih.[141] Amir-Entezam left the ILM and joined the INF in early 1990s.

After Bazargan's death and the assumption of ILM's leadership by Ibrahim Yazdi, the ILM moved away from the INF and became more and more reactionary and close to the fundamentalist regime. Many pro-democracy activists have criticized Yazdi for his reactionary policies saying that during his leadership of the ILM, the party became like a moat around the fundamentalist regime providing it with protection. After Yazdi's death, Mohammad Tavasoli has become the secretary-general of the ILM.

---

140 Houchange Chehabi, *Iranian Politics and Religious Modernism: The Liberation Movement of Iran Under the Shah and Khomeini* (Ithaca, NY: Cornell University Press, 1990).
141 Hassan Nazih, "Interview," Harvard University, Iranian Oral History Project, Paris, (April 3, 1984), https://curiosity.lib.harvard.edu/iranian-oral-history-project/catalog/32-nazih__hassan01, audio available at https://www.youtube.com/watch?v=B6uqIUHeMqs; https://www.youtube.com/watch?v=6chtiCr3Hr0; and https://www.youtube.com/watch?v=9rxR17G7qDE.

Chapter 4
The INF and the Revolution, 1977–1979

Many scholars consider the beginning of the Iranian Revolution to be the famous open letter written by three leaders of the INF to the Shah that was released on June 12, 1977.[142] More than 20,000 copies of the letter were distributed.[143] The politely worded letter was signed by Dr. Karim Sanjabi, Dr. Shapur Bakhtiar, and Dariush Forouhar. In early May 1977, a number of individuals including Sanjabi, Bakhtiar, Forouhar, Mehdi Bazargan, Dr. Sahabi, Hassan Nazih, and Ayatollah Reza Zanjani met to discuss what should be done. They made the decision to write an open letter to the Shah. Each wrote what they thought should be in the letter. Nazih was given the responsibility to put all the points into one letter. Bazargan wanted the letter to be signed by a large number of activists (e.g., 40–50). Sanjabi, Bakhtiar, and Forouhar wanted the letter to be signed by only a handful (e.g., 5 or so). Because of this disagreement, no action was taken for about four weeks. Finally, in early June, they asked Bazargan again to sign the letter. After Bazargan refused, the three INF leaders published the letter.[144] After this letter, the Shah unleashed a campaign of terror against the INF.

The Shah sent about 300 SAVAK agents in plainclothes to beat up INF members when they had gathered at a private garden called Bagh Golzar in Karvansarae Sangi in the outskirts of Tehran on November 22, 1977. SAVAK agents broke the windows of the building, severely damaged about 300 autos of the attendees in the parking lot. About thirty were seriously injured and were taken to hospitals. SAVAK agents broke Abdul-Karim Anvari's hip and knee, broke Bakhtiar's elbow, and bludgeoned Forouhar's head.[145] According to Dr. Mehrdad Arfazadeh, the plainclothes security forces were dressed as workers. They scaled the walls of the garden and systematically beat up the INF members. The regime claimed that

---

142 Ahmad Ashraf and Ali Banuazizi, "The State, Classes and Modes of Mobilization in the Iranian Revolution," in *State, Culture and Society*, Vol. 1, No. 3 (1985), pp. 3–40; Abrahamian, *Iran Between Two Revolutions*, pp. 496–529.

143 My translation of excerpts of the letter are available in Part II in this book. The full text in Persian is available at http://jebhemeliiran.org/?p=2101.

144 Khosrow Seif, "*Chegoonegi Tashkil Nehzat Moghavemat Melli Va Nameh 3 Emzae*" [How the National Resistance Movement Was Established and About the Letter Signed by 3], Melliun, (November 2020), https://melliun.org/v/wp-content/uploads/2020/11/chegunegi-tashkil-nehzat-moghavemat-melli.pdf.

145 Abdul-Karim Anvari, *Talash Baray Esteghlal: Khaterat Siasi* [Struggle for Independence: Political Memoirs] (London: Self-Publication, 2015), pp. 173–74. Anvari's injuries have been so severe that even today after 42 years, he has to walk with clutches.

https://doi.org/10.1515/9783110782158-006

the workers were upset that the INF members were drinking vodka on *Eid Fitr*. Arfazadeh added that the intension of the Shah was to intimidate the INF. According to Arfazadeh, the Shah's tactics did not work, and made the INF leaders become more determined to struggle against the regime.[146]

After President Carter praised the Shah profusely on December 31, 1977 at the New Year's Eve party in Niavaran Palace in Tehran,[147] the Shah's campaign of terror against the INF became more violent. On April 8, 1978, SAVAK, the Shah's secret police, bombed the homes and offices of Sanjabi, Dariush Forouhar, Mahmoud Manian as well as several close to INF such as Mehdi Bazargan.[148] SAVAK also bombed the homes and offices of other liberals close to the INF such as Dr. Matin-Daftari, Dr. Hassan Nazih, Dr. Abdol-Karim Lahiji, and Moghadam Maraghei.[149]

The Shah considered the liberal democrats of the INF and the Marxist left to be the main dangers to his regime and underestimated the significance of the right-wing Shia clerics (who had been his allies until June 1963). In July 1978, when asked by the press if he would be willing to negotiate with the secular opposition, the Shah rejected any such possibility and said that the INF was "even more traitorous than the Tudeh party."[150] Although the INF and ILM were the major parties organizing the people against the Shah during the early stages of the revolution (June 1977-August 1978), Khomeini and his supporters gradually gathered more support and eclipsed them.

Due to a variety of reasons, such as the brutal violent repression by the Shah in killing thousands of peaceful protesters and President Carter's public support for the Shah, the masses became more radicalized which increased the support for Khomeini and undermined the support for the INF. Moreover, the Shah ordered his cabinet to the reduce the inflation rate. The government orchestrated a mild recession by cutting government spending in order to reduce the inflation rate. The Shah was unwilling to cut military spending; therefore, the bulk of the cutbacks were in construction. This policy caused mass unemployment among construction workers – many of whom were recent migrants from rural areas

---

146 Personal interview with Dr. Mehrdad Arfazadeh, London, February 1995.
147 Andrew Glass, "Carter lauds shah of Iran, Dec. 31, 1977," Politico, (December 30, 2018), https://www.politico.com/story/2018/12/30/this-day-in-politics-december-31-1077103.
148 Azarang, *"Jebhe Melli Iran, Bozorgtarain."*
149 Abrahamian, *Iran Between Two Revolutions*, p. 508. Also see Hassan Nazih, "Interview," Harvard University, Iranian Oral History Project, Paris, (April 3, 1984), https://curiosity.lib.harvard.edu/iranian-oral-history-project/catalog/32-nazih__hassan01. All these individuals had been strong supporter of Dr. Mossadegh and had been a member of or close associate of the INF.
150 Abrahamian, *Iran Between Two Revolutions*, p. 508.

and were living in shanty towns in the outskirts of Tehran and other major cities – and sent them in to the streets with no state unemployment protection. This large and angry mass, with no previous political experience and hostile to the extravagance and the conspicuous consumption lifestyles of the Shah, his family, and his regime's nouveau riches base, became attracted to Khomeini's message of returning to the golden age of tradition and justice that Islam promises.

By September 1978, the Shah's policies allowed Khomeini to gain the upper hand in the opposition. By increasing political repression of the INF, the Shah further angered the modern middle classes who cared far more about political freedom and democracy than a few percentages off the inflation rate. The modern middle classes were the social base of the INF, and their opposition to the Shah was primarily political. By increasing unemployment among the recent migrants to the cities, the Shah further swelled the ranks of the right-wing traditional religious opposition, who until then were primarily comprised of Shia clerics (and their families) and the traditional (and religious) lower middle classes in small towns (what Marxists call traditional petite bourgeoisie).

The monarchy was overthrown on February 11, 1979. While in Paris, Ayatollah Khomeini promised freedom and democracy and declared that he would not accept any political power and that clerics would not become president. But soon after arriving in Tehran, he went back on his promises and established a dictatorship far more reactionary and brutal than that of the Shah's. Between October 1978 and early 1979, the INF leadership was split on what to do.

There were only a handful of individuals in mid-1978 who believed that Khomeini was reactionary, dictatorial, and dangerous. One was Dr. Gholam-Hussein Sadighi. A second individual was Dr. Shapour Bakhtiar.[151] A Sociology professor at the University of Tehran, Dr. Sadighi was considered the father of sociology in Iran. He had served in Mossadegh's cabinet as Minister of Interior. According to one of his students, during a lecture around 1977, one of his students named Mahdavi (who became a fundamentalist after the revolution), asked him why he was giving his usual lectures instead of talking about the revolution and joining the Shia clerics in the movement.[152] Professor Sadighi stops his lecture, and responds:

---

151 Shapour Bakhtiar, "Interview," Harvard University, Iranian Oral History Project, Paris, (March 7, 1984), audio also available at You Tube at: https://www.youtube.com/watch?v=t47-vBeVsdo; and https://www.youtube.com/watch?v=K2XP_uqjGDg. A large number of Dr. Bakhtiar's speeches are available at a Facebook account established by his supporters: https://www.facebook.com/ShapourBakhtiar/.

152 Mirzasen (pseudonym). "*Goftegoy Daneshjo Va Ostad*" [Dialogue Between Student and Professor], (May 2010), https://melliun.org/iran/204968.

Mr. Mahdavi, freedom and justice have not been the outcome of revolutions, revolutions are like civil wars, that when one side defeats the other side, the winning side represses the defeated side and then it will also represses any person who opposes them or criticizes them in order to eliminate them because with revolution neither justice is created nor there is the possibility of liberty, especially if the leaders of that revolution are the Shia clerics and their troops are the Muslim people of Iran, then the worst revolution in the world would occur. Mr. Mahdavi, do you know that if the gentlemen that you named, that is the Shia clerics, were able to capture the state, what would they do? I say that what the [atrocities] Arabs and the Mongols did [to Iran], these clerics would do all of those [atrocities].[153]

The Shah intensely hated the INF and spent much of June 1977 to mid-October 1978 repressing the INF. According to Abbas Milani, only after the Americans and the British told the Shah in late October or early November 1978 that he should negotiate with the INF and ask them to form a government did the Shah begin thinking of opening negotiations with the INF.[154]

On behalf of the INF, Dr. Sanjabi was invited to attend a meeting of the Socialist International (a group comprised of social democratic and socialist parties such as the Labour Party of the UK, Social Democratic Party of West Germany, Socialist Party of France) in Canada. At that time, Khomeini was in Paris. With approval of the INF, Sanjabi decided to stop in Paris and hold a meeting with Khomeini.[155] Sanjabi canceled his trip to the Socialist International and stayed in Paris. Along with several other INF members in Paris, Sanjabi wrote a brief 3-Point Declaration and after approval from colleagues in Tehran, he took it with him to the meeting with Khomeini. On November 5, 1978, the 3-Point Declaration was signed by Sanjabi.

Shortly after he arrived back in Tehran, there was a press conference at Sanjabi's house. Before the press conference, the Shah's security forces arrested Sanjabi and Forouhar in Sanjabi's house for threatening national security.[156] They

---

153 Ibid. My translation.

154 Dr. Abbas Milani is a political scientist. He is the Head of Iranian Studies at Stanford University.

155 Some have said that Sanjabi had made that decision by himself and without approval of the INF. Abdul-Karim Anvari clearly shows that Sanjabi had full support of the INF before, during, and after the Paris meeting and the 3-Poiny Declarations had the support of all the INF leadership. Anvari, *Talash Baray Esteghlal: Khaterat Siasi* [Struggle for Independence: Political Memoirs] (London: Self-Publishing, 2015), pp. 234 – 237.

156 For a video of the arrest, see Karim Sanjabi, "AP Video of the Arrest of Dr. Sanjabi and Dariush Forouhar at their Press Conference," (November 1978), Dr. Karim Sanjabi Facebook page, (2019), https://www.facebook.com/274402532665234/videos/375129523314074.

were taken to a prison for about a week. Then, they were sent to a luxurious SAVAK house in northern Tehran for about one month.[157]

The Shah entered negotiations with Sadighi to form a government. According to Sadighi, Dr. Ali Amini and Abdollah Entezam went to see Sadighi and told him that the Shah would like to meet with him and is interested in discussing the possibility of him forming a government.[158] Sadighi agrees to meet with the Shah. At the meeting, Sadighi criticizes the Shah for his actions against the INF and democracy. The Shah replies that he is willing to fully abide by the constitution and asks Sadighi to think about his conditions for forming a government. Sadighi agrees to think about his conditions and there is a second meeting between the Shah and Sadighi, when Sadighi presents his conditions.[159] First, he would take the post of prime minister after a vote from the Majles in order to revive the tradition of constitutionalism. Second, the Shah had to abide by the original 1906 Constitution and not the (anti-democratic) amendments that the Pahlavi kings had imposed to increase their powers such as dismissing parliament at will. Third, a regency council would be appointed to be in Tehran. Fourth, the Shah should not leave the country (where he could remain in clandestine contacts with his supporters to organize a coup). Rather, the Shah should go to place in Iran such as the Kish island for a while and would remain in constant contact would be with representatives from the government (to make certain that he would not engage in anti-constitutional conspiracies). When Sadighi was telling the Shah about this condition, the Shah said: "You want to control me."[160] Sadighi replies: "My intention is to prevent misunderstandings."[161] According to Sadighi: "If the Shah went outside the country it would not be possible to prevent his contacts and conspiracies. But if it was possible to do so if the Shah was inside the country, particularly if there was a group from the government that was in constant presence with him."[162] Fifth, the end of martial law as well as prosecution of those involved in crimes and corruption in the previous 25 years. The Shah did not call Sadighi back. Shortly afterwards, it was an-

157 Sanjabi, *Memoirs*, op. cit. p. 302.
158 Gholam-Hussein Sadighi, *"Chera Nokhost-vaziri Ra Napaziroftam?"* [Why Did Not Accept Becoming Prime Minister?], *Omid Iran* Weekly, (January 28, 1979), http://tarikhirani.ir/fa/news/4926.
159 Ibid.
160 Ibid.
161 Ibid.
162 Ibid.

nounced that Bakhtiar had accepted the Shah's offer to become prime minister.[163]

Sadighi had not informed other INF leaders and had not been attending INF meetings. The INF published a letter by Sanjabi to Sadighi informing him of the INF opposition to him forming the cabinet.

The Shah also entered negotiations with Sanjabi. Sanjabi told the Shah that his condition for accepting to become prime minister was that the Shah should leave Iran for a short period and that he would talk with Khomeini and gain his support as well. The Shah told Sanjabi that his condition to leave Iran is not acceptable.[164] Finally, the Shah entered negotiations with Dr. Bakhtiar several weeks later. Bakhtiar's conditions were that the Shah leave Iran briefly and that he would go to the Majles and take the oath of office to the 1906 constitution. The Shah accepted Bakhtiar's conditions.[165] Bakhtiar accepted the Shah's offer without informing or getting the consent of the INF. The INF expels Bakhtiar from the INF. Sadighi publicly supported Bakhtiar.[166]

A small group under the leadership of Bakhtiar believed that Khomeini was lying and that he would establish a theocratic dictatorship that would be far worse than the secular dictatorship of the Shah; he therefore, accepted to serve as the Shah's prime minister.[167] His government lasted 37 days. The majority of the INF leadership trusted Khomeini's words and joined the Provisional Government. The INF members constituted about one-third of the cabinet. However, the INF resigned after 60 days in protest against the violations of human rights committed by Khomeini and his associates such as kidnapping two sons of Ayatollah Taleghani as well as unfair trials, lack of due process, and summary executions of alleged monarchists, monarchists, and others.[168] Sadighi re-joined the INF after Sanjabi resigned from the post of foreign minister in April 1979.

---

163 Ibid.
164 Sanjabi, *Memoirs*, op. cit., pp. 306–310.
165 Shapour Bakhtiar, *37 Rooz Paas Az 37 Saal* [37 Days after 37 Years] (Los Angeles: Radio Iran Press, 1982), https://melliun.org/nehzat/n05/37rouz.htm.
166 Gholam-Hussein Sadighi, *"Mosahebeh Ba Etellaat 27 Dey 1357: Mardom Vatanparast Keshvar Beh Hemayat Az Bakhtiar Barkhizand"* [Interview with Daily *Etellaat* January 17, 1979: Patriotic People of the Country Should Support Bakhtiar], Melliun, (January 19, 2014), https://melliun.org/iran/34996.
167 Ibid.
168 Karim Sanjabi, "Video of Resignation from the Provisional Government," (April 1979), Dr. Karim Sanjabi Facebook page, (2019), https://www.facebook.com/274402532665234/videos/320665275317710.

It is necessary to emphasize that the Shah never agreed to abdicate. He only agreed to leave Iran for a brief vacation. In fact, the Shah never abdicated the throne. And after his death in exile in Egypt, his son, Reza Pahlavi, took a public oath as the next Pahlavi king. The monarchists have been struggling to restore the Pahlavi monarchy.

Chapter 5
The Struggle against Khomeini and the Fundamentalist Regime 1979 – 2021

Resistance to Khomeini's Dictatorship

The so-called *"Bahar Azadi"* [Spring of Freedom] after the overthrow of the Shah's dictatorship did not last long. During the brief interlude between the monarchist and fundamentalist dictatorships, the people expressed their desire for democracy, freedom, and secularism. In one of the largest gatherings in Iran's history, people went to Mossadegh's residence and grave on March 5, 1979, the 12th anniversary of Dr. Mossadegh death, to pay their respect. The INF estimates the number of the people to be around one million. The fundamentalists had not consolidated their power yet.

The INF opposed the fundamentalist constitution because of its terribly anti-democratic features such as imposing a Shia cleric as the Supreme Leader with dictatorial powers. The INF regards the fundamentalist regime as dictatorial, ultra-reactionary, and extremist. As early as May 1979, the INF leaders condemned the fundamentalist regime as reactionary and fascistic. Many INF leaders and intellectuals close to it consider the fundamentalist regime to be similar to European fascism of 1920s-1945. These intellectuals and leaders include Dr. Karim Sanjabi, Ali Asghar Haj Seyyed Javadi, Dr. Mansour Farhang, and Dr. Mehdi Mozaffari.

Sanjabi was among the original founders of the INF in 1949, the number one leader of INF during the revolution, and the former Dean of the College of Law and Political Science at the University of Tehran.[169] In the words of Dr. Sanjabi:

> We believe that a monopolizing and reactionary force is taking shape in this country. This force cannot ignore and deny Iran's past history. It cannot negate Mossadeq or the significance of the oil nationalization movement.... Accusations and intimidations are the mani-

---

169 Karim Sanjabi, *"Jebhe Melli Iran Ba Mellat Sokhan Migooyad"* [Iran National Front Speaks to the Nation], (November 24, 1980), https://melliun.org/v/wp-content/uploads/2019/09/baya nie-dr.-sanjabi-azar-1359.pdf; Masoud Kazemzadeh, "The Perils and Costs of a Grand Bargain with the Islamic Republic of Iran," *American Foreign Policy Interests*, Vol. 29, No. 5 (2007), pp. 301–327.

https://doi.org/10.1515/9783110782158-007

festations of this fascist and reactionary tendency. The National Front of Iran has the responsibility of resisting reaction and dictatorship.[170]

When it was announced that the Assembly of Experts had written a constitution giving Shiite clerics monopolistic powers, the INF issued a strongly worded 10-page analysis. The document repeatedly calls the system "religious dictatorship," and repeats the earlier warning about the emerging "fascism." The document states:

> Individual and social liberties and rights that have been the goals of the revolution have to be respected in practice. Today, all of these liberties are in serious threats, and our country is being taken towards a form of fascism. The offices of political parties and societies have been attacked and shot down. Such meetings have also been attacked and closed down. Safety and security of political and social activities of other groups have been eliminated.[171]

Haj Seyyed Javadi was a member of the Third Force Party and a prolific author whose articles were published at the INF paper during the first two years after the revolution. His famous "*Seday Paye Fashism*" [Sounds of Fascism's Steps] articles were among the first that publicly stated that Khomeini and his supporters were introducing fascism in Iran.[172] Farhang was a member of the Third Force and a professor of political science at Bennington College. He is currently an emeritus professor there. Mozaffari was a political science professor at the University of Tehran. He was a supporter of INF. During the revolution, he supported Dr. Bakhtiar. He left Iran and later became Chair of the Political Science Department at Aarhus University in Denmark. He is currently an emeritus professor there.[173]

Although the INF and many of its intellectuals were the first to consider the fundamentalist regime to be a form of fascism, many other Iranian political par-

---

170 *Peygham-e Emrouz* (31 May 1979), translated and cited in Ali Rahnema and Farhad Nomani, *The Secular Miracle: Religion, Politics and Economic Policy in Iran* (London: Zed Books, 1990), pp. 200, 232.
171 Jebhe Melli Iran, "*Nazar Jebhe Melli Iran dar bareh Shoraha va Majles Khobregan: Majles Khobregan bayad dar tasmimat khod betore asasi tajdid nazar konad*" [The Perspective of the Iran National Front on the Councils and the Assembly of Experts: The Assembly of Experts Has to Make Fundamental Changes in its Decisions] (Aban 1358) [October 1979]. My translation.
172 Ali Asghar Haj Seyyed Javadi, "*Ghool-e Fashism Dar Hal-e Tasalot Bar Iran Ast*" [The Fascist Monster is gaining Control Over Iran], (February 1981), republished in Mihan, (January 29, 2018), http://mihan.net/1396/11/09/1330/; and Ali Asghar Haj Seyyed Javadi, "*Seday Paye Fashism*" [Sounds of Fascism's Steps], (February 5, 1981), republished at Radio Zamaneh (July 1, 2018), https://www.radiozamaneh.com/401640.
173 Mehdi Mozaffari, *Islamism: A New Totalitarianism* (Boulder: CO: Lynne Rienner, 2017).

ties and groups have also come to the same analysis.[174] The Iran Liberal Organization regards the fundamentalist regime, "fascist."[175] The Workers Communist Party of Iran also calls the regime "fascist."[176] By and large, the parties that considered the fundamentalist regime to be a form of fascism tended to be Marxist (e. g., United Left Council for Democracy and Independence, Organization of Communist Unity, Worker's Path) or liberal democrat (e. g., National Movement of Iranian Resistance).[177]

The INF strongly opposed the anti-democratic, repressive, and reactionary policies of Khomeini and his supporters. First, when in April 1979, Khomeini ordered the dismissal of all female judges, the INF was the only party in Iran that publicly opposed and condemned the move as reactionary. The INF invited the people to attend a public rally at the University of Tehran on May 2, 1979 to oppose the firing of all female judges and restrictions on female lawyers.[178] The INF also condemned the fundamentalists' compulsory rules on how women should dress in public.[179]

Second, when in August 1979, Khomeini condemned the non-fundamentalist press and ordered the closing of *Ayandegan* daily, the INF was one of the few par-

---

174 Kazemzadeh, "The Perils and Costs."

175 See the analyses of two of the founders and leaders of Liberal Democrats of Iran: Hassan Behgar, "*Jojeh Fashistha Sar Az Tokhm Dar Miavarand!*" [Fascist Chicks Are Hatching], (July 3, 2005), www.iranliberal.com/Maghaleh-ha/Hassan_Behgar/jojeh.htm; and Ramin Kamran, "*Bohrani Ke Dar Raah Ast,*" [The Upcoming Crisis], www.iranliberal.com/Maghaleh-ha/Ramin_Kam ran/051123_Ahmadi_W_2_RaminK.htm.

176 See the article by one of its top leaders Hamid Taqvaee, "Round Two of The Election Puppet Show in Iran," (June 22, 2005), www.wpiran.org/English/wb183%20round%20two%20of% 20election%20show%20in%20Iran%20HT.htm.

177 The United Left Council for Democracy and Independence (*Shora-y Motehad Chap Baray Democracy Va Esteqlal*) was established in the early 1980s. Its views were close to the New Left, the Frankfurt School, and socialist feminism. Its leaders included Bahman Niroumand, Kambiz Rousta, Parvin Paidar (aka Nahid Yeganeh), and Mehdi Khanbaba Tehrani. The Organization of Communist Unity (*Sazeman-e Vahdat Kommonisti*) was established in 1979. Its views were close to council communism and Rosa Luxemburg. The Worker's Path (*Rah-e Kargar*) was a traditional Marxist-Leninist group, but in many ways it was less extreme and more thoughtful than other traditional leftists. Its leader has been Mohammad Reza Shalgooni. See BBC Persian, "Liberalism" (July 21, 2011), https://www.youtube.com/watch?v=PeK28o6HyIA. National Movement of Iranian Resistance (*Nehzat-e Moghavemat Melli Iran*) was established by Dr. Bakhtiar in 1979.

178 Azar Tabari and Nahid Yeganeh, *In the Shadow of Islam: The Women's Movement in Iran* (London: Zed Press, 1982), pp. 227–228.

179 Ibid., pp. 141–142.

ties that publicly condemned the order and called upon the people to oppose this dictatorial move.

Third, when the fundamentalist students invaded and took over the U.S. Embassy on November 4, 1979, the INF was the sole party in Iran that publicly opposed and condemned the embassy takeover and taking its personnel as hostage. Even the ILM, whose leaders had resigned from the Provisional Government, issued a statement strongly supporting the fundamentalist students taking over the U.S. embassy. Virtually all parties in Iran had strongly supported the U.S. embassy takeover.

Fourth, the INF strongly opposed and condemned the fundamentalist constitution as reactionary and anti-democratic. It called for mass protests against the fundamentalist constitution in December 1979.

Fifth, the INF presented its list of candidates for the Majles elections in March 1980. Several members won their constituencies: Dr. Karim Sanjabi (Kermanshah), Dr. Ali Ardalan (Toysirkan), Dr. Ahmad Madani (Kerman), Abolfazl Qassemi (Dargez), and Mohammad Nasser Qashqaee (Shiraz). None was allowed to take his seat. The fundamentalists threatened that if they showed up at the Majles, they would be killed. It is also believed that Kazem Hasibi won in Tehran but due to fraud, his votes were not counted. Only Ahmad Salamatian (Isfehan) was allowed to take his seat probably because he was also the head of President Bani Sadr's Office in Isfehan.[180] After the dismissal of President Bani Sadr in June 1981, the fundamentalists captured all powers in their own hands and went after all the non-fundamentalists. Sanjabi and Madani escaped Iran and passed away in the United States. Ardalan was arrested in 1989–90 and severely tortured. He suffered two heart attacks under torture. He passed away in Iran. Mohammad Nasser Qashqaee left Iran and passed away in the U.S. in 1984.[181] His brother Khosrow Qashqaee was executed by firing squad and then his corps was hanged in public in the Qashqaee region. Salamatian has escaped Iran and currently lives in France.

Sixth, in June 1981, the INF publicly criticized and condemned the Bill of Retribution as inhumane, reactionary, misogynist, and oppressive. The INF called upon the people to attend a mass rally on June 15, 1981 to oppose several bills

---

180 Hussein Moussavian, *"Dar Rooz 25 Khordad 1360 Bar Jebhe Melli Iran Cheh Gozasht? Gozidehee Az Khaterat Dr. Hussein Moussavian Dar Morede Aan Rooz"* [What Happened to the Iran National Front on June 15, 1981? Selections from the Memoirs of Dr. Hussein Moussavian], (June 11, 2016), http://melliun.org/iran/92885.

181 Mohammad Nasser Qashqaee, "Interview," Harvard University, Iranian Oral History Project, Las Vegas, Nevada, U.S., (January 1983), audio available at https://www.youtube.com/watch?v=wuLYQKUGIMO&list=PL-PRP1hqq8eLx_zqkyCtgKws5FpAU84j3.

under consideration at the Majles. On the morning of June 15, Khomeini declared the INF and Dr. Mossadegh (who had passed away in 1967) as apostates.[182] Video footage shows that large numbers of people attended the non-violent peaceful INF rally and that a very large crowd of the Islamic Revolutionary Guards Corps (IRGC) and Basij viciously and violently attacked them with clubs, knifes, and guns.[183]

As time went on, Khomeini and the fundamentalists were becoming stronger. They created the Islamic Republican Party (IRP) as their vehicle for organizing supporters of Khomeini, concentrating all power in their own hands, eliminating the non-fundamentalists, and creating a totalitarian right-wing clerical theocratic regime. They organized and armed their supporters in the IRGC. They also created the *Basij* and plain-cloths club-wielding violent extremists called *Hezbollahis*. One of the main slogans of the fundamentalists between February 1979 and late 1980s was: *"Hezb Faghat Hezbollah, Rahbar Faghat Ruhollah"* [Sole Party Is Party of God, Sole Leader Is Ruhollah].[184]

As the fundamentalists became stronger, Ruhollah Khomeini began eliminating non-fundamentalists one by one. First, they went after the feminists and female judges. Then, the free press. Then, the religious and ethnic minorities. Then, the secular, liberal, and leftist university professors and students. The IRGC, Basij, and Hezbollahis attacked the non-fundamentalists with knifes, clubs, and guns in order to beat up, injure or murder them. The fundamentalists routinely took non-fundamentalist political activists hostage and tortured them. By June 1981, the fundamentalists had murdered many members of the PMOI and Marxist organizations.

Soon after the triumph of the revolution, Khomeini went after the moderate liberal Islamists such as the prime minister of the provisional government Bazargan and the first elected president Bani Sadr.[185] After the elimination of the moderates in June 1981, the fundamentalist regime engaged in wholesale massacres of opponents and political prisoners many of whom were supporters of Bani Sadr, the Islamist leftist People's Mojahedin Organization of Iran (PMOI), and the Marxist left.

---

182 Ibid.

183 You Tube, "Jebhe Melli Iran," https://www.youtube.com/watch?v=JkEcUjqUTlo.

184 During this period, the supporters of the fundamentalist regime were called "Hezbollahis" and Falangists.

185 For an excellent and highly sympathetic book on Bani Sadr see Ali Gharib, *Istad-e Bar Arman* [Standing on Principles], (2006), https://www.enghelabe-eslami.com/pdf/Gharib-Istade-bar-Arman.pdf?fbclid=IwAR2UjiHF0eHH03iyfTbTH6G81gZ8xdnfy6GcJnAHNXEm10wUZ-Iv2knFhAU.

During the First Reign of Terror between June 1981 and December 1982 some-where between 12,000 and 20,000 political prisoners were executed. *The Economist* (October 23, 1982) provided the figure of 12,000 while the higher number was given by opposition groups.[186] Thousands more were killed in armed clashes between the regime and the opposition groups.

During the Second Reign of Terror in August and September 1988, about 5,000 political prisoners were executed.[187] About 4,000 were members and supporters of the PMOI, many of whom teenage boys and girls, who had already gone through unfair trials and given prison sentences. About 1,000 were members of various Marxist groups (who had been born into Muslim families). PMOI prisoners were asked whether they still were supportive of their positions, would they be willing to execute members of the PMOI, or would be willing to walk over mines in minefields. Those PMOI political prisoners who refused to an-swer or gave the "wrong" answer were executed within hours or days. The members of Marxist groups were asked if they believed in god, if they were Muslim, if they believed that the Koran was the word of God. Those who refused to answer or said "no," were considered apostates and were executed within hours or days.[188]

The corpses were buried in unmarked mass graves throughout Iran. These gravesites became known as "*Khavaran.*" The regime has refused to provide de-tails to families about the whereabouts of the corpses of their loved ones. On sev-eral occasions when mass graves were discovered many years later, the regime destroyed the remains. Grieving mothers of the victims have been asking for in-formation about their children. They became known as "*Madaran-e Khavaran*" [Mothers of Khavaran]. Among officials directly responsible are: Ayatollah Ru-hollah Khomeini (Supreme Leader), Ahmad Khomeini (Chief of Staff for Supreme Leader), Ayatollah Abdol-Karim Moussavi Ardabili (Chief of the Judicia Branch), Ebrahim Raisi (a member of the "Death Board" and later Chief of the Judicial

---

186 Ramy Nima, *The Wrath of Allah: Islamic Revolution and Reaction in Iran* (London: Pluto Press, 1983), pp. 115, 158.
187 Paul Lewis, "U.N. Inquiry Says Iran Still Abuses Human Rights," *The New York Times*, (No-vember 19, 1989); and *Iran Times*, (December 7, 1990), p. 1.
188 Geoffrey Robertson, *The Massacre of Political Prisoners in Iran, 1988, Report of An Inquiry*, Abdorrahman Boroumand Foundation, (April 18, 2011), https://www.iranrights.org/library/document/1380/the-massacre-of-political-prisoners-in-iran-1988-report-of-an-inquiry; Amnesty International, *Blood-soaked Secrets: Why Iran's 1988 Prison Massacres Are Ongoing Crimes Against Humanity* (London: 2017), https://www.amnesty.org/download/Documents/MDE139421 2018ENGLISH.PDF, p. 10.

Branch, and President), and Mostafa Pour-Mohammadi (Rouhani's Minister of Justice).[189]

Amnesty International considers the 1988 massacres of political prisoners to constitute "crimes against humanity."[190] Moreover, according to Amnesty International, the regime officials have lied about the massacres or justifies them, refused to give the corpses of those executed to their families or tell them where the graves are, and threatened the families with violence. In September 2020, a U.N. human rights group stated that the 1988 massacre of political prisoners may constitute "crimes against humanity."[191]

The fundamentalists attacked the offices of the INF, ransacked, and took them over.[192] By June 1981, the fundamentalists were discussing a bill in the parliament to dismiss President Bani Sadr.[193] The INF leaders and members knew that they would be a major target soon. They had the option of either ceasing all activities or resist the oncoming violent onslaught. After intense deliberations, the INF leadership decided that they would stand up for their principles.[194] The INF called for a mass protest on June 15, 1981 to protest about four bills under consideration at Majles including the Bill of Retribution.

The Bill of Retribution was a long bill on a range of issues. It had made the punishment of simple theft cutting-off of hands and feet, stoning for adultery, and executions for a number of crimes (including vague crimes of promoting corruption on earth and undermining of the regime). It gave full custody of children (boys after 2 years old and girls after 7 years old) to the father or the paternal grandfather even if the father was in jail for drug dealing and the mother was

---

189 Iran Human Rights Documentation Center, *Deadly Fatwa: Iran's 1988 Prison Massacre* (February 5, 2011), https://iranhrdc.org/deadly-fatwa-irans-1988-prison-massacre/.
190 Amnesty International, *Blood-soaked Secrets: Why Iran's 1988 Prison Massacres Are Ongoing Crimes Against Humanity* (London: 2017), https://www.amnesty.org/download/Documents/MDE1394212018ENGLISH.PDF.
191 U.N. Letter to the Iranian Government (Geneva, Switzerland: September 3, 2020), https://spcommreports.ohchr.org/TMResultsBase/DownLoadPublicCommunicationFile?gId=25503.
192 Moussavian, *"Dar Rooz 25 Khordad."*
193 Although Bani Sadr was not a member of the INF, many INF leaders and members supported him for the presidency. Bani Sadr received over 75% of the votes cast. Dr. Madani, a member of the INF Central Committee, received 15% of the votes. The IRP candidate, Hassan Habibi, received only 4.9% of the votes. Bani Sadr passed away in Paris on October 9, 2021. Stephen Kinzer, "Abol-hassan Bani Sadr, Former Iranian President Dies at 88," *The New York Times*, (October 9, 2021), https://www.nytimes.com/2021/10/09/obituaries/abolhassan-bani-sadr-dead.html.
194 Mehdi Moayedzadeh, *"Dar Daheh Shast Cheh Gozasht?"* [What Happened During the Decade of the 1360s], (June 15, 2007), http://www.melliun.org/didgah/d09/09/05moayadz.htm. This is an official report of the INF. The study was carried out under the direction of Mehdi Moayedzadeh, who was a member of the Executive Committee of the INF.

a fully law-abiding person. It totally disallowed women to be witnesses at courts for first-degree murder. For lesser crimes, the testimony of one male was equal to the testimony of two females. The bill reinstituted polygyny (four permanent wives and unlimited temporary wives) unconditionally. It states that punishment for drinking alcoholic beverages is lashes. It stated that it is permissible to kill anyone who insults the Prophet and the Shia Imams. Khomeini declared that all these were part of Sharia law and the Koran and anyone (who was born a Muslim) who criticizes them is apostate (and thus should be killed).

The INF made the decision the hold its protest rally. On the morning of June 15, 1981, Khomeini made his declaration that the INF and Dr. Mossadegh were apostates. Other groups that had told the INF leaders that they would join, changed their mind on the morning of June 15. The only group that stood by its promise to join the INF protest march was *Hezb Ranjbaran Iran* [Iran Laborers' Party].[195] The non-violent protest was violently suppressed by the fundamentalists.

The number one and two INF leaders, Dr. Sanjabi and Dr. Mehdi Azar, went underground.[196] After living underground for 14 months, Sanjabi was able to escape Iran. Number three and four, Asghar Parsa and Dr. Masoud Hejazi as well as other leaders such as Dr. Parviz Varjavand, Dr. Ali Ardalan, and Manuchehr Etminani were arrested. All were severely tortured. None recanted their support for the INF. Parsa proudly took responsibility for all the policies and positions taken by the INF and was sentenced to death. Despite horrendous torture, he did not recant.[197] Parsa's family took his case to Grand Ayatollah Hussein-Ali Montazeri, who was at that time, the designated successor to Supreme Leader

---

195 The *Ranjbaran* was a Maoist Party. It argued that Iran had a "semi-feudal, semi-colonial" mode of production, the Shah was the representative of comprador bourgeoise, and Ayatollah Khomeini was the representative of reactionary feudalism. The *Ranjbaran* argued that liberal democrats, such as the INF and President Bani Sadr, were representatives of the national bourgeoise. The *Ranjbaran* argued that the main contradiction in Iran was between the reactionary feudalistic dictatorship of Khomeini and the bourgeois democratic opposition by liberal democrats. Because Iran was at the stage of democratic revolution, the *Ranjbaran* argued that the communists should support democratic forces and oppose reactionary feudal forces.

196 Mehdi Moayedzadeh, *"Dar Daheh Shast Cheh Gozasht?"* [What Happened During the Decade of the 1360s], op. cit. Mehdi Azar, "Interview," Harvard University, Iranian Oral History Project, Norfolk, Virginia, U.S., (March 31, 1983), https://curiosity.lib.harvard.edu/iranian-oral-history-project/catalog/32-azar_mehdi01.

197 Moayedzadeh, *"Dar Daheh Shast Cheh Gozasht?."*

Khomeini. Montazeri told the revolutionary judge to give Parsa a fair trial. Parsa was then acquitted and freed.[198]

Among the leaders executed are Khosrow Qashqaee, Haj Karim Dastmalchi (bazaar leader), Haj Ali-Akbar Zahtabchi (bazaar leader), and Manuchehr Masoudi (Bani Sadr's legal adviser).[199] Other top leaders who were jailed are: Houshang Eatesamifar (labor leader), Abolfazl Qassemi, Farhad Aarabi, Hussein Beikzadeh, Abbas Abedi Tajrishi (teachers leader), Mohammad Shahedi (white-collar employees leader), Hassan Khoramshahi (merchants leader), Mehdi Qazanfari (merchants leader), Sadegh Toosi (merchant), Alinaghi Soozani (bazaar), Assadollah Mobasheri, Col. Mojalleli (ret.), Hussein Naeb Husseini, Mohammad Yeganeh (merchant), Samad Maleki (white-collar employees leader). Many others who had gone into hiding were able to escape Iran such as Dr. Azar and Abolghassem Lebaschi.[200] During the so-called "Chain Murders," whereby the Ministry of Intelligence systematically assassinated dissidents, many INF members were killed. Among them was Shamsaldin Amir-Alaee, who was murdered on August 11, 1994. Amir-Alaee had served as Minister of Interior, Minister of Economy, and Minister of Justice in Mossadegh's cabinet.

In a comprehensive study of its policies during the above period, particularly in regard to its policy in June 1981, the INF has officially stated that it believes that its decision to stand up to the fundamentalist regime and continue resistance was the correct policy.[201] In a private conversation, the late Hassan Lebaschi told me that he was very proud of the INF for the decision to stand up to Khomeini and not to retract its views after Khomeini's fatwa against the INF and Dr. Mossadegh. Mr. Lebaschi added that he was proud that Khomeini issued his fatwa against the INF.[202] Mr. Lebaschi was a member of the Central Committee and the Executive Committee of the INF after the revolution. He was also the INF's Spokesman.

----

198 Jebhe Melli Iran. *Asghar Parsa Farzand Delavar Nehzat Melli Iran; Be Hamrah Khaterat Montasher Nashodeh Va Yadnameh Asghar Parsa* [Asghar Parsa the Brave Child of the National Movement of Iran; Along with the Unpublished Memoirs and Remembrances of Asghar Parsa], (October 23, 2019), https://melliun.org/v/wp-content/uploads/2020/06/ketab-asghar-parsa.pdf.
199 Ervand Abrahamian, *The Iranian Mojahedin* (New Haven: Yale University Press, 1989), p. 68.
200 Moayedzadeh, *"Dar Daheh Shast Cheh."* Abolghassem Lebaschi, "Interview," Harvard University, Iranian Oral History Project, Paris, (February 28, 1983), https://curiosity.lib.harvard.edu/iranian-oral-history-project/catalog/32-lebaschi__abolghassem01, audio available at https://www.youtube.com/watch?v=Nn3UeWm8tpY.
201 Moayedzadeh, op. cit.
202 Personal conversation with Hassan Lebaschi at his home in the San Francisco Bay Area, January 2001.

Resistance, Protests, Repression, and the Tipping Point

There have been major pro-democracy protests against the regime in 1999, 2003, 2009 – 2010, December 2017-January 2018, November 2019, and January 2020. Mass protests have become more frequent and more widespread in recent years.[203] With the exception of the mass protests during 2009 – 2010 that were under the leadership of the reformist factions of the fundamentalist oligarchy, all the other protests were by the democratic opponents. Despite mass executions and mass repression, vast number of the people continue to resist.

The fundamentalist regime has been using increasing levels of lethal violence against unarmed protesters to suppress dissent and protests. For example, during November 2019 protests, the regime used direct shots to the heads of protesters and used machine guns to put down peaceful protests. A report from officials stated that about 23% of those who were shot were shot in the head from short distance.[204] The regime has refused to release official numbers but officials have said that about 200 protesters died. Reuters put the numbers of killed at 1,500 and the U.S. government said more than 1,000.[205] A recent scholarly study conducted by three epidemiologists investigating the number of deaths due to Covid-19 looked at the number of registered deaths in each province before and after the Covid-19 epidemic emerged in Iran. Their research shows that during November 2019 the number of registered deaths spiked greatly. There were 4,201 more deaths in November 2019 than those in October 2019. There

---

203 Radio Farda, "Fresh Wave of Protests Starting From Universities Spread to Several Cities in Iran," (January 12, 2020), https://en.radiofarda.com/a/fresh-wave-of-protests-starting-from-uni versities-spread-to-several-cities-in-iran/30373141.html; Masoud Kazemzadeh, "Protests in Iran: Characteristics, Causes, and Policy Ramifications," *Small Wars Journal* (January 3, 2018), http://smallwarsjournal.com/jrnl/art/protests-iran-characteristics-causes-and-policy-ram ifications; Kazemzadeh, "Five Possible Outcomes Following the Mass Protests in Iran," Radio Farda, (February 6, 2018), https://en.radiofarda.com/a/iran-unrest-scenarios-war-revolution-up rising/29023446.html; and Reuters, "Special Report: Iran's leader ordered crackdown on unrest – 'Do whatever it takes to end it'," (December 23. 2019), https://www.reuters.com/article/us-iran-protests-specialreport/special-report-irans-leader-ordered-crackdown-on-unrest-do-whatever-it-takes-to-end-it-idUSKBN1YR0QR.

204 Iran International, "*Vakonesh Magham Dowlati Beh Koshtar Aban Mah*" [Reaction of the Government Official to the Massacre of November 2019], (April 24, 2021), https://www.you tube.com/watch?v=FiNvX16SF1M,

205 Radio Farda, "*Enteshar Amar Marg O Mir Dar Aban 98*" [Publication on the Statistics on Deaths During November 2019], (May 27, 2021), https://www.radiofarda.com/a/31276567.html; Zeitoon, "*Abaad Jadidi Az Koshtar Aban 98*" [New Dimensions of the Massacre of November 2019], (May 27, 2021), https://www.zeitoons.com/87839; and Reuters, "Special Report: Iran's leader ordered crackdown," op. cit.

were 4,902 more deaths in November 2019 than those in December 2019. There were 6,302 more deaths in November 2019 than those in November 2018. All these deaths occurred before the emergence of the epidemic of Covid-19 in Iran in early 2020.[206] An exhaustive scholarly research indicates that no known factor explains the spike in deaths in November 2019.[207] The sole factor during November 2019 was the deaths due to the protests against the fundamentalist regime. These numbers suggest that the number of killed during the November 2019 protests might be somewhere between 4,000 and 6,000.

On the Nature of the Fundamentalist Regime

The fundamentalist regime has not been a one-man dictatorship. Rather, it has been an oligarchy of fundamentalist clerics and lay. The fundamentalist regime that was established after the revolution by Khomeini and his followers is a theocratic oligarchy. It is theocratic because its top rulers have to be Shia clerics. Increasingly, lay fundamentalists – members of the IRGC, who dominate the military, intelligence, and security apparatuses – have become extremely powerful. With exception of Khomeini, who was very old and terribly ill and thus unable to rule personally and had to delegate the day to day running of the regime to his lieutenants, no one person has been able to have total power in the sense that Reza Shah Pahlavi, Mohammad Reza Shah Pahlavi had in their rule (or Saddam Hussein in Iraq or Hafiz al-Assad in Syria, or Mao in China, or Hitler in Germany). The regime has thus been an oligarchy.

Khomeini and the fundamentalists themselves have used the term "*Velayat Faghih*" [Rule of a High-Ranking Shia Cleric] between 1979 and 1989 to refer to their regime. After 1989, they have used the term "*Velayat Motlagh Faghih*" [Absolute Rule of a High-Ranking Shia Cleric] for their regime. Since 1997, the fundamentalists tend to also use the terms "*democracy dini*" [religious democracy] and "*democracy Islami*" [Islamic democracy] to refer to their regime. These terms

---

206 Mahan Ghafari, Alireza Kadivar, and Aris Katzourakis, "Excess deaths associated with the Iranian COVID-19 epidemic: A province-level analysis," *International Journal of Infectious Diseases*, Vol. 107, (June 2021), pp. 101–115, https://www.sciencedirect.com/science/article/pii/S120197122100326X.
207 Mahan Ghafari, "*Marg O Mir Aban 98: Moamae Chand Hezar Nafari Keh Ezafeand?*" [Deaths of November 2019: The Puzzle of Several Thousand Additional Deaths?], Radio Farda, (May 28, 2021), https://www.radiofarda.com/a/commentary-on-death-toll-report-of-november-2019/31276714.html. Also see Ghafari, Kadivar, and Katzourakis, op. cit.

are Orwellian double-speak for a regime that has little relationship to democracy.

In this book, I use the term "fundamentalist regime" for "*Nizam Velayat Faqih*." The literal translation would be the "system of rule by a high-ranking Shia cleric." This system was established by Ayatollah Ruhollah Khomeini in Iran after the 1979 revolution.

I use the term "fundamentalists" for the supporters of Khomeini and his regime. This includes the officials and supporters of the Islamic Republican Party (IRP). Between February 1979 and June 1981, many non-fundamentalists were part of the post-revolution governing structure. For example, the Liberation Movement of Iran, under the leadership of Mehdi Bazargan, who served as the prime minister in the provisional government, was a main element within the governing structure. Also, the first elected president was Dr. Abol-Hassan Bani Sadr, a progressive liberal Islamist. The non-fundamentalists also included the secular liberal democrats and secular social democrats of the Iran National Front under the leadership of Dr. Karim Sanjabi. All the non-fundamentalists were purged from positions of power by June 1981. The fundamentalists then eliminated many non-fundamentalist groups and individuals (e. g., Marxists, left-wing Islamists, and ethnic minority parties) through violence and mass executions.

I use the term "fundamentalist oligarchy" to refer to those who supported Khomeini's interpretation of Islam and were officials in the post-June 1981 regime. The IRP soon split into three main factions: left, center, and right. Around 1997, the left faction of the fundamentalist oligarchy (e. g., Mohammad Khatami, Mir Hussein Moussavi, and Mehdi Karoobi) chose the name "reformist," while the right faction (e. g., Ali Khamenei) became known as "hard-liners" or "principlists." The center faction (e. g., Ali Akbar Rafsanjani and Hassan Rouhani) became known as "moderates," or "pragmatic conservatives," or "expedients."

The fundamentalist regime's ideology is a far-right totalitarian ideology. In the words of Supreme Leader Khamenei:

> One cannot assume that Islam to demand a form of social system, but does not specify the issues of governance, as well as the rule of religion and the world. When religion becomes regime, a regime that is related to individual and the society, it become a constellation which has views on all individual and social issues, has an opinion, and demands; therefore, it is necessary to specify who will be on the top of this society, what should be done, and choose the Imam [Religious-Political Leader].[208]

---

208 Imam Ali Khamenei, "*Bayanat Dar Didar Mehmanan Konferance Vahdat Islami Va Jamee Az Masoulan Nezam*" [Speech at the Islamic Unity Conference and a Group of Regime Officials],

Khamenei goes on to say that Islam is all-inclusive and has rules for both individual and the society including for politics, economy, domestic security, national security, and foreign policy.[209] Khamenei adds that anyone who disagrees with him is anti-Islamic. According to Khamenei: "What I want to say is that first, this movement is in reality anti-Islamic, and primarily from the Great Powers in the world..."[210]

Islamic fundamentalism is ideologically opposed to the Enlightenment thought, secularism, liberalism, Marxism, feminism, and universal human rights. Islamic fundamentalism opposes the Enlightenment on the grounds that knowledge comes from revelation and not materialistic, scientific, and rational bases of knowledge. Islamic fundamentalism opposes secularism arguing that God has revealed the Truth and God's Truth is superior to any human knowledge. Islamic fundamentalists want to impose (their version of) Sharia as the primary law of the land. Islamic fundamentalists oppose liberalism because (modern) liberalism respects: individual rights; civil liberties; *de jure* equality of all citizens; freedoms of expression, the press, and political parties; pluralism; religious pluralism; democracy; and secular form of government. Islamic fundamentalists argue that according to Sharia, there should be different laws for Muslims and non-Muslims as well as men and women. Islamic fundamentalism opposes Marxism because of Marxism's egalitarianism. Islamic fundamentalists oppose feminists because feminists advocate equality between men and women. Islamic fundamentalists oppose universal human rights because such universal declarations are not based on Sharia but rather based on secular and Western values.[211]

There are similarities between Islamic fundamentalism and European fascisms of 1920s-1945.[212] Many Western and Iranian scholars consider the funda-

---

(October 24, 2021), https://farsi.khamenei.ir/speech-content?id=48891. My translation. Brief excerpts of Khamenei's speech in English is available at his site https://english.khamenei.ir/news/8739/Muslims-unity-necessary-for-realization-of-new-Islamic-Civilization. The English translation does not include some of the most significant segments. From the mid-2021, the regime and Khamenei's own site refer to him with the title of "Imam."

209 Ibid.

210 Ibid.

211 Ayatollah Ali Khamenei, "Speech," (January 17, 2020), http://english.khamenei.ir/news/7318/Our-Islamic-power-will-overcome-the-superficial-grandeur-of-material.

212 On characteristics of European fascisms see Roger Griffin, ed. *Fascism* (Oxford: Oxford University Press, 1995), pp. 1–12. For the classic structuralist work on the social class basis of fascism in Germany and Italy see Barrington Moore, Jr., *Social Origins of Dictatorship and Democracy: Lord and Peasant in the Making of the Modern World* (Boston: Beacon Press, 1966). For the classic psychoanalytic analysis of fascism see Erich Fromm, *Escape from Freedom* (NY: Farrar &

mentalist regime to have similarities with fascism.[213] One of the most prominent Western scholars who very early came to consider Islamic fundamentalists to be similar to fascists was the preeminent French Marxist scholar Maxime Rodinson.[214] In a major review of Rodinson's works, Professor Jean Batou analyzed Rodinson's views.[215] Batou wrote:

> In three articles published in December 1978 for *Le Monde*, he [Rodinson] described Islamic fundamentalism as a kind of "archaizing fascism" based on "the will to establish an authoritarian and totalitarian state whose political police would ferociously maintain the moral and social order," while also imposing "conformity to the norms of religious tradition as interpreted in the most conservative sense."[216]

Another great Western scholar of Iran, who very early came to recognize the fascistic nature of Islamic fundamentalism was Fred Halliday.[217] Paraphrasing Karl Kautsky's description of Nazim as the socialism of fools, Halliday describes Islamic fundamentalism as "the anti-imperialism of fools."[218] According to Walter Posch (historian and Iran expert at the National Defense Academy of the Austrian Army in Vienna), the IRGC has many similarities with the Nazi Party's Waffen-SS.[219] The role of the *Basij* for the fundamentalist regime is similar to the role of the SA Brown Shirts for the Nazi regime. Members of the *Basij* have been mobi-

---

Rinehart, 1941), ch. 6. Also see Benito Mussolini, "The Doctrine of Fascism," (1932), https://sjsu. edu/faculty/wooda/2B-HUM/Readings/The-Doctrine-of-Fascism.pdf.

213 Masoud Kazemzadeh, "Teaching the Politics of Islamic Fundamentalism," *PS: Political Science and Politics*, Vol. 31, No. 1 (1998), pp. 52–59. Some of the most sophisticated scholarly works considering the fundamentalist regime as similar to European fascism are: Said Amir Arjomand, *The Turban for the Crown: The Islamic Revolution in Iran* (Oxford and New York: Oxford University Pres, 1988); and Sharif Arani, "Iran: From the Shah's Dictatorship to Khomeini's Demagogic Theocracy," *Dissent*, No. 27 (Winter 1980), pp. 9–26.

214 Jean Batou, "Maxime Rodinson Was a Revolutionary Historian of the Muslim World," Jacobin, (January 31, 2021), https://www.jacobinmag.com/2021/01/maxime-rodinson-islam-middle-east. Professor Rodinson was one of the greatest scholars of Islam and the Middle East. Both of his parents (of Russian-Polish Jewish descent) died at the Auschwitz concentration camp. Professor Rodinson passed away in 2004.

215 Batou, ibid.

216 Ibid.

217 Of Irish descent, Halliday became a professor of political science and international relations at the School of Oriental and African Studies, University of London. Halliday passed away in 2010.

218 Fred Halliday, "The Iranian Revolution and Its Implications," *New Left Review*, No. 166 (November/December 1987), p. 37.

219 Walter Posch, "Ideology and Strategy in the Middle East: The Case of Iran," *Survival*, Vol. 59, No. 5 (October-November 2017), p. 96, endnote 50.

lized to beat up and suppress dissidents and opponents of the regime such as liberal democrats, Marxists, feminists, labor activists, pro-democracy university students, dissident Shia clerics, and secular women.

Increasingly, observers and scholars from diverse perspectives have also described the fundamentalist regime as similar to European fascism.[220] Many university professors inside Iran (on condition of anonymity) as well as the public use the term "banality of evil" coined by Hannah Arendt in her work *Eichmann in Jerusalem*, to describe the fundamentalist regime. Many Iranians consider President Ebrahim Raisi to be very similar to Adolf Eichmann.[221] Persian translation of Arendt's *Eichmann in Jerusalem* has been a top seller in Iran.[222]

Even some European officials have recently compared fundamentalist officials with Nazi officials. In December 2020, in his speech at the European Parliament, Radoslaw Sikorski, Poland's representative to the European Parliament and former Polish foreign minister (2007– 2014), described Iran's foreign minister Mohammad Javad Zarif as similar to Nazi regime's foreign minister von Ribben-

---

220 For a recent left-liberal observer see Bijan Ghoghnoos, *"Aya 'Jomhuri Velayat Faghih' Regimi Fashisti Ast?"* [Is the "Rule of Shia Cleric Republic" a Fascist Regime?], Iran Emrooz, (January 31, 2021), http://www.iran-emrooz.net/index.php/politic/more/87667/. Utilizing Hannah Arendt's definition of totalitarianism, Ghoghnoos argues that the fundamentalist regime is a form of right-wing totalitarianism similar to European fascism. In an scholarly article in a journal published by an Israeli university, Eliot Assoudeh argues that the fundamentalist regime is similar to Eastern European fascism of the 1930s-1940s. Eliot Assoudeh, "Shia Phoenix: Is Iran's Islamic Republic a Variety of Political Religion?" *The Journal for Interdisciplinary Middle Eastern Studies*, Vol. 4 (2019), pp. 57– 95, https://www.ariel.ac.il/wp/jimes/shia-phoenix-is-irans-islamic-republic-a-variety-of-political-religion/.

221 Ghazal Golshiri, "L'incroyable succès d'Hannah Arendt en Iran," *Le Monde*, (August 6, 2021), https://www.lemonde.fr/series-d-ete/article/2021/08/06/l-incroyable-succes-d-hannah-arendt-en-iran_6090745_3451060.html; and Nasser Etemadi, *"Chera Mardom Iran Ebrahim Raisi Va Ozaeh Keshvareshan Ra Shabih Eichmann Va Alman Nazi Midanand?"* [Why the Iranian People Consider Ebrahim Raisi and the Condition of Their Country to Be Similar to Eichmann and Nazi Germany?], Radio France International, (August 6, 2021), https://www.rfi.fr/%D8%A7% DB%8C%D8%B1%D8%A7%D9%86/20210806-%DA%86%D8%B1%D8%A7-%D9%85%D8%B1% D8%AF%D9%85-%D8%A7%DB%8C%D8%B1%D8%A7%D9%86-%D8%A7%D8%A8%D8% B1%D8%A7%D9%87%DB%8C%D9%85-%D8%B1%D8%A6%DB%8C%D8%B3%DB%8C-%D9% 88-%D8%A7%D9%88%D8%B6%D8%A7%D8%B9-%DA%A9%D8%B4%D9%88%D8%B1% D8%B4%D8%A7%D9%86-%D8%B1%D8%A7-%D8%B4%D8%A8%DB%8C%D9%87-%D8% A2%DB%8C%D8%B4%D9%85%D9%86-%D9%88-%D8%A2%D9%84%D9%85%D8%A7%D9% 86-%D9%86%D8%A7%D8%B2%DB%8C-%D9%85%DB%8C-%D8%AF%D8%A7%D9%86% D9%86%D8%AF.

222 Golshiri, ibid.; and Etemadi, ibid.

trop.[223] This is perhaps the most apt description of Zarif. As Nazi Germany's ambassador to the U.K., Ribbentrop had successfully kept the British out of war against Germany when Nazis invaded Czechoslovakia and then as Nazi Germany's foreign minister, he signed the Nazi-Soviet non-aggression pact with Molotov, which was used to invade Poland. Zarif, similarly, was highly successful in manipulating and fooling Western policy makers and the public.[224]

The analysis that Islamic fundamentalism has similarities with European fascism should not come as a surprise. Both Khomeini and Khamenei were greatly influenced by the Muslim Brotherhood's Hassan al-Banna and Seyed Qotb.[225] Al-Banna was strongly influenced by Benito Mussolini and his fascist movement.[226]

Like fascism, Islamic fundamentalism is a reaction to modernity. They attract individuals and strata that feel that the processes of modernization have caused decline in their economic well-being, power, social status, and security. These individuals and strata become attracted to the use of violence and mass movement to go back to a romanticized and mythologized golden past when things were superior to the current situation. They call their advocacy and use of mass violence for rapid change a "revolution."

Like fascists, Islamic fundamentalists organize the disaffected into para-military organizations. Members in these para-military organizations get economic and psychological benefits from such memberships. They absolutely obey the Leader and they get to have power over segments of the population that are considered enemies.

Like fascists, Islamic fundamentalists are against legal equality of all citizens and peoples. Fascists and Islamic fundamentalists argue that a particular group is superior and that they want a system whereby that particular group holds positions of power and privilege. Italian fascists considered the Italian people to be such a group, German Nazis considered the Aryan race to be such a group, and

---

223 Radio Farda, *"Namayandeh Lahestan Dar Parleman Eropa, Zarif Ra Beh Vazir Omor Kharejeh Alman Nazi Tashbih Kard"* [The Representative to the European Parliament from Poland, Considered Zarif to be Similar to the Foreign Minister of Nazi Germany], (December 18, 2020), https://www.radiofarda.com/a/31008036.html; Radoslaw Sikorski, "Speech," (December 18, 2020), posted on You Tube https://www.youtube.com/watch?v=YjrnThhS7ZY (December 21, 2020).

224 Masoud Kazemzadeh, *The Grand Strategy of the Islamic Republic of Iran* (Forthcoming).

225 Masoud Kazemzadeh, *Iran's Foreign Policy: Elite Factionalism, Ideology, the Nuclear Weapons Program, and the United States* (London: Routledge, 2020), Chapters 1, 2, and 5.

226 Ana Belen Soage, "Hasan al-Banna or the Politicisation of Islam," *Totalitarian Movements and Political Religions*, Vol. 9, No. 1 (March 2008), pp. 21–42, https://www.researchgate.net/publication/233003241_Hasan_al-Banna_or_the_Politicisation_of_Islam.

the Shia fundamentalists consider the Shia fundamentalists to be such a group. As mentioned earlier, the fundamentalists use the term *"khodi"* [of one's own] to refer to Shia fundamentalists. They use the term *"ghereh khodi"* [not of one's own, the others] to refer to those who are not Shia fundamentalists. The fundamentalist constitution and laws make distinctions between Shia Muslims and others. The positions of power are designated in the fundamentalist constitution solely for the Shia. For example, the position of Supreme Leader, Head of the Judicial Branch, and Minister of Intelligence are solely for Shia clerics. The position of president is only for male Shia. Positions of power are only for *khodi* individuals. Through *de jure* and *de facto* discriminations, *ghereh khodi* Iranians are oppressed and privilege is provided to *khodi* individuals.

Although fascism and Islamic fundamentalism contain atavistic and obscurantist elements, they are not total rejections of all things modern. Both fascists and Islamic fundamentalists strongly admire and embrace the most advanced military technologies (e.g., missiles, jetfighters, nuclear weapons, and tanks). Fascism and Islamic fundamentalism are reactionary adaptations to the modern world. Fascists and Islamic fundamentalists feel threatened by certain aspects of modernity and globalization, and they are mass violent movements to forcefully change the situation to their benefits.

Like fascism, Islamic fundamentalist ideology is explicitly corporatist and organic (i.e., society is conceived of an organic body where all parts have to cooperate in order to ensure the healthy functioning of the system). Such political system regards its leader as the brain of the polity that has the right to order others and others have to obey. This form of corporatist ideology explicitly denies civil liberties and the right of dissent. Thus, individuals are crushed for the sake of the Islamic state. Like fascism, Islamic fundamentalism attempts to create a cult of personality of its leader. Like fascism, Islamic fundamentalism denies the saliency of class struggle and class consciousness and utilizes class-derived rhetoric to mobilize certain classes against certain groups and scapegoats.

Islamic fundamentalists excel in manipulating prejudices (usually against religious and ethnic minorities) and xenophobic fears of the masses. Islamic fundamentalists have succeeded in mobilizing the masses not through appealing to their best and most noble desires (e.g., tolerance, coexistence, amity, compassion, mercy), but rather to their basest (e.g., hate, prejudice, revenge, envy).

The fundamentalist regime, under the auspices of the Ministry of Foreign Affairs, has organized seminars on the Holocaust inviting Europeans who deny the Holocaust. For example, the regime held an official conference on the Holocaust on December 11–12, 2006.[227] It is significant to add that the conference was organized by Mohammad Ali Ramin, who was a top advisor to then-President Mahmoud Ahmadinejad and was the Secretary of *"Rayeheh Khosh Khedmat"* the electoral list of supporters of Ahmadinejad for the 2006 elections.[228] In a lecture at the University of Gilan on May 30, 2006, Mr. Ramin said:

> Among the Jews there have always been harmful and wicked elements who killed God's prophets and stood against justice and rights, and this ethnic group has done the most damage to the human society throughout history, and another group among them has engaged in conspiracies, inflicting harm and cruelties on other nations and ethnic groups.... There are many accusations against the Jews throughout history, among them that they are the cause of spreading of diseases such as plague and typhus, because the Jews are very dirty persons.[229]

Like fascism, Islamic fundamentalism views political violence not as a necessary evil, but as a desirable tool to subjugate and intimidate domestic and foreign opponents. Religious rituals and liturgy have been manipulated to create a cult of violence that glamorizes violence. Like fascists, Islamic fundamentalists violently attack ethnic and religious minorities, feminists, liberals, leftists, labor unions, professional associations, and homosexuals.

In several speeches Khomeini criticized *"democratha va melliun"* [democrats and nationalists] for being under the influence of the West by criticizing violence against dissidents as violations of human rights. Khomeini said that these people are wrong and do not understand Islam. Khomeini said: "Islam includes teachings and punishments... For example, the Prophet Mohammad told Imam Ali to behead 700 Jews of Banu Qarayza."[230]

---

227 See www.adelaideinstitute.org/2006December/contents_program1.htm.

228 For some of Mr. Ramin's views see www.memri.org/bin/opener_latest.cgi?ID=SD140807.

229 BBC Persian, *"Taasis Bonyad Jahani Holocast Dar Tehran"* [Establishment of the Global Foundation of the Holocaust in Tehran], (December 14, 2006), www.bbc.co.uk/persian/iran/story/2006/12/061214_mf_holocaust.shtml. My translation.

230 Grand Ayatollah Ruhollah Khomeini, "Speech," (1984), the video of the speech available on You Tube, (May 18, 2014), https://www.youtube.com/watch?v=0EmAxl1Ksv0&list=RD0Em Axl1Ksv0&start_radio=1&rv=0EmAxl1Ksv0&t=399. Also see Grand Ayatollah Ruhollah Khomeini, "Speech," (no date), posted at You Tube (August 31, 2014), https://www.youtube.com/watch?v=C8nX-IZiWFY. Banu Qurayza or Bani Quraizah was a Jewish tribe in Medina. The tribe was defeated in a war against the Prophet Mohammad's forces. The Shia believe that Imam Ali personally cut off the heads of 700 male members of the group. It is not clear how true or exaggerated the story is. What is analytically significant here is that Khomeini used this story several times to argue that those who say that Islam is a religion of peace are wrong. Khomeini argues that Islam includes the use of great violence.

Like European fascists in Germany and Italy, Islamic fundamentalists pursue extremely bellicose, militarist, and expansionist foreign policies. Khomeini and Khamenei have been attempting to export their fundamentalist revolution and political system to other countries using violence and terrorist proxies. The Shia fundamentalists want to dominate the region and bring their governments under their control.[231] Khomeini famously said that Islam says "*Jang Jang Ta Raf'ah Fitna*" [War, War Until the Elimination of Rebellion].[232] Khomeini justified the continuance of war against Saddam Hussein with the slogan of "*Jang Jang Ta Raf'ah In Fitna*" [War, War Until the Elimination of This Fitna], and "*Rah-e Qods Az Karbala Migozarad*" [The Road to Jerusalem Goes Through Karbala].[233]

Islam enjoys a rich tradition that includes both mercifulness and peace as well as violence and aggressive war. Moderate and liberal Muslims regard the merciful and peaceful aspects of Islam to constitute Islam's primary message and soul, while violence is interpreted as exceptional and historical. Islamic fundamentalists, on the contrary, regard jihad and violence to be primary aspects of Islam, while peace and mercifulness are interpreted as minor aspects practiced only after infidels have been vanquished and dominated.

It is necessary to emphasize that the highest-ranking clerics in Shia Islam have opposed the fundamentalists. For example, the highest-ranking Shia cleric in Iran during the revolutionary period was Grand Ayatollah Kazem Shariatmadari who strongly opposed Khomeini, the fundamentalist regime, and the fundamentalist constitution. The two highest ranking Shia clerics in the Shia world since 1979 have been Grand Ayatollah Abol-Qassem Khoi and Grand Ayatollah Ali Sistani. Both Khoi and Sistani have been of Iranian origins, strongly opposed Khomeini and the fundamentalist regime, lived in Najaf, Iraq, and refused to move to Iran.

There are some major differences between European fascism and Islamic fundamentalism. European fascists are extreme nationalists. Ideologically, Islamic fundamentalists are pre-modern, pre-Westphalian, anti-Westphalian, and

---

231 IRGC Gen. Qassem Soleymani, "Speech," Fars News, (March 29, 2014). The speech was delivered on February 16, 2014, http://www.farsnews.com/newstext.php?nn=13930108000154. Kayhan, "*Ma'muriyat-e niru-ye qods towse'eh-ye enghelab-e eslami dar jahan ast*" [The Quds Force's Mission is to Expand the Islamic Revolution Throughout the World], (October 2, 2014), http://kayhan.ir/fa/news/24370. For translations of excerpts of the above see Masoud Kazemzadeh, *The Grand Strategy of the Islamic Republic of Iran*, (Forthcoming).
232 In this context, "*fitna*" or "*fitnah*" refers to opposition to Islam, or discord, or rebellion.
233 Grand Ayatollah Ruhollah Khomeini, "Speech," (1985), You Tube, (May 27, 2015), https://www.youtube.com/watch?v=8uhI1FUeVxA.

pan-Islamists. Ideologically, Islamic fundamentalists do not recognize the legitimacy of the nation-state and nationalism, although they have made pragmatic adjustments. Ideologically, the fundamentalists regard the only legitimate entity to be the *Ummah* (the Islamic community). For the Shia fundamentalists, the theocratic leader is called *Vali Faghih* or Imam. In the West, the term Supreme Leader is used to refer to the *Vali Faghih*, or *Rahbar Moazam Enghelab*.[234] For the Sunni fundamentalists, the theocratic leader is called *Khalifah* or Caliph. For example, the Shia fundamentalists regard the Supreme Leader Ali Khamenei (and before him, Ruhollah Khomeini) to be the leader of all Muslims. When Shia fundamentalists talk about Islamic unity, they mean that all Muslims (Sunni and Shia alike) should follow the leadership of the Supreme Leader. The fundamentalist constitution emphasizes this notion.[235] The fundamentalists emphasize that the Islamic Revolutionary Guard Corps (IRGC) purposefully does not contain the word "Iran" in its title.[236] In fact, the membership of the IRGC includes Shia from many nationalities such as Lebanese, Iraqi, Pakistani, and Afghans.[237] Khomeini's "Last Will and Testament" goes even further and argues that Sunni Islam is theologically false, that the only true Islam is the Shia denomination, and thus all Muslims should embrace Shia Islam.[238] There are *de jure* and *de facto* discriminations against Sunni Muslims by the Shia fundamentalist regime in Iran. Sunni fundamentalists (e.g., ISIS, Taliban) discriminate against Shia Muslims under their control.

---

234 The term *"Vali"* means "leader." The term *"Faghih"* refers to a high-ranking Shia cleric who has specialized in Islamic law. The term *"Rahbar"* means "leader." The term *"Moazam"* means "Supreme" or "Great." The term *"Enghelab"* means "Revolution."

235 See the fundamentalist constitution at https://www.constituteproject.org/constitution/Iran_1989.pdf?lang=en.

236 Fadavi, IRGC Gen. Ali. *"Sardar Fadavi: 'Sepah Pasdaran Enghelab Islami' Hich Kalamee Dar Edameh Khod Nadarad Hatta Iran"* [Gen. Fadavi: "The Islamic Revolutionary Guards Corps" Does Not Have Any Words After its Title, Even Iran], Bahar News, (April 22, 2018), https://www.baharnews.ir/news/148310/.

237 IRGC, *"Razmandegan Bedon-e Marz Ra Behtar Beshnasid: Niroyeh Qods Sepah Chegoneh Shekl Gereft?"* [Get to Know Better the Fighters Without Borders: How Was the Qods Force Formed?], Fars News (January 25, 2020), https://www.farsnews.ir/news/13981105000470/; and IRGC, *"'Razmandegan Bedon-e Marz' Dar Meydan Razm: Niroyeh Qods Dar Kodam Jang-ha Hozoor Yaft?"* ["Fighters Without Borders" on the Battlefield: Qods Force Was Present in Which Wars?], Fars News (January 26, 2020), https://www.farsnews.ir/news/13981106000522/. Also see Ayatollah Ali Khamenei, "Speech," (January 17, 2020), http://english.khamenei.ir/news/7318/Our-Islamic-power-will-overcome-the-superficial-grandeur-of-material.

238 Ayatollah Ruhollah Khomeini, "Last Will and Testament," (February 15, 1983), released after his death in June 1989, https://www.al-islam.org/imam-khomeini-s-last-will-and-testament.

Although the fundamentalist regime has many similarities with European fascist regimes, it has not been successful in imposing a stable system. One reason is the oligarchic nature of the regime. The fundamentalist regime tried to create a fascistic party (the Islamic Republican Party), but due to intense factional differences as well as Ayatollah Ruhollah Khomeini's old age and illness, the regime had to dismantle the party in 1987. A second reason is the lack of stature by Ali Khamenei to create a successful cult of personality and impose his personal rule. A third reason is the regime's failures in economy, culture, and governance. A fourth reason is technological changes such as the internet, satellite television, and cell phones, which have enabled and empowered the people to undermine the regime's ability to impose its monopoly of news and analysis. A fifth reason is the resistance by the people to the regime's ideology (e. g., female hejab). And sixth, the resistance by the various opposition groups and parties (e. g., the INF) to the regime and their providing hope for the people for an alternative and better future.

Intra-Elite Factionalism

Intra-elite factionalism is fueled by class differences, policy preferences, and personal ambitions for power. There are three main factions among the fundamentalists: right (hardline), center (moderate), and left (reformist).[239]

The right faction is better known in the West as hardliners. Their leader is the Supreme Leader Ali Khamenei. The center faction of the fundamentalist oligarchy has also been called "*Kargozaran Sazandegi*" [Executives of Construction]. This faction is also referred to as "moderates." The leaders of this faction include Ali Akbar Hashemi Rafsanjani and Hassan Rouhani.

The left faction of the fundamentalist oligarchy was called "*Peyrove Khate Imam*" [Supporters of Imam Khomeini's Line]. Since 1997, the left faction of the fundamentalist oligarchy is called reformist. The left faction was the most anti-democratic, violent, anti-American, and repressive faction between 1979 and early 1990s. The leaders of this faction have included: Ahmad Khomeini (responsible for the massacre of political prisoners in 1988); Ayatollah Sadegh Khalkhali (the head of the revolutionary courts, known in the West as the "hanging judge," the leader of Fadaian Islam, one of Khomeini's closest confidents before and after the revolution)[240]; Ayatollah Hadi Ghaffari; Ayatollah Abdol-Karim

---

239 Kazemzadeh, *Iran's Foreign Policy*, op. cit., pp. 1–45.
240 Ayatollah Sadegh Khalkhali, "All the People Who Are Opposed to Our Revolution Must Die," Interview, *MERIP Reports*, No. 104 (March-April 1982), pp. 30–31.

Moussavi Ardabili; Ayatollah Mohammad Moussavi Khoeiniha (the leaders of fundamentalist students who took over American embassy and their liaison with Ayatollah Khomeini); Hojatolislam Mohammad Khatami (president 1997–2005); Mir-Hussein Moussavi (prime minister 1981–1989); Hojatolislam Mehdi Karoobi (Speaker of Majles); and Ayatollah Ali Akbar Mohtashami-pour (ambassador to Syria, one of the main founders of the Lebanese Hezbollah, Interior Minister for Mir-Hussein Moussavi's government, members of Majles, top official for Mir-Hussein Moussavi's presidential campaign in 2009).

Most of the fundamentalist students who attacked the U.S. Embassy on November 4, 1979 and took its diplomats hostage for 444 days were members of the reformist faction.[241] The top three fundamentalist student leaders who planned, organized, and carried out the takeover of the American Embassy were Habibollah Bitaraf, Mohsen Mirdamadi, and Ebrahim Asgharzadeh. The number one leader of the fundamentalist students, Bitaraf, became governor of the province of Yazd and Minister of Energy under President Khatami (1997–2005). The number two, Mirdamadi, became governor of the Khuzestan province, member of Majles, and the secretary-general of the largest reformist fundamentalist party, Islamic Iran Participation Front (IIPF). The number three, Asgharzadeh, became member of Majles and top official at *"Vezarat Ershad Va Tablighat Islami"* [the Ministry of Islamic Guidance and Propaganda]. Asgharzadeh is one of the few fundamentalists who has apologized to Abbas Amir-Entezam for the false allegations. Saeed Hajjarian became one of the founders of the Ministry of Intelligence, Deputy Minister of Intelligence, and the theoretician of the reformist faction in 1997. Mohsen Aminzadeh became Deputy Foreign Minister (1997–2005) during President Khatami and the most influential foreign policy official during that period. Reza Khatami, the younger brother of President Khatami, became the Secretary General of the IIPF. Masoumeh Ebtekar, the spokeswoman of the hostage takers, became Deputy to the President on environmental affairs under Khatami and Rouhani. She continues to strongly support the hostage taking.[242] Mohammad Hashemi Isfehani (Ebtekar's husband) became the Foreign Operations Head of the Ministry of Intelligence. He was personally tasked with leading a group of assassins to assassinate Hadi Khorsandi (Iran's leading satirist and a supporter of Dr. Bakhtiar) who was living in exile in Britain. The British security

---

241 ISNA, *"Sarnevesht Daneshjooyan Eshghalkonandeh Sefarat America"* [What Became of the Students Occupying the American Embassy], (November 3, 2016), https://www.isna.ir/news/95081309267.
242 Ibid.

forces foiled the operations.[243] Abbas Abdi, one of the more outspoken funda-mentalist students, has been a top adviser to Karoobi. Abdi remains a strong supporter of the hostage taking and continues to make false allegation against Amir-Entezam. Abdi is one of the most reactionary and dictatorial leaders of the reformist fundamentalist faction. Abdi was among the top reformist leaders during 2018 and 2019 that publicly condemned the protesters and publicly called for the violent suppression of the protests.

Other reformist members of the fundamentalist oligarchy have also played very violent and dictatorial roles when the left faction of the fundamentalist oli-garchy had the upper hand. Mostafa Tajzadeh was a top prosecutor in revolu-tionary courts in 1980s, during the worst violations of human rights in the fun-damentalist regime. Sadegh Zibakalam was a top fundamentalist official in the Cultural Revolution when the fundamentalists violently attacked the universities and purged secular, liberal, and leftist professors, students, and staff.

Between 1981 and 1989, Supreme Leader Ruhollah Khomeini was ill and was able to only occasionally intervene is detail of policy. Five top members of the oligarchy ruled the country: Ahmad Khomeini, Rafsanjani, Khamenei, Mir-Hussein Moussavi, and Moussavi Ardabili. Until Khomeini's death in 1989, the left (or reformist) faction had the upper hand in the regime. Between 1989 and mid-1990s Rafsanjani and his expedient faction had the upper hand. The years between 1981 and 1989, the left fundamentalists had the upper hand. These years are by far the most repressive years of the regime.[244] Between 1989 and 1995, expedients (Rafsanjani) had the upper hand. This period is the second worst period in term of repression and dictatorship. Since 1995, Khamenei and the hardline faction have gained the upper hand. This period has been the least repressive period under the fundamentalists. Khamenei has been far more tolerant of criticisms than either Khomeini (1979–1989) or Rafsanjani (when he was the most powerful figure 1989–1995). Mass executions and assas-sination of dissidents were far more prevalent under Khomeini and Rafsanjani periods than under Khamenei's period.

---

243 Shappi Khorsandi, "My Family Values," *The Guardian*, (October 23, 2015), interview, https://www.theguardian.com/lifeandstyle/2015/oct/23/shappi-khorsandi-my-family-values. The would-be assassin, Abol-Qassem Mesbahi, defected and gave the information to Bani Sadr, the former president in exile in France. The court testimony of Mr. Mesbahi was crucial in con-victing top officials of the fundamentalist regime in the Mykonos restaurant trial in Berlin for assassination of dissidents in Europe.
244 Masoud Kazemzadeh, "Ayatollah Rafsanjani's Death and Trump Policy on Iran," *Small Wars Journal*, (January 18, 2017), https://smallwarsjournal.com/jrnl/art/ayatollah-rafsanjani%E2%80%99s-death-and-trump-policy-on-iran.

Each faction believes that its policies would better serve the interests of the fundamentalist regime. The reformist faction proposes to reduce political repression, reduce cultural repression, make less adventurist and violent foreign policies. The reformists want to make (minor) reforms in order to preserve the fundamentalist regime and the fundamentalist constitution. The reformists oppose replacing the ruling fundamentalist dictatorship with democracy. They continue to support the fundamentalist regime, the extremely anti-democratic fundamentalist constitution (which grants a Shia cleric enormous powers as Vali Faghih), and strongly support Khomeini (under whom they had the upper hand in most state institution). Mohammad Khatami has explicitly said that he opposes democracy, that the Iranian people are not capable of democracy, and that he strongly supports the fundamentalist constitution.[245] Mehdi Karoobi, too, has repeatedly supported the fundamentalist constitution, the fundamentalist rule, and Khomeini's rule. On October 5, 2021, in a gathering at Gholam-Hussein Karbaschi's home, Karoobi said: "I ask the Holy and Supreme God, to provide victory to all the supporters of Islam, to put this great movement that the Imam [Khomeini] created, on a path that Inshallah will continue. To preserve the basic principle of the regime and Inshallah get rid of its shortcomings."[246] Mir-Hussein Moussavi, infamously referred to Khomeini's period as *"Dowran Talaee Imam"* [The Golden Period of the Imam]. Moussavi was prime minister for about eight years under Khomeini when the regime's worst atrocities were occurring including mass executions of teenagers. According to Amnesty International, Moussavi played a role in distorting the truth about the massacre of political prisoners in August-September 1988, during the Second Reign of Terror.[247]

---

245 Mohammad Khatami, "Speech," You Tube, (2014), https://www.youtube.com/watch?v= KiygQj96DrQ.

246 Mehdi Karoobi, "Speech," *"Avalin Sokhanrani Karrubi Pas Az 11 Sal"* [The First Speech by Karrubi After 11 Years], Ensafnews, (October 5, 2021), http://www.ensafnews.com/312263/% D8%A7%D9%88%D9%84%DB%8C%D9%86-%D8%B3%D8%AE%D9%86%D8%B1%D8%A7% D9%86%DB%8C-%DA%A9%D8%B1%D9%88%D8%A8%DB%8C-%D9%BE%D8%B3-%D8% A7%D8%B2-%DB%B1%DB%B1-%D8%B3%D8%A7%D9%84-%D8%B9%DB%8C%D9%88% D8%A8-%D9%86/. Karbaschi is the Secretary-General of Executives of Construction Party, the party created by Rafsanjani. Karbaschi has been a top supporter of Karrubi since 2008. The words chosen by Karoobi are: *"Asl nezam mahfooz bemanad."* Karoobi's words unambiguously and strongly mean that one should work to preserve the basics and principles of the regime such as its constitution and the fundamentalist clerical supreme power.

247 Amnesty International, "Iran: Top government officials distorted the truth about 1988 prison massacres," (December 12, 2018), https://www.amnesty.org/en/latest/press-release/2018/12/ iran-top-government-officials-distorted-the-truth-about-1988-prison-massacres/.

The expedient faction proposes what is called the Chinese model: increase political repression, reduce cultural repression, make IMF-style economic policies, and reduce confrontation with the United States. The hardline faction proposes to increase political repression, increase cultural repression, increase confrontation with the U.S. and EU, as well as expand the IRI's influence in the Middle East region through violent proxies. The hardline faction believes that reduction of repression would results in collapse of the regime in Iran as it occurred in the former Soviet Union. The crises engulfing the regime have further inflamed intra-elite struggles.

The Election of Ebrahim Raisi to Presidency: Hard-Line Solution to Crises or the Final Nail in the Coffin

The hardliners orchestrated the election on June 18, 2021 to make certain that Ebrahim Raisi would become president. Raisi is one of the more extreme members of the hardline faction. Raisi was born on December 14, 1960.[248] His father was a mid-ranking cleric. He attended only six years of primary school. Then he began attending seminaries. When the revolution occurred in 1979, he was 18 years old. He began working with the fundamentalists after the revolution. Raisi held a series of positions in the judiciary from revolutionary prosecutor to judge. He was responsible for execution of thousands. He was a member of the so-called "Death Board" in Tehran and Karaj during the Second Reign of Terror in August-September 1988 when about 5,000 political prisoners were summarily mass executed. The "Death Boards" consisted of three individuals who would ask several questions and then decide whether the political prisoners would live or executed. On Saturday June 19, 2021, when the regime announced that Raisi had won the election to presidency, Amnesty International and Human Rights Watch called for probes for crimes against humanity committed by Raisi.[249]

By August 2021, the hardline faction controls all levers of power in Iran: Supreme Leader, President, Majles, Council of Guardians, Assembly of Experts, Council for Expediency of the System, and IRGC. This not only cements hardline control of the regime in the short-term but also eliminates the likelihood of a

---

248 Raisi's biography at his website https://raisi.ir/page/biography.
249 Reuters, "Rights groups call for prob into Iran's Raisi for crimes against humanity," (June 19, 2021), https://www.reuters.com/world/middle-east/amnesty-calls-investigation-into-irans-raisi-crimes-against-humanity-2021-06-19/.

non-hardline candidate to become the next Supreme Leader after Khamenei dies for the long-term.

The expulsion of reformist and expedient factions from the top positions of power and the monopolization of power in the hands of hardliners has advantages and disadvantages for the fundamentalist regime both domestically and internationally. The marginalization of reformists and expedients eliminates the hope by many inside Iran that gradual and small changes are possible. This would benefit the opposition (e. g., democratic opposition) that wants to replace the ruling fundamentalist regime with another form of political system (e. g., democracy). When another uprising such as those that occurred in 2017 and 2019, the likelihood of more people going to the streets and joining the uprising increases. Ebrahim Raisi's presidency indicates that Khamenei and hardliners have reached the conclusion that they fear mass uprisings and believe the best way to keep power is through brute force.

Raisi's presidency also makes it harder for the U.S. and Europeans to make concessions to the fundamentalist regime. One of the main arguments for the appeasement of the fundamentalist regime has been that by doing so, the U.S. and EU would increase the power of the reformists and moderates (expedients) within the fundamentalist regime. Presidencies of Khatami and Rouhani had made those arguments plausible for many. Raisi's presidency undermines the plausibility of such arguments.

The INF had called for boycott of this election as it had all the elections since 1980, with only two exceptions. The INF had called the people to vote for Mohammad Khatami for reelection to presidency in 2001 and for reformists for Majles elections in 1998. The INF argued that the people have moved on from choosing between "bad" (i. e., reformists, expedients, or less extremist hardliners) and "worse" (i. e., hardliners or more extreme hardliners). The INF believes that the Iranian people deserve freedom, democracy, and human rights. The INF advocates changing the current dictatorship with a democracy. By participating and voting, one would be providing legitimacy to the fundamentalist regime. Therefore, the INF called for boycott of the elections.[250]

---

250 Jebhe Melli Iran, "*Mellat Iran Az Entekhab Bein Bad Va Badtar Oboor Kardeh Ast*" [The Iranian Nation Has Moved On From Choosing Between Bad and Worse], (April 7, 2021), https://melliun.org/iran/257087. Also see Hussein Moussavian, "Interview," Iran National Front-Organizations Abroad TV, Channel One, (June 20, 2021), https://www.youtube.com/watch?v=Xfl RlCIejVk.

Chapter 6
INF, the Soviet Union, and the Far Left

The Soviet Union and the Tudeh Party

Joseph Stalin had an extremely hostile view of the INF and Mossadegh.[251] There are several reasons for this hostility. In 1944, while the Soviet Army (along with British and American armed forces) were occupying Iran during WWII, Stalin wanted Iran to grant the Soviet Union an oil concession in northern Iran similar to that which the British had in southern Iran. The Tudeh Party strongly supported Stalin's demand. The Tudeh Party argued that by granting the Soviet Union such an exclusive concession, Iran would create a *"movazeneh mosbat"* [positive balance or positive equilibrium] between the British and the Soviet Union in Iran.

Mossadegh was a member of the Majles in 1944. He was one of the most influential members of the parliament. Mossadegh was the leader of the opposition in 1944–45 in granting oil concession to the Soviet Union. Mossadegh galvanized support for a bill banning any discussion of granting any oil concession to any power anywhere in Iran, while foreign troops were stationed in Iran.[252] With huge popular support, Mossadegh succeeded in this effort. This was considered a major defeat for Stalin personally, the USSR, and the Tudeh Party.[253]

During 1945–1946, Stalin refused to withdraw the Soviet troops from Iranian provinces of Azerbaijan and Kurdistan. Again, the Soviet Union ordered the Tudeh Party to support Stalin's policy.[254] Mossadegh and Fatemi (who in 1949 founded the INF and were the top two leaders of it) strongly opposed the secession of Azerbaijan and Kurdistan.[255] Nationalist and progressive intellectuals

---

251 Cosroe Chaqueri, *"Naghdi Bar Pareh-e Az Nazarat Piramoon Naghsh Hezb Tudeh"* [Critique on Some Views on the Role of the Tudeh Party], Melliun (August 30, 2013), https://melliun.org/iran/26615.

252 Abrahamian, *Khomeinism*, p. 104.

253 Chaqueri, *"Naghdi Bar Pareh-e Az Nazarat Piramoon Naghsh Hezb Tudeh"* [Critique on Some Views on the Role of the Tudeh Party], op. cit.

254 Maziar Behrooz, "The 1953 Coup in Iran and the Legacy of the Tudeh," in Mark J. Gasiorowski and Malcolm Byrne, eds. *Mohammad Mosaddeq and the 1953 Coup in Iran.* (Syracuse: Syracuse University Press, 2005), p. 125.

255 Hussein Fatemi, *Neveshteh-hay Makhfigah Va Zendan: 28 Mordad 1332–19 Aban 1333* [Writings from the Hideout and Prison: 19 August 1953–10 November 1954], (London: Daftar-hay

https://doi.org/10.1515/9783110782158-008

condemned the Tudeh Party and *Fergheh Democrat Azerbaijan* (Azerbaijan Democratic Party) for collaborating with the Soviet Union in dismembering Iran.[256]

After the collapse of the Soviet Union, Soviet archives were opened for about a year or two. One of Iran's top historians, Cosroe Chaqueri (Khosrow Shakeri), had an opportunity to research the Comintern archives in 1992 and 1993. In his seminal article, Chaqueri showed how the Red Army Intelligence Division Brigade Commissar Il'ichev and Colonel Seliukov in secret meeting with Sulayman Eskandari formed the Tudeh Party. On September 29, 1941 Sulayman Eskandari met with other leftists to officially establish the Tudeh party.[257] There was a core group of cadres that were absolutely subservient to Moscow.[258] Among these were Abdol-Samad Kambakhsh and Nureddin Kianouri, both of whom closely collaborated with the Soviet intelligence and both were made general secretaries (at different periods) of the Tudeh Party under direct pressure from Soviet officials.[259] In 1941, the Soviet Union did not want to establish a radical communist party in Iran that might have antagonized the British and the Americans in the middle of WWII. Therefore, the Tudeh Party, was intended to be similar to popular front organizations. It did not demand communism, but merely progressive and democratic reforms. It also did not officially oppose monarchy or Islam. The Soviets intended to use the Tudeh Party as a vehicle for advancing the foreign policy goals of the Soviet Union in Iran. The Soviets provided the Tudeh Party substantial resources, and it grew greatly.[260] By 1947, great tensions grew between those who were socialist and progressive and those who were pro-Soviet Communist. In 1947, under the leadership of Khalil Maleki, about 100 top mem-

---

Azadi, 2004), https://melliun.org/v/wp-content/uploads/2017/06/yaddasht-haye-dr.-Fatemi.pdf, p. 23.

256 Richard Cottam, *Iran and the United States: A Cold War Case Study* (Pittsburgh: University of Pittsburgh Press, 1988); and Sepehr Zabih, *The Communist Movement in Iran* (Berkeley and Los Angeles: University of California Press, 1966).

257 Cosroe Chaqueri, "Did the Soviets play a role in founding the Tudeh party in Iran?," *Cahiers du Monde russe*, Vol. 40, No. 3 (1999), pp. 497–528.

258 Fereydoon Keshavarz, *Man Moteham Mikonam Kommiteh Markazi Hezb Tudeh Iran Ra* [I Accuse the Central Committee of the Tudeh Party of Iran], (Tehran, 1979), https://www.iran-archive.com/node/17392. Keshavarz was one of the top leaders of the Tudeh Party. He was a member of the Central Committee and one of three Tudeh Party ministers in Ahmad Qavam's cabinet in 1946.

259 Cosroe Chaqueri, "*53 Nafar Beh Ravayat Kambakhsh: Gozaresh Serri Beh Rofaghay Ruus*" [Group of 53 According to Kambakhsh: The Secret Report to Russian Comrades], Melliun (January 2, 2014), https://melliun.org/iran/33964.

260 Azimi, "On Shaky Ground," op. cit., pp. 60–62; Chaqueri, "Did the Soviets play," op. cit.; and Keshavarz, *Man Moteham Mikonam Kommiteh*, op. cit.; Zabih, *The Communist Movement in Iran*, op. cit.

bers and intellectuals split from the Tudeh Party.[261] Maleki was Iran's foremost democratic socialist intellectual. Maleki and his supporters presented a devastating criticism of the Tudeh Party, its absolute subservience to the Soviet Union, Stalin's brutal dictatorship, its imperialist policies towards Iran, and the subjugation of Eastern Europeans countries.[262] Radio Moscow began a campaign of vicious personal attacks against Maleki. The Tudeh Party and its supporters followed Moscow's line by making slanderous personal attacks on Maleki.[263] Stalin and the Tudeh Party failed to crush or intimidate Maleki into silence. Maleki succeeded in establishing a vibrant socialist party called the Third Force Party. Maleki and his supporters joined the INF and strongly supported Mossadegh. This further enraged Stalin and the Soviet Union.

Maleki's theory of third force argued that it was possible and desirable to create a movement that was both socialist and democratic as well as being independent from all superpowers (the U.S., U.K., and the USSR), was a challenge to the Soviet Union. Maleki's "third force" was complementary to Mossadegh's foreign policy doctrine of "*movazeneh manfi*" [negative balance] that he had announced in 1944. Stalin wanted to have oil concession of Iran's oil in the north and the Tudeh Party was fully supporting giving away Iran's northern oil to the Soviet Union. Mossadegh argued that if Iran gave to the Soviet Union its northern oil, what would be left for the Iranian people. On the floor of the 14th session of the Majles, Mossadegh said, if a man has a broken arm, do we break the other arm to create a positive balance or do we try to repair the broken arm.[264]

By 1947, the Cold War between the U.S. and the USSR was in full force. Stalin believed that the U.K. was in decline and the U.S. was the major superpower standing up to the Soviet Union; therefore, the main enemy of the Soviet Union was the United States.[265] Stalin further believed that there was a major contradiction between the interests of the U.S. and the U.K., and he intended to widen that gap. Stalin believed that the Shah was a puppet of the British and Mossadegh and the INF were pro-U.S. Stalin further believed that Mossa-

261 Homa Katouzian, *Khalil Maleki: The Human Face of Iranian Socialism* (London: Oneworld Academic, 2018); and Maziar Behrooz, *Rebels with A Cause: The Failure of the Left in Iran* (London: I.B. Tauris, 1999).
262 Katouzian, *Khalil Maleki, The Human Face of*; BBC Persian, "*Aya Khalil Maleki 1 Estesna Ast?*" [Is Khalil Maleki One Exception?], (May 10, 2018), https://www.youtube.com/watch?v=ACQ2EBXHwX0; and Behrooz, *Rebels with A Cause*.
263 Azimi, "On Shaky Ground" op. cit., p. 64.
264 Hussein Moussavian, "Interview with Radio Asr Jadid," (March 12, 2021), https://melliun.org/iran/255058.
265 Cottam, *Iran and the United States*.

degh's oil nationalization movement was a reflection of the antagonism between the U.S. and the U.K. over access to Iran's oil.[266] The Tudeh Party considered its "international proletarian duty" to be to make decisions that would override Iran's sovereignty and national interests.[267] Thus, the Tudeh Party considered Mossadegh and the INF as its primary enemies.[268]

Mossadegh, in fact, did have positive views of the U.S. and of President Franklin D. Roosevelt's New Deal programs. William O. Douglass, associate justice of the U.S. Supreme Court, was a long-time friend of Mossadegh's. Mossadegh also developed friendships with President Harry S. Truman and his Secretary of State Dean Acheson. However, Mossadegh's policy was to be a friend of the U.S. and not its subservient puppet. Mossadegh's policy was full independence from all superpowers. He wanted to have cordial relations with both the U.S. and the Soviet Union, but not be subservient to any of them.

Until 1955, the Soviet Union was strongly hostile to the notion of neutralism (which later became known as the non-align movement). For Stalin, a country was either friends with the Soviet Union or it was part of the imperialist camp. In 1955, the Soviet Union officially changed that policy and began supporting national liberation movements that were under the leadership of nationalists such as Col. Gamal Abdul Nasser.[269] According to Cosroe Chaqueri, Khrushchev supported nationalists in the Third World struggling for their independence from European or American domination. Chaqueri attributes the extremely hostile policies of the Soviet Union and the Tudeh Party toward Mossadegh due to Stalin. Between March and August 1953, the Soviet leaders were preoccupied with other matters and the Tudeh Party leaders had more leeway to make their own policy. Chaqueri attributed the hostility of the Tudeh Party during this period to Kianouri, who was extremely hostile to Mossadegh and the INF and publicly embraced Stalin's hostile view of "the national bourgeoisie" the classification that the Soviet Union and the Tudeh Party attributed to the INF.[270]

President Eisenhower's foreign policy team (Secretary of State John Foster Dulles and CIA Director Allen Dulles) held the view that a country is either part of the Communist bloc or part of the Western bloc. Much later, the Americans also began recognizing the non-align movement. From August 1953 until

---

266 Behrooz, "The 1953 Coup in Iran and the Legacy of the Tudeh," pp. 107–108.
267 Ibid., pp. 106–109.
268 Ibid., pp. 106–110, 120–125.
269 I owe this paragraph to the late Cosroe Chaqueri. He attributed the change of policy to Nikita Khrushchev.
270 Chaqueri, "*Naghdi Bar Pareh-e Az Nazarat Piramoon Naghsh Hezb Tudeh*" [Critique on Some Views on the Role of the Tudeh Party], op. cit.

1979 (perhaps with partial exception of the Kennedy administration), the U.S. supported the Shah as a reliable and subservient client regime.[271]

Moreover, in January 1953, Mossadegh refused to renew the concession of the Northern Fisheries and Shipping, a concession that was initially granted to Russia and then to the Soviet Union whereby the Soviets had exclusive rights to fish in the Caspian Sea depriving Iranians of the enormous employment and financial benefits. Despite tremendous pressure from Moscow, Mossadegh refused to renew the concession. Mossadegh's nationalization of the Northern Fisheries further antagonized the Soviets.[272] The Tudeh party viciously attacked Mossadegh.[273]

Stalin considered Mossadegh and the INF to be pro-U.S. and opposed to the Soviet domination of Iran. Thus, Stalin wanted Mossadegh to fail. Despite repeated demands, Stalin refused to return Iran's gold that had been placed in safe keeping in the Soviet Union during WWII. The Soviet Union returned Iran's gold (over 10 tons) after the August coup to the Shah's regime. Stalin passed away on March 5, 1953. Stalin's successors were busy with struggles over succession, the situation in East Germany, and the peace initiative in Korea. When the CIA and the MI6 were busy plotting the coup against Mossadegh, the Soviets did not want to challenge the U.S.[274]

In March 1953, the Tudeh Party began approaching Mossadegh. Maziar Behrooz attributes this primarily to factionalism in the Tudeh Party and the ascendency of the moderate faction that advocated close cooperation with the INF and Mossadegh.[275] However, March 1953 is when Stalin died. As Behrooz and Chaqueri argue, after July 1952, the Tudeh Party attacks on the INF and Mossadegh declined but did not disappear.[276] In fact, both scholars show that such attacks continued until after the coup in August 1953. Mossadegh did not believe that the Tudeh Party was strong enough to pose a real threat. Recent scholarship, based on declassified American and British documents, vindicate Mossadegh's view that the Americans and the British were publicly exaggerating the threat from

---

271 James A. Bill, *The Eagle and the Lion: The Tragedy of American-Iranian Relations* (New Haven and London: Yale University Press, 1988).

272 Katouzian, *Musaddiq and the Struggle*, pp. 133–136.

273 Ibid., p. 135.

274 Chaqueri, "*Naghdi Bar Pareh-e Az Nazarat Piramoon Naghsh Hezb Tudeh*" [Critique on Some Views on the Role of the Tudeh Party], op. cit.

275 Behrooz, "The 1953 Coup in Iran and the Legacy of the Tudeh."

276 Ibid., p. 110.

the Tudeh Party.[277] Mossadegh did not trust the Tudeh Party. Mossadegh also believed that the MI6 had infiltrated the Tudeh Party. Declassified documents show that in fact the British and the Americans had agents in the Tudeh Party acting as *agents provocateurs*.[278] One such person, Ehsan Lankarani, under instructions from the CIA bombed the home of a religious leader and spread rumors that atheist communists were about to take over Iran.[279] The CIA plan was to scare the conservative religious elements, a policy that actually did succeed in scarring conservative elements.[280]

After the coup, many members of the Tudeh Party strongly criticized the Tudeh Party's hostile policies toward the INF and Mossadegh. Due to these pressures, the Tudeh Party publicly criticized some of its policies against Mossadegh although Kianouri and the Tudeh Party continued to blame Mossadegh for the success of the coup.[281] In their plenum held in Moscow in July 1957, the Tudeh Party admitted that its views and policies toward the INF and Mossadegh were wrong.[282] Between 1957 and 1978, there were little tension between the INF and the Tudeh Party. Supporters of both parties outside Iran cooperated in establishing the Confederation of Iranian Students in Europe and the U.S. In June 1963, the INF and Mossadegh did not support Khomeini's uprising. The Tudeh Party issued a statement supporting Khomeini's uprising.

After February 1979, the Tudeh Party began a vicious campaign against the INF and other liberals and began strongly supporting Ayatollah Khomeini and the fundamentalists. The KGB in Tehran, the Tudeh Party, and the Fadaian-Majority began a campaign of vicious attacks and demonization against the INF, Mehdi Bazargan, Abbas Amir-Entezam, Sadegh Ghotbzadeh, and Abol-Hassan Bani-Sadr. The Tudeh Party publicly supported Ayatollah Sadegh Khalkhali's

---

277 Mark J. Gasiorowski, "U.S. Perceptions of the Communist Threat in Iran during the Mossadegh Era," *Journal of Cold War Studies*, Vol. 21, No. 3 (Summer 2019), pp. 185–221. https://www.mitpressjournals.org/doi/pdf/10.1162/jcws_a_00898.

278 Ervand Abrahamian, "The 1953 Coup in Iran," *Science & Society*, Vol. 65, No. 2 (Summer 2001), pp. 182–215; Behrooz, "The 1953 Coup in Iran," pp. 116, 118.

279 Abrahamian, "The 1953 Coup in Iran," pp. 201, 204.

280 Ibid., p. 204.

281 Babak Amir-Khosravi, *Hasel Yek Omr: Zendeginameh Siasi Babak Amir-Khosravi* [Results of a Life: Political Memoirs of Babak Amir-Khosravi], (Sweden, 2020), p. 153. Both Amir-Khosravi and Chaqueri say that Kianouri has lied about his accounts of the coup and his role during that period. Many believe that Kianouri is lying. Other members of the Tudeh Party also agree with Amir-Khosravi about Kianouri's lies. See Chaqueri, *"Naghdi Bar Pareh-e Az Nazarat Piramoon Naghsh Hezb Tudeh"* [Critique on Some Views on the Role of the Tudeh Party], op. cit. Also see Behrooz, "The 1953 Coup in Iran," p. 117, and endnote 60.

282 Behrooz, "The 1953 Coup in Iran," p. 123.

summary executions, supported him for presidency in 1980, and called upon him to execute liberals. The Tudeh Party called for arrest and execution of Amir-Entezam and other liberal democrats as agents and supporters of American imperialism.[283]

Babak Amir-Khosravi was a prominent member of the Tudeh Party Central Committee before and after the revolution.[284] His 900-page book is one of the best sources on the policies of the Tudeh Party.[285] In late 1978, in a meeting of the Central Committee that was held in East Germany, the representative from the International Department of the Central Committee of the Communist Party of Soviet Union (ID CC CPSU) told members that his order is to inform them that they should change the secretary general of the party from Iraj Eskandari to Kianouri. The ID CC CPSU is the entity (and usually not the KGB) the directly handles "foreign communists." The ID CC CPSU is more secretive and clandestine than the KGB. It has conducts the training of top foreign communist leaders usually in the USSR and trains them in how to send their reports to Moscow using various clandestine methods.[286] Eskandari was mild-mannered and

---

283 Radio Farda, *"Bazjui Amir-Entezam: Jasosi Oo Esbat Nashod Va Ghorbani Maarekeh Amrika-Setizi Shod"* [Amir-Entezam's Interrogator: His Espionage was not Proven and Became a Victim of Anti-Americanism], (July 14, 2020), https://www.radiofarda.com/a/motaghi-on-amirentezam/30726246.html; BBC Persian, *"Bazjoe Abbas Amir-Entezam: Eteham Jasosi Beh Oo Hargez Sabet Nashod"* [Abbas Amir-Entezam's Interrogator: The Accusation of Espionage Was Never Proven], (July 14, 2020), https://www.bbc.com/persian/iran-53404949; BBC Persian, *"Hezb Tudeh"* [Tudeh Party], (January 31, 2012), https://www.youtube.com/watch?v=m5rJtrrRlks; BBC Persian, *"Karnameh Fadian Khalq, Aksariyat"* [History of Fadaian, Majority], (February 16, 2011), https://www.youtube.com/watch?v=RLwMFzWZMmg; BBC Persian, *"Mostenad Farzand Enghelab: Dastan Zendegi Va Marg Sadegh Ghotbzadeh Ghesmat 1"* [Documentary Child of the Revolution: Story of Life and Death of Sadegh Ghotbzadeh Part 1] (February 9, 2020), https://www.youtube.com/watch?v=PWB0lM8-cQo; BBC Persian, *"Mostenad Farzand Enghelab: Dastan Zendegi Va Marg Sadegh Ghotbzadeh Ghesmat 2"* [Documentary Child of the Revolution: Story of Life and Death of Sadegh Ghotbzadeh Part 2] (February 10, 2020), https://www.youtube.com/watch?v=vpyLiEUtT_o; and BBC Persian, *"Mostenad Farzand Enghelab: Dastan Zendegi Va Marg Sadegh Ghotbzadeh Ghesmat 3"* [Documentary Child of the Revolution: Story of Life and Death of Sadegh Ghotbzadeh Part 3] (February 10, 2020), https://www.youtube.com/watch?v=HiyOu4fkR2I.
284 His website is http://www.babakamirkhosrovi.com/.
285 Babak Amir-Khosravi, *Nazar Az Doroon Beh Naghsh Hezb Tudeh Iran* [Inside Perspective on the Role of the Tudeh Party] (Tehran: Etellaat, 1996), https://www.iran-archive.com/start/230. Also see Babak Amir-Khosravi, *"Goftogo"* [Interview], (no date) http://www.rezafani.com/index.php?/site/comments/amirkhosravi/.
286 Denis V. Volkov, "The USSR and the Tudeh Party after the Islamic Revolution of 1979: Ideological Cohesion and Operative Controversies," paper presentation at Tudeh Party of Iran at 80 Conference, (April 1, 2021), http://www.mihan.org.uk/TudehAt80/, video at https://www.youtube.com/watch?v=aqrgkjaMXdE. Professor Volkov is one of Russia's the top experts on the

moderate and was sympathetic to the liberal democrats of the INF. Kianouri was the grandson of Sheikh Fazlollah Nouri (the highest-ranking Shia cleric during the Constitutional Revolution, who opposed the Constitution and was hanged by the constitutionalists). Sheikh Fazlollah Nouri was one of the main heroes of Khomeini. Both clerics opposed democracy and demanded the rule of Shariah. Kianouri was extremist, adventurist, and violent. For example, in 1949, without getting permission from other leaders of the Tudeh Party, Kianouri was involved in an assassination attempt on Mohammad Reza Shah Pahlavi on February 4, 1949.

The Soviets considered the overthrow of the Shah's regime and the establishment of the fundamentalist regime to have been a major strategic victory for the USSR. The Soviets wanted to use the Tudeh Party primarily to gather intelligence on Iran's political situation and to establish contacts with Khomeini and his lieutenants.[287] Under Kianouri's leadership, the Tudeh Party strongly supported Khomeini. The Tudeh Party argued that Khomeini is the leader of the anti-imperialist camp, and the liberals are friends of the U.S. and wish to have good relations with the U.S. and Western Europe. Thus, the Tudeh Party advocated the arrest and executions of liberals as agents of American imperialism. Kianouri directly reported to the ID CC CPSU usually using the KGB in Tehran to forward his encrypted messages.[288]

Babak Amir-Khosravi and a large number of Tudeh Party members split from the Tudeh Party and established *"Hezb Democratic Mardom Iran"* [Democratic Party of the Iranian People].[289] Amir-Khosravi and his party have published articles in which they have criticized the subservience of the Tudeh Party on the Soviet Union, and its hostile policies on the liberals democrats and social democrats. Amir-Khosravi, himself, has praised Mossadegh and criticized the policies of the Tudeh Party towards Mossadegh.[290] Amir-Khosravi has said that if the Soviets did not orchestrate the removal of Eskandari and the imposition of Kianouri, then the Tudeh Party would have allied with the INF and the liberals and not with Khomeini and the fundamentalists.

Tudeh Party and Iran. He is one of the few scholars, who has conducted research on Soviet archives on Iran.

287 Ibid.

288 Ibid.

289 For some of the founding documents of the party see https://www.iran-archive.com/node/2160.

290 Babak Amir-Khosravi, *Hasel Yek Omr: Zendeginameh Siasi Babak Amir-Khosravi* [Results of a Life: Political Memoirs of Babak Amir-Khosravi], (Sweden, 2020), pp. 150–156.

In 1983, the fundamentalist regime arrested members of the Tudeh Party and the Fadaian-Majority and executed a few. Many more were executed during the Second Reign of Terror in August-September 1988. Many leaders and cadres of the Tudeh Party and Fadaian-Majority escaped to the Soviet Union. According to a former leader of the Fadaian-Majority, the KGB then used them for intelligence gathering as it had done before.[291]

After the 1983 mass arrests of the members of the Tudeh Party and the Fadaian-Majority, many of its leaders and members went to Afghanistan and began close cooperation with the ruling Communist regime there.[292] The Afghan Communist regime provided the Tudeh Party and the Fadaian-Majority (under Farrokh Negahdar's leadership) various forms of support including a huge radio complex to broadcast into Iran. The Tudeh Party and Fadaian-Majority reciprocated with assisting the Afghan regime with propaganda and many began serving as university professors.[293]

In 1985 Iraj Eskandari (the former Secretary-General of the Tudeh Party), who had become a critic of Kianouri's collaboration with the fundamentalist regime, passed away. Many other leaders of the Tudeh Party were arrested by 1983. Other leaders such as Babak Amir-Khosravi and Mohsen Heydarian split and formed *"Hezb Democratic Mardom Iran"* [Democratic Party of the Iranian People], which also criticized Kianouri's policies. Under such conditions, Ali Khavari, who was residing outside Iran became the number one leader of the Tudeh Party. Under Ali Khavari's leadership, the Tudeh Party refused to change and remained as it has always been: traditional Communist, fully supportive of the USSR (prior to Gorbachev's reforms), and continued its close collaboration with the KGB.[294] The only time it appears that the Tudeh Party refused to do what the USSR ordered it to do was to make some reforms during the last years of Gorbachev's rule. Khavari died in Berlin on March 19, 2021, at age 98. Khavari's main accomplishment is that the Tudeh Party is still recognized by traditional pro-Soviet Communists such as the Vietnamese Communist regime and

---

291 Atabak Fathollahzadeh, *Khane Daee Yuusef: Vaghae Tekandahandeh Az Mohajerat Fadaian Aksariyat Beh Shoravi* [Uncle Joseph's House: Shocking Reports from the Emigration of Fadaiyan-Majority to the Soviet Union] (Tehran: Nashr Ghatreh, 2002), pp. 149–164, https://melliun.org/v/wp-content/uploads/2020/04/Khaneye-Daei-Yusof.pdf.
292 Arash Azizi, *"Ali Khavari, Rahbar Hezb Tudeh Iran Keh Bood Va Chegoneh Beh Rahbari Resid?"* [Ali Khavari, Who Was the Leader of the Tudeh Party of Iran and How Did He Become Its Leader?], Iran Wire, (March 23, 2021), https://iranwire.com/fa/features/47298.
293 Ibid.
294 H. Azin, *"Beh Bahaneh Dargozasht Ali Khavari"* [On the Occasion of the Passing Away of Ali Khavari], Gooya News, (March 24, 2021), https://news.gooya.com/2021/03/post-49972.php.

the Communist Party of Greece. The Tudeh Party has very few members. Several very small and insignificant groups which call themselves Tudeh Party continue to exist.[295]

The Tudeh Party was the largest and most organized political party in Iran between 1941 and 1950.[296] It was a major party between 1951 and 1953. It experienced a revival in 1979 and played a role in assisting Khomeini as well as against pro-democracy and leftist forces. Since 1992 it has atrophied to insignificance. The Tudeh Party has a website and publishes its views periodically.[297] Since the late 1990s, one could no longer use the term "real political party" to describe the Tudeh Party.

In a major statement published on August 16, 2021, the Tudeh Party officially responded to the INF's public call that was made on August 12, 2021 for all pro-democracy forces to cooperate in creating a broad-based alliance against the fundamentalist regime.[298] The Tudeh Party's detailed statement profusely praised the INF and Mossadegh, as well as strongly condemned the Shah and the fundamentalist regimes. It blamed the rise of the fundamentalist regime on the Shah's policies of repressing secular liberal, and leftist forces as well as allowing room for right-wing reactionary fundamentalist forces to operate. The statement criticized the Tudeh Party for its attacks on the INF and Mossadegh in the 1950s. The statement remained silent on the Tudeh Party's attacks on the INF after the revolution and for the Tudeh Party's strong support for Khomeini and the fundamentalists. The statement called for replacement of the fundamentalist regime's dictatorship with secular democracy. It stated the Tudeh Party's strong support for the INF.[299]

The INF and the INF-OA did not respond to the Tudeh Party. It does not appear that the INF would accept to form a formal coalition with the Tudeh Party. The strong rejection of the fundamentalist regime by the Tudeh Party is significant. The Tudeh Party's public support for the INF and the establishment of a

---

295 Azizi, op. cit.

296 For a highly sympathetic view of the Tudeh Party see Abrahamian, *Iran Between Two Revolutions* (Princeton: Princeton University Press, 1982): chapters 6 – 8. For a critical analysis of the Tudeh Party see the seminal article by Chaqueri, "Did the Soviets play a role in founding the Tudeh party in Iran?," op. cit. Chaqueri was a Marxian independent democratic socialist, highly sympathetic to Mossadegh, and a member of the INF in Europe.

297 The website of the Tudeh Party is at https://www.tudehpartyiran.org/en/home/.

298 Tudeh Party, "*Sokhani Ba Jebhe Melli Iran Be Monesabat Kodeta-e Nangin 28 Mordad 1332: Ma Az 'Etehad Melli Baray Tahaghogh Hakemiyat Melli' Esteghbal Mikonim*" [A Talk with the Iran National Front on the Occasion of the Infamous Coup of August 19, 1953: We Welcome the "National Unity for Realization of National Sovereignty"], (August 16, 2021), http://www. ensafnews.com/312263/. For INF's statement see Chapter 8.

299 Tudeh Party, ibid.

democratic secular republic under the leadership of the INF is also positive for the prospects of democracy in Iran. The cooperation between the pro-democracy forces and the far left against the fundamentalist regime is reminiscent of the coalition between the Western democracy and the Soviet Union against fascist powers during World War Two. It remains to be seen how the INF would handle the support from the far left.

Organization of the People's Fadaian Guerrillas of Iran

In 1979, the largest leftist group in Iran was the Organization of the People's Fadaian Guerrillas of Iran. It was established in 1963 by young activists who were frustrated by the brutal repression of the Shah's regime and the lack of activities by the INF and the Tudeh Party. Inspired by the Cuban revolution and embracing the theories of French Marxist Régis Debray, they began guerrilla operations. They believed that a small group of revolutionaries can use violence against a tyrannical regime, and thus show the masses that the ruling dictatorship is vulnerable. The small group then can encourage the large masses to enter the struggle and overthrow the tyrannical regime.[300]

Some of the leaders had been members of the Tudeh Party or their parents were members of the Tudeh Party, others had been members of the INF or their parents were members of the INF. Bijan Jazani was a member of the Tudeh Party in the 1950s. A brilliant philosophy student at the University of Tehran, he wanted to work with the INF in 1960 – 63. He opposed the Tudeh Party's subservience to Moscow. Jazani strongly condemned the Tudeh Party's attacks and opposition to Dr. Mossadegh and the INF. He wanted to establish an independent socialist movement. He was a Leninist and there exists no evidence that he opposed Stalinism. A close friend of Jazani was Hassan Zia-Zarifi. Zia-Zarifi was a supporter of the Tudeh Party in the early 1950s and joined the INF in 1960 – 63. Mostafa Shoaiyan had been a member of the INF. He became a Marxist who was strongly anti-Stalinist, critical of Leninism, highly critical of the Soviet Union, and the

---

300 Rangin-Kaman TV, "*Jame-e Shenasi Siasi Opposision Iran: Sazeman Cherikhay Fadaian Khalq Iran*" [Political Sociology of the Opposition in Iran: Organization of the People's Fadaian Guerrillas of Iran], (June 11, 2020), https://www.youtube.com/watch?v=aepF_I_ENcc; and Rangin-Kaman TV, "*Jame-e Shenasi Opposision Iran: Sazeman Aksariyat Va Sazeman Rah-e Kargar, Bakhsh 1*" [Political Sociology of the Opposition in Iran: Fadaian-Majority and Rah-e Kargar, Part 1], (July 17, 2020), https://www.youtube.com/watch?v=6j_b9EL2nr4.

Tudeh Party's subservience to the Soviet Union.[301] Shoaiyan was also critical of the Fadaian's silence toward the Tudeh Party and the Soviet Union. Shoaiyan wanted to develop an independent, democratic socialist, guerrilla movement. As was the practice among Iran's guerrillas, he took cyanide capsule seconds before being captured by the Shah's security forces.[302] Masoud Ahmadzadeh came from a famous INF family. Jazani and Zia-Zarifi along with seven other political prisoners were murdered by SAVAK outside the Evin Prison in April 1975. SAVAK claimed that they were escaping from the prison, a claim that few believe. Ahmadzadeh was killed in armed clashes with the Shah's security forces. Jazani, Zia-Zarifi, Shoaiyan, and Ahmadzadeh held very positive views of the INF and were highly critical of the Tudeh Party, its subservience to the Soviet Union, and were concerned about the Soviet Union's negative intentions toward Iran. Had they lived after the victory of the 1979 revolution, in all likelihood they would have developed the Fadaian organization as an independent leftist group siding with pro-democracy parties such as the INF, rather than allying with the Tudeh Party and collaborating with the Soviet Union and the KGB as the Fadaian-Majority did.[303] Other Marxist guerrillas who had been members of the INF before joining leftist guerrillas, tended to values democracy and liberal democrats, whereas those who emerged from the Tudeh Party tended to hold strongly anti-democratic views. For example, Shokrollah Paknejad, was one of the most prominent and brave Marxist guerrillas before the revolution who had been a member of the INF before becoming Marxist. After the revolution, Paknejad worked with other liberal democrats and established the National Democratic Front, which strongly opposed Khomeini and the fundamentalists and supported civil liberties.

In 1979, the number one leader of the Fadaian was Farrokh Negahdar. Negahdar told me that many members of his family were members of the Tudeh Party.[304] He had served many years in the Evin prison under the Shah. A close friend and collaborator of Kianouri after the 1979 Revolution, he moved the Fadaian towards close alliance with the Tudeh Party. The Tudeh Party made a huge effort to infiltrate the Fadaian and bring it to alliance with itself. With assistance from Negahdar, the Tudeh Party succeeded. Many in the Fadaian opposed this

---

301 Peyman Vahabzadeh, *A Rebel's Journey: Mostafa Sho'aiyan and Revolutionary Theory in Iran* (London: Oneworld Academic, 2020).

302 SAVAK would use extreme torture to extract intelligence from the guerrillas they would capture in order to find out about others and their safe houses. In order to protect others, members of various guerrillas were instructed to carry cyanide capsules with them.

303 See below.

304 Personal interview with Farrokh Negahdar, London, February 1995.

move.[305] The Fadaian in early 1979 had organized a rally of about 500,000 but soon fractured into 10 small groups. Fadaian-Majority (under the leadership of Negahdar) along with the Tudeh Party began strongly supporting Ayatollah Khomeini, the Islamic Republican Party, and the fundamentalist regime.[306] By 1983, Fadaian-Majority ranks shrank to only a few thousands. According to a former top leader, in a region where he was operating, its members and supporters shrank from over 5,000 in early 1979 to only about 30 in 1983.[307] In 1983, the regime arrested about 2,000 members of the Tudeh Party and the Fadaian-Majority and executed many of them by 1988. Many Fadaian-Majority members escaped to the former Soviet Union, where the KGB recruited them to work for them. According to many former leaders, Negahdar and Kianouri supported the policy of collaborating with the KGB.[308] After the collapse of the Soviet Union, Fadaian-Majority has gone through major transformations. The rank and file changed their leaders and strongly criticized the organization's collaboration with the fundamentalist regime.

Left Party of Iran

Fadaian-Majority is the largest left-wing group today and is highly active.[309] Since 2017, along with few other Fadaian groups, it formed the *"Hezb Chap Iran (Fadaian)"* [Left Party of Iran (Fadaian)].[310] It says that it is not a social democratic party; rather it is a "former communist party" along the lines of the Left Party of Germany. The Left Party of Iran (LPI) has publicly criticized itself (e. g., Fadaian-Majority) for its dictatorial past, its support for Khomeini, and its vicious attacks against the INF. It has privately and publicly apologized to Abbas Amir-Entezam. The LPI says that today it supports democracy, civil liberties, and accepts capi-

---

305 Rangin-Kaman TV, *"Jame-e Shenasi Siasi Opposision Iran: Sazeman Cherikhay Fadaian Khalq Iran"* [Political Sociology of the Opposition in Iran: Organization of the People's Fadaian Guerrillas of Iran], (June 11, 2020), https://www.youtube.com/watch?v=aepF_I_ENcc; Rangin-Kaman TV, *"Jame-e Shenasi Opposision Iran: Sazeman Aksariyat Va Sazeman Rah-e Kargar, Bakhsh 1"* [Political Sociology of the Opposition in Iran: Fadaian-Majority and Rah-e Kargar, Part 1], (July 17, 2020), https://www.youtube.com/watch?v=6j_b9EL2nr4.
306 Ibid.
307 Atabak Fathollahzadeh, *Khane Daee Yuusef: Vaghae Tekandahandeh Az Mohajerat Fadaian Aksariyat Beh Shoravi* [Uncle Joseph's House: Shocking Reports from the Emigration of Fadaiyan-Majority to the Soviet Union] (Tehran: Nashr Ghatreh, 2002), p. 16.
308 Ibid.
309 The organization's website is at http://fadai.org/index.html.
310 The organization's website is at https://bepish.org/.

talism. It wishes to represent the working class and participate democratically in politics.

The Fadaian-Majority had assisted in establishing *"Ettehad Jomhurikhahan Iran"* [United Republicans of Iran][311] in a coalition with a large number of progressives and former leftists. The LPI is the dominant group in the United Republicans of Iran, and many groups that have had disagreements with the LPI have left the United Republicans of Iran. Another group of mostly former leftists has been established called *Hambastegi Jomhurikahahn Iran* [Solidarity of Iranian Republicans].[312]

The LPI appears to lack a consistent policy. One faction, under the leadership of Farrokh Negahdar, advocates following the leadership of the reformist faction of the fundamentalist regime. A second faction advocates working with the pro-democracy opposition groups such as the INF. Before the mass protests of December 2017-January 2018, the LPI was strongly supportive of the reformist faction of the fundamentalist regime. After the mass protests of December 2017-Janaury 2018 and November 2019, it appeared that the second faction gained the upper-hand and the LPI distanced itself from the regime and began close cooperation with the INF-OA. Between 2018 and December 2020, the LPI, United Republicans of Iran, and Solidarity of Iranian Republicans were cooperating closely with the INF-OA. During this period, they issued about two dozen joint statements, sent messages of solidarity to each other's congresses, and organized rallies outside Iran in support of the mass protests inside Iran.

From January 2021, the LPI and the United Republicans of Iran again changed their policy and began following the reformist faction of the fundamentalist regime. By April 2021, it appeared that Negahdar's faction had gained the upper hand again. The reasons for these changes are not clear. Perhaps, between 2018 and 2020, it appeared that the regime was on the verge of collapse; therefore, it made more sense to distance themselves from the regime. After Joe Biden's election to presidency in the U.S., the possibility of regime collapse appeared less likely (due to possible American return to the JCPOA and sale of oil); therefore, it made more sense to get close to the fundamentalist regime again.

---

311 The organization's website is at http://jomhouri.com/jomhouri/.
312 The organization's website is at https://iranian-republic.org/fa/home.

Chapter 7
Religion, Politics, and the INF

The 20th century witnessed many efforts around the globe to combine religion and politics. For example, there have been Christian Democratic parties in European democracies (e. g., Italy, Germany) and in Latin America (e. g., Chile, Venezuela). There has also been the Liberation Theology in Latin America attempting to combine Marxism and Catholicism. Religious leaders such as Dr. Martin Luther King, Jr., and Archbishop Desmond Tutu were influential and inspiring political figures. Similar attempts have been made in both the Sunni and Shia worlds during the 20th and 21st centuries.

What is the "proper" role of religion in politics? What is the "proper" role of clerics in politics? In the case of contemporary Iran, what should be the proper roles of Islam, Shia clerics, Islamism, and Islamists in politics? By "Islamist," I refer to those who transform Islam into a political ideology. They might be liberal Islamist, socialist Islamist, communist Islamist, or fundamentalist Islamists. Bazargan attempted to both modernize Islam and to articulate a liberal democratic Islamism. Dr. Shariati attempted to articulate socialist Islamism. The PMOI attempted to articulate communist Islamism.[313] The Fadaian Islam and Ayatollah Khomeini articulated an extreme-right-wing totalitarian ideology and system that have great similarities with European fascisms of 1920s – 1945.

These issues on the proper relationship between religion and politics have animated Iranian politics since at least the Constitutional revolution (1905). Islamic fundamentalists played a major role in the Iranian Revolution (1977–1979) and by July 1981 were able to defeat all other forces that had participated in the revolution against the monarchy. Since July 1981, the fundamentalists have had complete political power in Iran.

The atrocities committed by the Shia fundamentalists (e. g., Khomeini and his regime in Iran, Lebanese Hezbollah, Kataib Hezbollah in Iraq) and Sunni fundamentalists (e. g., ISIS, al Qaeda, Taliban, Hamas, Muslim Brotherhood) have made many Islamist and Moslem thinkers and activists to reassess such

---

313 The PMOI called its goal as the establishment of *"Jame'e Bi-Tabagheh Towhidi"* (classless divine society). For a critical view of the PMOI see Abrahamian, *The Iranian Mojahedin*, op. cit.; for a sympathetic view of the PMOI see Suroosh Irfani, *Iran's Islamic Revolution: Popular Liberation or Religious Dictatorship?* (London: Zed Press, 1983). The PMOI's website is at https://english.mojahedin.org/. Other acronyms of the PMOI are MKO and MEK. The PMOI is the main group within the National Council of Resistance of Iran (NCRI). The group's site is at https://www.ncr-iran.org/en/.

https://doi.org/10.1515/9783110782158-009

projects. Many blame the coming to power of the fundamentalists in Iran to the attempts by Islamic reformers like Mehdi Bazargan and Dr. Ali Shariati. In this chapter, I discuss the history and views of the INF on the roles of Islam and clerics in politics.

Mossadegh and Religion

One of the charges against Mossadegh in his trial after the 1953 coup was apostacy. On June 15, 1981, Ayatollah Khomeini declared Mossadegh "*mortad*" [apostate] and declared the INF to have committed apostasy for its opposition to the Bill of Retribution. The punishment for apostasy in Shia Islam is execution. Both the Shah and Khomeini were using Islam for their political objectives. Like the Shah and Khomeini, Ayatollah Kashani had also called Mossadegh apostate after they became political opponents in early 1953.

Mossadegh believed in Shia Islam. Moreover, he paid his religious taxes (*Zakat* and *Khoms*). Mossadegh considered his religious beliefs to be a private matter. As prime minister, Mossadegh considered his job to be establishment of democracy and nationalization of oil. Mossadegh did not consider his job as prime minister to be the implementation of Shia Sharia as the law of the country.[314] In addition, Mossadegh stated that as prime minister, his job was to legally treat all Iranian citizens equally before the law and not to discriminate against any citizens due to his religion. Mossadegh's views and policies brought him into conflict with right-wing Islamic forces (e. g., Ayatollah Behbahani, Ayatollah Falsafi, Fadaian Islam) who wanted to use the government to discriminate and oppress religious minorities in Iran.

Dr. Hussein Mesr-Oghli, a prominent member of the INF, has described one of Mossadegh's decisions. Dr. Mesr-Oghli was an Azerbaijani and was from Tabriz. He was a prominent member of the Iran Party and the INF in Tabriz during Mossadegh's premiership. He was also one of the founders of the INF-OA in Europe in the 1960s. According to Dr. Mesr-Oghli, during Mossadegh's government, an official from the Treasury Ministry was appointed the Head of the Treasury Ministry in Tabriz the capital of the Azerbaijan province. This new official was Jewish and many bazaaris in Tabriz objected to his appointment due to his religion. The bazaaris asked Ayatollah Khosrowshahi, a prominent cleric and sup-

---

314 Ayatollah Mahmoud Taleghani, "*Sokhanrani Dar Mazar Doktor Mossadegh*" [Speech at Dr. Mossadegh's Grave], (March 5, 1979), https://www.youtube.com/watch?v=gJUXNP7yMiE (posted on You Tube September 11, 2019).

porter of the Mossadegh government, to go and talk with Dr. Mossadegh and ask for his dismissal from his new position.[315] After returning from Tehran, Ayatollah Khosrowshahi tells the bazaaris: "No matter how much I insisted, Dr. Mossadegh did not accept to dismiss him and said that he is Jewish so he is and this is not an issue. He is an honest, competent, and honorable Iranian. Whatever religion and denomination he may have. He is an Iranian and possess all the rights of other Iranian citizens that is equal to all other Iranians."[316] And based on this principle, that competent Head of the Treasury remained at his post.[317]

According to Ayatollah Falsafi's memoirs, Falsafi went to see Mossadegh when he was prime minister. Falsafi says that he was bringing a message from Grand Ayatollah Brujerdi for Mossadegh. Falsafi tells Mossadegh that many Moslems are complaining that Bahais are engaging in propaganda and are bothering the Moslem faithful in numerous towns. And that Ayatollah Brujerdi founds it necessary that you take action against them.[318] Falsafi says that after hearing this, Mossadegh sarcastically chuckled and laughed out hard. Mossadegh replied: "Mr. Falsafi, from my point of view, there is no difference between a Moslem and a Bahai, they are from one nation and are Iranian."[319] What Mossadegh was saying is that from the point of view as the prime minister, the government has to treat all citizens similarly and not engage in religious inquisition, discrimination, and oppressive actions against any religious group.

Ayatollahs Brujerdi, Falsafi, Kashani, and Behbahani supported the Shah during and after the 1953 coup. As reward, the Shah allowed them to attack the Bahais. Ayatollah Falsafi was extremely anti-Bahai and a popular preacher. The Shah allowed him a program on Radio Tehran during the month of Rama-

---

315 Ali Rasekh-Afshar, Parviz Davarpanah, Ali Shakeri-Zand, and Mehdi Moghadaszadeh, *"Baray Melliun Hoghogh Shahrvandi Asl Asl Va Azadi Aghideh Az Osol Zirbanaee Va Gheir Ghabel Tagheer Mast"* [For the Nationalists Rights of Citizenship Are Principles And Freedom of Belief Are Our Foundational and Unchanging Principles], (December 4, 2014), https://ehterameazadi. blogspot.com/2014/12/blog-post_4.html.

316 Ibid.

317 Ibid.

318 Tasnim News Agency, *"Khatereh Ayatollah Falsafi Az Mossadegh Va Masaleh Oo Ba Islam"* [Memoirs of Ayatollah Falsafi on Mossadegh and His Problem with Islam], (August 19, 2017), https://www.tasnimnews.com/fa/news/1396/05/28/1495651/%D8%AE%D8%A7%D8%B7%D8% B1%D9%87-%D8%A2%DB%8C%D8%AA-%D8%A7%D9%84%D9%84%D9%87-%D9%81%D9% 84%D8%B3%D9%81%DB%8C-%D8%A7%D8%B2-%D9%85%D8%B5%D8%AF%D9%82-%D9% 88-%D9%85%D8%B3%D8%A6%D9%84%D9%87-%D8%A7%D9%88-%D8%A8%D8%A7-% D8%A7%D8%B3%D9%84%D8%A7%D9%85.

319 Ibid. My translation.

dan in 1955 with permission to broadcast extremely vicious anti-Bahai sermons. Falsafi had the full support of Brujerdi and Kashani. The clerics attacked and destroyed the Bahai Center in Tehran in 1955. The violent attacks on Bahais in 1955 included murders, rapes, and burning of homes of Bahais. Bahais in the U.S. lobbied the U.S. government to tell the Shah to stop the attacks. After the U.S. government told the Shah to stop these attacks, the Shah ordered a halt of the attacks on Bahais.[320] In 1963, Falsafi abandoned the Shah's side and allied with Khomeini. Falsafi was also a strong supporter and ally of Khomeini during and after the 1979 revolution.

In late 1952, conflict arose between Mossadegh and Ayatollah Kashani. According to Abrahamian, one of the issues was over the release of assassins from the Fadaian Islam, Navab Safavi and Khalil Tahmasebi. Kashani wanted to release them while Mossadegh opposed their release from prison. Navab Safavi (real name is Sayyed Mojtaba Mir-Lohi) had founded the Fadaian Islam in 1946. The Fadaian Islam was the Shia version of the Egyptian Muslim Brothers, a Sunni organization founded in 1918 by Hassan al-Banna in Egypt. The Fadaian Islam advocated the establishment of an Islamic government and the implementation of (Shia) Shariah as the law of the land.

Navab Safavi was responsible for assassinations of historian Ahmad Kasravi, prime minister Abdol-Hussein Hazhir, and Gen. Haj-Ali Razmara. During Mossadegh's government, Navab Safavi was kept in jail. After the coup in 1953, the Shah rewarded the Fadaian Islam with releasing Navab Safavi.[321] Navab Safavi was very close to both Seyyed Zia al-Din Tabatabae and Gen. Fazlollah Zahedi. Khalil Tahmasebi was a member of the Fadaian Islam as well. The Shah was behind the assassination of Gen. Razmara, and the person who was sent to assassinate Gen. Razmara was Khalil Tahmasebi. In 1952, Ayatollah Kashani and Hojatol-Islam Shams Ghanat-Abadi passed a bill in the Majles freeing Tahmasebi. The Shah signed the bill. Mossadegh was opposed to the bill releasing Tahmasebi.[322] After Mossadegh became prime minister, with his support both Navab Safavi and Tahmasebi were put in jail.[323] The Fadaian Islam was one of the main

---

320 Mina Yazdani, "Towards a History of Iran's Baha'i Community During the Reign of Mohammad Reza Shah, 1941–1979," *Iran Namag*, Vol. 2, No. 1 (Spring 2017), pp. 63–68, https://encompass.eku.edu/cgi/viewcontent.cgi?article=1076&context=fs_research.

321 Abrahamian, *Khomeinism*, p. 109.

322 Mohammad Amini in interview with Hussein Mohri, (August 16, 2011), https://www.youtube.com/watch?v=VoKkbC6sChc&feature=.

323 Yasser Mirdamadi, "*Terrorhay Fadiyan Islam: Az Ahmad Kasravi Ta Hussein Ala*" [The Assassinations of Fadaian Islam: From Ahmad Kasravi to Hussein Ala], BBC Persian, (March 14, 2012), https://www.bbc.com/persian/iran/2012/03/120313_144_islam_fadaiyan.shtml.

groups that supported the 1953 coup against Mossadegh. The Fadaian Islam worked closely with Gen. Zahedi. However, the honeymoon between the Shah and the Fadaian Islam did not last long. After the assassination of prime minister Hussein Ala in 1955, the Shah executed the top leaders of the Fadaian Islam including both Safavi and Tahmasebi.[324]

The Fadaian Islam made an assassination attempt on the life of Mossadegh's foreign minister Dr. Hussein Fatemi and had plans to assassinate Mossadegh.[325] Mr. Mohammad Mehdi Abd-Khodaee, the person who shot Fatemi in the stomach, became one of the leaders of the Fadaian Islam after the revolution, a top member of the fundamentalist oligarchy, and a member of the Majles in 1980.[326] He was close to Ayatollah Ali Akbar Rafsanjani. The Fadaian Islam's top leader after the revolution was Ayatollah Sadegh Khalkhali, a close friend and ally of Khomeini. Khalkhali became the Revolutionary Judge, responsible for the execution of somewhere between 1,000 and 2,000 individuals.[327] Ayatollah Ali Khamenei considers Navab Safavi, the founder of the Fadaian Islam, to be one of his heroes.[328]

The INF and Religion Today

As mentioned in Chapters 2 and 4, conflicts between the INF and the fundamentalists increased in June 1981. On June 15, 1981, Ayatollah Khomeini declared the INF apostate.[329] The INF is a secular (non-religious) party. It is not an anti-religious party. It opposes mixing religion and the state. In other words, the INF op-

---

324 Ibid.

325 Farhad Kazemi, "The *Fada'iyan-e Islam:* Fanaticism, Politics and Terror," in Said Amir Arjomand, ed. *From Nationalism to Revolutionary Islam* (Albany: State University of New York Press, 1984), pp. 158–176; and Abrahamian, *Khomeinism*, p. 105.

326 Mohammad Mehdi Abd-Khodaee, "*Goftogo-e Hussein Dehbashi Ba Mohammad Mehdi Abd-Khodaee*" [Hussein Dehbashi Interview with Mohammad Mehdi Abd-Khodaee], Khesht Kham, No. 42 (2018), https://www.aparat.com/v/LxJpW/ت‌شخ_ماخ_%2F_تبون_لهچ_و_مود_%2F‌یوگتفگ_نیسح.

327 After his death, then-president Mohammad Khatami profusely praised Ayatollah Khalkhali and his work for the revolution.

328 Ayatollah Ali Khamenei, "Navab Safavi Triggered the First Sparks of the Islamic Revolution," www.Khamenei-ir (January 17, 2018), https://english.khamenei.ir/news/5409/Nawab-Safawi-triggered-the-first-sparks-of-the-Islamic-Revolution. Also see Masoud Kazemzadeh, "Ayatollah Khamenei's Foreign Policy Orientation," *Comparative Strategy*, Vol. 32, No. 5 (2013), pp. 443–458.

329 Ayatollah Ruhollah Khomeini, *Sahifeh Noor*, vol. 14, (June 15, 1981), https://emam.com/posts/view/2645.

poses any position in the state to be exclusively reserved for clerics such as the position of *Vali Faghih* [Supreme Shia Cleric Leader], or Assembly of Experts, Council of Guardian, or Head of the Judiciary. The INF wants the constitution and state institutions to be secular.

Historically, however, the INF did not oppose the mixing of religion and politics. In other words, the INF believed that people have the right to organize based on their religious views. For the INF, clerics should have the same right as all other citizens to run for office.

The INF has always had devout members and leaders. In fact, many clerics have been its members and leaders, such as Ayatollahs Mahmoud Taleghani, Grand Ayatollah Reza Zanjani, Ayatollah Abolfazl Zanjani, Ayatollah Haj Ziaaldin Haj Seyyed Javadi, Ayatollah Seyyed Bagher Jalali Moussavi, and Ayatollah Milani.[330] Ayatollah Taleghani and Ayatollah Jalali Moussavi were elected to the INF Central Committee in the Tehranpars congress in January 1963. During and after the 1979 revolution, the highest-ranking Shia cleric in Iran, Grand Ayatollah Kazem Shariatmadari closely and publicly cooperated and coordinated with the INF, including the opposition to the fundamentalist constitution.

Ayatollah Taleghani, was a strong supporter of Mossadegh and had been a member of the INF. In 1953, he was one of the founding members of the *Nehzat Moghavemat Melli*, the organization founded to resist the coup. A close ally and friend of Bazargan, Taleghani was one of the founders of the Liberation Movement of Iran in 1961. He was a member of the Assembly of Experts, which wrote the 1979 constitution. Taleghani strongly and publicly opposed the notion of *Velayat Faghih* [rule of a high-ranking Shia cleric]. Taleghani was one of five members of the assembly that opposed the position of the *Vali Faghih* [Supreme Leader that is a Shia Cleric]. Taleghani publicly and strongly condemned the emerging clerical dictatorship in his last sermon on September 6, 1979.[331] Taleghani died under mysterious circumstances three days later on September 9, 1979. Although Taleghani had heart problems and was a heavy cigarette smoker, nevertheless he was too healthy and young to die so suddenly. On the video of Taleghani delivering his speech on September 6, he appears healthy and vigorous. His widow and son have publicly blamed the death as murder by the fun-

---

330 Hussein Moussavian, "*Goftogo Ba Doktor Hussein Moussavian*" [Interview with Dr. Hussein Moussavian], Rangarang TV, (October 2, 2019), https://melliun.org/iran/215417.
331 Ayatollah Mahmoud Taleghani, "*Akharin Namaz Jomeh Ayatollah Taleghani*" [The Last Friday Prayer Sermon of Ayatollah Taleghani], (originally September 6, 1979), https://www.youtube.com/watch?v=t25EPRObOZQ.

damentalists. The fundamentalists refused to allow an autopsy to determine the cause of death.[332]

Ayatollah Reza Zanjani was a member of the INF leadership.[333] After the 1953 coup, he organized the resistance to the coup. He sold his hazelnut orchard in order to fund the resistance to the coup regime.[334] He was arrested many times after the coup. He became a prison cell mate with Dr. Fatemi. After Fatemi was given sentence of execution, he asked Ayatollah Zanjani to serve as guardian of his family and young son. And Ayatollah Zanjani did so exemplary. Ayatollah Zanjani also provided financial support to the family of many who had been killed during the 1953 coup and under torture after the coup whether they were supporters of the INF or any other group. For example, Ayatollah Zanjani provided support to the family of Vartan Salakhanian, who was an Armenian member of the Tudeh Party who had died under torture. When Mossadegh passed away on March 5, 1967, Ayatollah Zanjani delivered the funeral prayer. Ayatollah Zanjani passed away on January 4, 1984. During his funeral, gangs of fundamentalists shouted slogans such as "Death to Opponent of *Velayat Faghih*," "Death to Hypocrite," and "Death to America."[335]

Ayatollah Reza Zanjani was strongly and publicly against the notion of *Velayat Faghih*. He believed that the clerics should not accept any executive positions in government. He believed that the role of the clerics is to support politicians or oppose them but not become politicians themselves. Zanjani strongly defended Mossadegh and said that he was more a Muslim than any prime minister or cabinet minister before and after his government. That Mossadegh was a statesman and not a religious preacher. In June 1981 he publicly supported President Dr. Bani Sadr and opposed the efforts of Khomeini and fundamentalists in removing him from power.[336]

There have been members and former members of the INF who have attempted to combine liberal democracy with Islam (Mehdi Bazargan) or to combine social democracy with Islam (Mohammad Nakhshab, Hussein Razi, and

---

332 VOA, "*Ayatollah Taleghani Va Ghatelan Oo Ra Behtar Beshenasim*" [To Know Better Ayatollah Taleghani and His Murderers], (December 27, 2019), https://www.youtube.com/watch?v=8d_G8vgbJBw.

333 Jebhe Melli Iran, "*Seyyed Reza Zanjani, Mojtahed Melli-gara*" [Seyyed Reza Zanjani, Nationalist Cleric], (January 2021), http://jebhemeliiran.org/?p=2516.

334 Ibid.

335 Ibid.

336 Ibid.

Ayatollah Taleghani), or to combine Marxism with Islam (Dr. Ali Shariati).[337] It is noteworthy to emphasize that their public efforts to articulate an Islamist ideology occurred after they left the INF and were the leaders of the LMI. Many Iranians, including many in the INF, believe that such efforts were mistaken. Many activists, including INF members, argue that religion should not be transformed into political ideology even benign ideologies such as liberal democracy and social democracy. The horrific experience of the fundamentalist regime, according to these thinkers, shows that mixing Islam and politics is a recipe for disaster. [338] For some of these thinkers, the fundamentalist regime has terribly harmed both the Iranian people and Islam.[339]

The thinkers of the *"Melli-Mazhabi"* [Nationalist-Religious] group consider themselves to constitute the political and intellectual heirs of Bazargan, Nakhshab, Razi, Shariati, and Taleghani.[340] Before the 1979 revolution, they tended to work on transforming Islam into their liberal democratic Islamist or social democratic Islamist ideology, that is (re)interpreting Islam to constitute a political ideology. Today, however, they explicitly say that they support separation between religion and the state.[341]

The Iran People Party has been a member of the INF (see Chapter 3). It attempts to combine social democracy and Islam. It also opposes mixing Islam and the state. In other words, it mixes Islam and politics for its inspiration but supports a secular state.

Because of the painful experiences of the Iranian people under the fundamentalist dictatorship, many Iranians are reassessing their earlier views. The

---

337 For a sophisticated analysis of the views of Bazargan, Taleghani, and Shariati see Chehabi, *Iranian Politics and Religious Modernism*, op. cit., pp. 42–84. Chehabi argues, convincingly, that Bazargan did not turn Islam into an ideology. His efforts were mostly to argue that Islam is compatible with science, democracy, and modernity. Chehabi argues that Shariati did articulate an Islamist ideology, one that combined Third-Worldist Marxism and Shia Islam.

338 See the views of Dr. Mohsen Ghaemmagham, Ali Gosheh, Dr. Houmayun Mehmaneche, Esfandiar Khalaf, and Dr. Farhang Ghassemi at Rangin-Kaman TV, *"Hamsooe Social Demokrat-hay Secular, Bakhsh 2"* [Cooperation Among Secular Social Democrats], (November 3, 2020), https://www.youtube.com/watch?v=9emWTuJ-sO8. Also see the views of members of the INF and INF-Abroad at Rangin-Kaman TV, *"Jame-e Shenasi Siasi Opposision Iran: Jebhe Melli Iran, Bakhsh 1"* [Political Sociology of the Opposition in Iran: Iran National Front, Part 1], (July 2, 2020), https://www.youtube.com/watch?v=Td4STdpQYTU and Rangin-Kaman TV, *"Jame-e Shenasi Siasi Opposision Iran: Jebhe Melli Iran, Bakhsh 2"* [Political Sociology of the Opposition in Iran: Iran National Front, Part 2], (July 9, 2020), https://www.youtube.com/watch?v=lLC4ypIeVYw.

339 Ibid.

340 The group's website is at https://melimazhabi.com/.

341 See the "About Us" section of the group at https://melimazhabi.com/%d8%af%d8%b1%d8%a8%d8%a7%d8%b1%d9%87-%d9%85%d8%a7/.

fundamentalist rule has given rise to a massive backlash against not only against theocracy (rule by the clerics) but also against Islamism among large segments of the Iranian population. Many have come to the conclusion that the best policy is to have a secular political system. Many others argue that the experience of the fundamentalist regime has shown that mixing of Islam and politics is also dangerous.

These reassessments come not merely from observing the cruelties and oppression by the fundamentalists but more significantly because many of these atrocities have been justified by Islamic or Shia doctrines and beliefs. For example, Khomeini lied in Paris about the nature of the post-Shah regime that he would establish. After coming to power, Khomeini justified his lies with reference to Shia concepts of *"taghieh"* [lying] and *"khodeh"* [deception]. The defamations against opponents and dissidents have been justified with the Shia concept of *"bohtan"* [defamation], which allows slandering and or libeling a person who presents effective criticisms of Islam, and defenders of Islam are not able to provide logical answers to.[342] The fundamentalist regime has engaged in mass rape of female political prisoners and has justified it on Shia grounds. The fundamentalist regime has also engaged in rape of male political prisoners although no religious concept was found to present as justification. The ISIS also used Islamic concepts to justify taking slaves, mass beheadings, and rape of female prisoners. The mass atrocities committed by the fundamentalist regime in Iran and their justifications based on Shia concepts have caused cognitive dissonance among not only the Iranian people in general but also among Islamist thinkers. Some scholars have referred to this phenomenon as "secular miracle."[343] Rahnema and Nomani also mention the many changes of what was *"haram"* [forbidden] into *"halal"* [not forbidden] and vice versa as showing to the population the opportunism of Islamist rulers and the weaknesses of Islam as a doctrine to deliver what it has promised for over a millennium.[344]

---

342 For an excellent documentary on Shia concepts of *"bohtan"* and *"taghieh"* with specific examples that the fundamentalist regime used against opponents and dissidents see BBC Persian, *"Bohtan Barayeh Hefz Nezam"* [Defamation for Preserving the Regime], (December 18, 2018), with English subtitles, https://www.youtube.com/watch?v=qIwgrSnxwLI. *"Bohtan"* is best translated as defamation, but also refers to slander (oral form of defamation) or libel (written form of defamation).
343 Ali Rahnema and Farhad Nomani, *The Secular Miracle: Religion, Politics & Economic Policy in Iran* (London: Zed Books, 1990).
344 Ibid.

The fundamentalist regime is a totalitarian theocratic regime. It *de jure* and *de facto* discriminates against religious minorities. It considers fundamentalist Shia clerics to be superior to all other segments of the population. The regime's ideology considers the fundamentalist Shia clerics to be the representative of Allah on earth. Any opposition to them is opposition to Allah himself and apostasy and thus should be physically eliminated. The regime considers Christians, Jews, and Zoroastrians as second-class citizens. The regime actively oppresses Bahais. It has executed many merely for believing or practicing their religion. The regime also discriminates against Sunni citizens, including destroying their mosques and refusing permits to build mosques.

The regime also discriminates against Sufis. The regime has violently been oppressing the Gonabadi Darwishes, who are a non-violent Shia Sufi group.[345] The late Dr. Nour-Ali Tabandeh, a lawyer, was the leader of the Gonabadi Darwishes. Despite long prison terms and harsh treatment, he remained a supporter of democracy. Mr. Tabandeh was a strong supporter of Dr. Mossadegh, the INF, Bazargan, Amir-Entezam, and the provisional government.[346] Mr. Tabandeh served as defense attorney during Amir-Entezam's trial for spying. Tabandeh was also a member of the Board of Directors of Dr. Mossadegh's House in Ahmadabad. In late February 2021, Mr. Behnam Mahjoobi, a young member of the group died in the Evin prison.[347] The regime then increased repression of the Sufis.[348] The INF and the INF-OA have condemned the fundamentalist regime's violent repression of the Sufis.[349]

Since 1949, the INF has been a secular political party. It has been the subject of demagogic attacks by both the Shah's regime and the fundamentalist regime

---

345 Morteza Kazemian, *"Chera Jomhuri Islami Darawish Gonabadi Ra Khatari Aleh Khod Modanad?"* [Why Does the Islamic Republic Considers the Gonabadi Darwishes a Threat Against Itself?], Iran International, (March 5, 2021), https://www.youtube.com/watch?v=MOpDfhr-VKo.
346 Ibid.
347 Radio Farda, *"Payam Panj Darwish Zendani Dar Mored Marg Behnam Mahjoobi"* [The Message of Five Darwishes in Jail on the Death of Behnam Mahjoobi], (February 22, 2021), https://melliun.org/iran/253855.
348 Iran International, "Report on the Suppression of Gonabadi Darwishes," (March 5, 2021), https://www.youtube.com/watch?v=v-607PvwpGs; Iran International, "Report on the Suppression of Gonabadi Darwishes," (March 5, 2021), https://www.youtube.com/watch?v=sWoyOiJZk jU; and Vahid Beheshti, "Interview," Iran International, (March 5, 2021), https://www.youtube.com/watch?v=M-eWP9AUmiY.
349 Iran National Front, Organizations Abroad. *"Sarkoob Darawish Keshvar Va Aparthied Mazhabi Jomhuri Islami Ra Mahkoom Mikonim"* [We Condemn the Suppression of the Country's Darwishes and the Religious Apartheid of the Islamic Republic], (February 26, 2018), https://iranazad.info/jebhehkharej/jkh18/02/26%20daravish.htm.

accusing it and its leaders of apostacy. Although the INF has been a politically secular political party it has always defended the rights of all individuals and groups to hold any religious views or no religious views. It holds that religion should not be mixed with government. The INF has had members who have been Zoroastrian, Shia, Sunni, Christian, Jewish, Sufis, agnostic, and atheist. For the INF, religion is a private matter.

In 2015, the INF published its latest Platform (see Chapter 7). In Article Three, the Platform states: "In order to preserve respect for the religion of Islam and to provide opportunity to utilize the capabilities of all the people of Iran, the Iran National Front emphasizes the principle of the separation of religion from the state." There are discussions within the leadership to revise the wording in order to make the wall of separation between the state and religion even more clear. There are debates among the INF members as well as among Iranian intellectuals about the lessons of the fundamentalist regime and whether it is wise to also avoid mixing Islam and politics.

Chapter 8
The INF Today

Platform

The INF struggles to establish democracy, civil liberties, civil rights, and human rights in Iran. The INF Charter includes the following eight articles:

Article One. Preservation of territorial integrity, and establishment of democracy and political independence arising from the public will of the Iranian nation within a system based on a republican form of government built upon principles of democracy, human rights, and the rule of law.

Article Two. Emphasis on gaining and protecting basic liberties and rights of the people of Iran, especially freedom of political parties, elections, and the press as well as equal rights for women and men and struggling against any abridgments of human rights.

Article Three. In order to preserve respect for the religion of Islam and to provide opportunity to utilize the capabilities of all the people of Iran, the Iran National Front emphasizes the principle of the separation of religion from the state.

Article Four. Establishing social justice and raising the standard of living based on scientific worldviews, increasing [domestic] production, increasing employment, and promoting the just distribution of the national wealth.

Article Five. Respect for equal rights for all citizens, all religious beliefs, and customs, cultures and languages of all the ethnic groups and the people of the land of Iran.

Article Six. Strengthening, guarding, and spreading the national and shared Persian language and national arts and culture of Iran.

Article Seven. Adoption of an independent Iranian foreign policy based on the national interests and preservation of the territorial integrity of the country, support for the objectives and principles of the Charter of the United Nations, promotion of friendship and mutual respect with all the nations and countries, especially countries in the [Middle East] region, and struggle against all forms of individual, group, and state terrorism.[350]

Article Eight. Protection and security of the country's environment, meaning protection for jungles, pastures, rivers, and wetlands, as well as utilization of scientific and scholarly works to prevent air pollution.[351]

---

350 Jebhe Melli Iran, *Asasnameh Jebhe Melli Iran* [The Charter of the Iran National Front], (2015), http://jebhemeliiran.org/wp-content/uploads/2015/11/JMI-Statute.pdf, my translation.
351 Article Eight was added in early 2019.

https://doi.org/10.1515/9783110782158-010

Ideology

From 1949 to today, the INF has considered the establishment of democracy as its primary goal.[352] From Mossadegh to Moussavian, INF leaders have emphasized the primary significance of the establishment of democracy. They have argued that with the establishment of democracy in Iran, the Iranians would also gain independence because with their true representatives the people would demand independence from powerful foreign powers (U.K., USSR, U.S., Russia, China). It is easier for a foreign power to nefariously control a dictator than an entire nation.[353] According to the INF, with democracy, one would also be able to get social justice because the people can vote for those who advocate social justice.[354] According to the INF, with democracy and various liberties (e. g., freedoms of expression, press, parties, associations), the people could better monitor and counter financial corruption.[355] According to the INF, with democracy, a nation could also gain progress and development.[356] From Mossadegh to Moussavian, INF leaders have argued that principles such as democracy, freedom, social justice, economic development, social progress, modernity, and human rights are universal principles.[357]

The INF considers itself not only a democratic organization but also a nationalist one. The INF defines its nationalism as the struggle for *de facto* independence from colonial powers. The INF embraces moderate nationalism and patriotism. The INF has explicitly condemned all forms of extreme nationalism such as chauvinism, racism, fascism, xenophobia, and jingoism.[358]

In an article, entitled "What is the Nationalism of the Iran National Front?," published in its official publication, the INF describes its version of nationalism as "constructive patriotism."[359] From the very beginning, the INF argues, "Mossa-

---

352 Hussein Moussavian, "Interview with Radio Asr Jadid," (March 12, 2021), https://melliun.org/iran/255058.
353 Ibid.
354 Ibid.
355 Ibid.
356 Ibid.
357 Ibid.
358 Jebhe Melli Iran, "*Sokhani Dar Bab Melligaraee (Nationalism) Va Mihanparastee Efrati (Chauvinism)*" [Some Words Regarding Nationalism and Chauvinism], *Payam Jebhe Melli Iran*, (December 22, 2017), p. 3, http://jebhemeliiran.org/wp-content/uploads/2017/12/PAYAME-JMI-191-PAGE3.pdf.
359 Jebhe Melli Iran, "*Melli-Garay-e Jebhe Melli Iran Chegoneh Ast?*" [What is the Nationalism of the Iran National Front?], *Payam Jebhe Melli Iran*, No. 199 (December 5, 2019), p. 3, https://melliun.org/v/wp-content/uploads/2019/12/payam-jebhe-melli-iran-199.pdf.

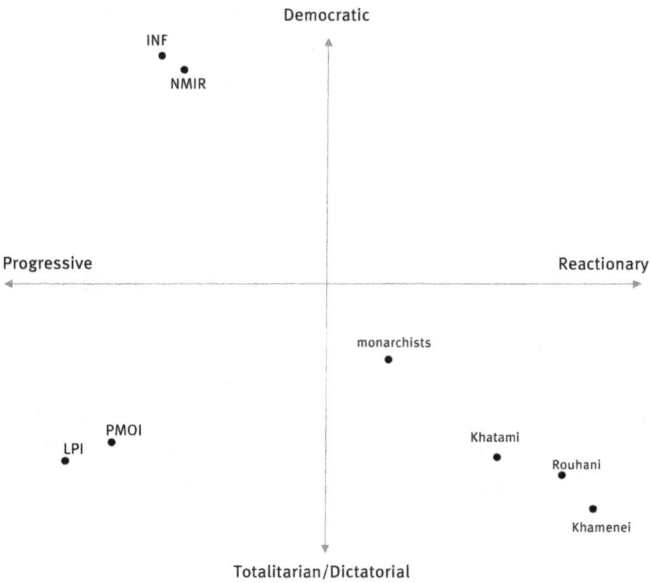

Figure 1: Ideologies of Political Parties and Politicians in Iran, 2020.

degh formulated Iran's nationalism as based upon freedoms of thought, expression, democracy, and the rule of law promulgated by [democratically-elected] representatives of the people."[360] Mossadegh, INF argues, "did not consider the nation to be comprised of peasants in need of a shepherd, but rights-owning citizens and not duty-bound [persons]."[361] The INF regards its ethical criteria to be "human dignity and condemns oppression of human beings...."[362] The INF adds: "The Mossadeghi constructive patriotism is unity within diversity. Iran's culture is like a plural rainbow containing beautiful, diverse, autonomous and connected, a beautiful unity of diverse pieces."[363] The INF condemns all forms of discrimination against women and ethnic, linguistic, and religious minorities. The INF promotes peace and friendship with all the nations and countries of the world.[364]

---

360 Ibid.
361 Ibid.
362 Ibid.
363 Ibid.
364 Jebhe Melli Iran, "*Sharhi Bar Osol-e Eateghadi Hasht-ganeh Jebhe Melli Iran*" [An Elaboration on the Eight Articles of the Charter of the Iran National Front], *Payam Jebhe Melli Iran*,

The INF has criticized reactionary, misogynist, and xenophobic policies and proposals of the fundamentalist regime. The INF considers itself to be an anti-imperialist party, which it defines as defending the independence of Iran and the interests of the Iranian people.

Economic Policy

The INF promotes an economic system that includes both state and private ownership in the economy. It argues that certain industries such as oil, steel, and rail roads should remain under state ownership. The state should develop infrastructures such as roads and bridges. The INF argues that state ownership, however, destroys incentive and innovation and thus undermines economic growth and prosperity. It argues that small and medium size enterprises and industries should be in private hands (individuals, corporations).[365] Iran has historically suffered greatly from arbitrary rule and lack of security for private property, which have thwarted economic and political development and long-term planning.[366] Both the Pahlavi dictatorship and the fundamentalist regime have continued arbitrary rule and lack of security for private property. The INF believes that social democratic economic policies in combination with political democracy and freedom of the press would pave the way for political and economic development of Iran.[367]

Foreign Policy

The INF has strongly condemned the foreign policies of both the Shah's regime and the fundamentalist regime. The INF condemned the Shah as fully subservient to the British and the U.S. The INF also strongly condemns the foreign policy of the fundamentalist regime as being ideological and undermining Iran's national interests. According to the INF, the fundamentalist regime's jingoistic foreign policy of attempting to export its fundamentalist system to neighboring

No. 199 (December 5, 2019), p. 4, https://melliun.org/v/wp-content/uploads/2019/12/payam-jebhe-melli-iran-199.pdf.

365 Hussein Moussavian, "Interview with Dr. Mehmaneche," Channel One TV, (December 10, 2020), https://melliun.org/iran/248202.

366 Homa Katouzian, *The Persians: Ancient, Mediaeval and Modern Iran* (New Haven: Yale University Press, 2009).

367 Hussein Moussavian, "Interview with Dr. Mehmaneche," Channel One TV, (December 10, 2020), https://melliun.org/iran/248202.

countries by organizing extremist violent groups is intervening in the internal affairs of other countries. The fundamentalist regime's ideological policies of violent opposition to the U.S. and Israel have undermined Iran's national interest. The INF has consistently condemned the fundamentalist regime's violations of international law and norms such as invasions and occupations of the embassies of the U.S., U.K., and Saudi Arabia in Tehran. Moreover, the fundamentalist regime has attempted to make "strategic" alliances with China and Russia. According to the INF, in order to gain the support of Russia and China in its confrontations with the U.S., the fundamentalist regime has granted these two countries numerous concessions that have undermined Iran's national interests.[368]

The INF advocates a non-aligned foreign policy based on promoting Iran's national interests. It opposes interventions in the internal affairs of other countries. It advocates respect for international laws and norms. It supports working through international organizations and respect for the Universal Declaration of Human Rights. It advocates amity and comity with all the countries in the world.[369]

The INF has consistently and strongly condemned the terrorist policies of the fundamentalist regime such as assassinations of dissidents in Europe and Turkey, as well as support for terrorist groups in the Middle East (e.g., Lebanese Hezbollah, Iraqi Kataib Hezbollah, Palestinian Islamic Jihad, Hamas).

Strategy

The fundamentalist regime's domestic and foreign policies are driving Iran into cataclysmic conflicts with the overwhelming majority of the Iranian people as well as regional and world powers.[370] The mass protests during December 2017-January 2018, November 2019, and January 2020 are indications of the cri-

---

368 For the condemnation of the agreement with China see Jebhe Melli Iran, "*Gharardadi Ra Keh Hagh Hakemiyat Melli Iran Ra Makhdoosh Konad Mahkoom Mikonim*" [We Condemn Any Agreement that Undermines Iran's National Sovereignty], (July 13, 2020), http://jebhemeliiran. org/?p=2083; and Jebhe Melli Iran, "*Gharardad Hokumat Jomhuri Islami Ba Chin Ba Manafe Melli Iran Dar Tazad Ast*" [The Agreement Between the Islamic Republic Regime And China Is Against the National Interests of Iran], *Payam Jebhe Melli Iran*, (April 23, 2021), http://jebhemeliiran.org/?p=2670. For the condemnation on the agreement with Russia see Jebhe Melli Iran, "*Jahat Sabt Dar Tarikh*" [For Documenting History], (August 30, 2016), http://jebhemeliiran.org/?p=1129.
369 Hussein Moussavian, "Interview with Dr. Mehmaneche," Channel One TV, (December 10, 2020), https://melliun.org/iran/248202.
370 Masoud Kazemzadeh, "Five Possible Outcomes Following the Mass Protests in Iran," Radio Farda, (February 6, 2018), https://en.radiofarda.com/a/iran-unrest-scenarios-war-revolution-up rising/29023446.html.

ses.[371] On January 30, 2018, the INF issued an open letter to President Rouhani demanding its right to hold a public rally to be recognized.[372] The INF stated that it wants to share its views and policies with the people at the rally on March 5, the anniversary of the passing of Dr. Mossadegh. On February 28, 2018, the INF released a statement saying that it had not heard anything from the regime on its request for the protest and thus was not holding the rally. The statement, then, presented six proposals as solution to the crisis:

1. The political prisoners and prisoners of conscience from the whole country should be freed right away.

2. The basic liberties of the Iranian people, such as freedoms of political parties, assemblies, expression, the pen, as well as free and fair elections consistent with international standards should be established.

3. Financial corruption should be uprooted with full force and the looted wealth returned to the nation's treasury.

4. Iran's foreign policy should be based on an independent Iranian policy, non-alignment, non-interference in the regional and global conflicts, establishing friendly and respectful relations with all the countries of the world, and adherence to the Charter of the United Nations.

5. With reducing of unnecessary imports and paying attention to increasing domestic production and preventing of the waste of financial resources of the country outside of the borders, the deterioration of the people's financial and economic situation and the crippling unemployment should be ended.

6. The principles of the Universal Declaration of Human Rights such as political freedoms, religious liberties, freedom of thought, as well as ethnic, racial, and gender equality has to be respected.[373]

---

371 Masoud Kazemzadeh, "Protests in Iran: Characteristics, Causes, and Policy Ramifications," *Small Wars Journal*, (January 3, 2018), http://smallwarsjournal.com/jrnl/art/protests-iran-characteristics-causes-and-policy-ramifications.

372 For the translation of the INF call, see Iran National Front, Organizations Abroad, "Iranian Democrats Ask Pro-Democracy Forces Around the World for Solidarity," (February 18, 2018), https://iranazad.info/jebhehkharej/jkh18/02/18%20az%20azadikhahan%20jahan%20english.htm.

373 Jebhe Melli Iran, "*Dowlat Jomhuri Islami Mojavez Baray Bargozarae Gerdehamaee Beh Jebhe Melli Iran Nadad*" [The Government of the Islamic Republic Did Not Provide Permission for the Holding of a Rally by the Iran National Front], (February 28, 2018), http://jebhemeliiran.org/?p=1374, my translation.

On July 27, 2018, the INF released its proposals to the ruling regime on the solution to the grave situation confronting Iran and the Iranian people. The proposals contained the following three elements:

(1) The regime should announce reconciliation with the Iranian people, release all political prisoners and prisoners of conscious from all over the country, and cease all violence against the Iranian people who oppose the regime and have had enough.

(2) The regime should in a real manner establish political freedoms such as freedoms of expression, the pen, political parties, and assemblies.

(3) The regime should acquiesce to free elections for a real Constituent Assembly to write a new constitution and choose the form of the new government. The regime should accept holding this election and accept that the ruling [fundamentalist] entities would not interfere and accept supervision by committees that are acceptable to the people. The regime should respect and acquiesce the decisions of the Constituent Assembly on all the areas whatever they are.[374]

According to Dr. Hussein Moussavian, the number one leader of the INF, "The strategy of the Iran National Front for achieving its goal of establishing democracy is exclusively political struggles, exposing the mistakes of the rulers, and suggesting constructive proposals to the people of Iran. The three-elements proposal to the regime is actually a roadmap for the struggles of the Iranian people as well, meaning that the Iranian people can use these demands as their main and primary demands."[375] The INF strategy is to use non-violent methods of struggle to (further) delegitimize the regime. Then to put pressure on the regime to allow freedom of expression and protests. The INF supports strikes and protests against the regime. The objective of the INF is to force the dictatorial rulers to accept free and democratic elections and leave power. The INF supported and participated in the mass protests during 1979–1981, 1998, 2003, and 2009 as well as those in December 2017 and January 2018.

There have not been any free and democratic elections in Iran since 1980. Only members of the fundamentalist oligarchy have been allowed to run for offices. Non-fundamentalists are not only are not allowed to run, but have been arrested, tortured, executed, and assassinated since 1979. The Iranian people obviously know this fact. The dilemma has been whether to participate in these fundamentalist-only elections and vote for less extremist members of the funda-

---

374 Jebhe Melli Iran, *"Pishnehadat Jebhe Melli Iran Beh Hayat Hakemeh Jomhuri Islami"* [Proposals of the Iran National Front to the Ruling Regime of the Islamic Republic], (July 27, 2018), http://jebhemeliiran.org/?p=1374, my translation.
375 Personal e-mail interview with Dr. Hussein Moussavian, February 5, 2019. See Part III, for the complete interview.

mentalist oligarchy or to boycott these elections. By participating in these fundamentalist-only elections, one would provide legitimacy to the regime. Moreover,
the fundamentalist regime and its supporters engage in massive propaganda outside Iran to deceive the world about the terribly totalitarian and anti-democratic
nature of the fundamentalist regime by arguing that the participation of the population in these elections show support for the regime. By not participating in
these elections, the more extremist members of the oligarchy gain those offices.

Since 1981, the INF and INF-OA have called for boycott of these sham elections except for a handful of them. Only when there has been a meaningful
difference between the fundamentalist candidates – such as the presidential
election in 2001 when Mohammad Khatami was running against extremist candidates and in the 2000 Majles elections when reformists promised reductions of
repression – have the INF and INF-OA called upon the people to participate and
vote for the reformist candidates.

This strategy intends to encourage and reward those members of the fundamentalist oligarchy who promise reforms such as reductions of repression and
keep their promises. The reformist members of the oligarchy want minor reforms
in order to preserve and prolong the rule of the extremely anti-democratic system. The democratic opposition (e. g., the INF) wants to replace the ruling dictatorship with democracy. Therefore, the ultimate objective of the reformist fundamentalists and the pro-democracy forces are very different. However, their short-
term objectives of countering the most authoritarian elements of the fundamentalist oligarchy coincide on some occasions. The reformist factions of the fundamentalist oligarchy benefit when the INF calls upon the people to participate in
elections. The INF and INF-OA are willing to call on the people to vote only if the
reformists are willing to stand up to the hardline elements and reduce repression. This strategy also intends to develop a democratic discourse within Iranian
political sphere. Moreover, this strategy signals to both reformist elements and
their social base that if the hardline elements do not allow them to participate
in the pseudo-elections, they should leave the fundamentalist regime and support the democratic alternative.

The INF believes that in order to increase the likelihood of a non-violent
transition to democracy, some members of the ruling oligarchy have to be con-
vinced that it is in their best interests to leave the ruling dictatorship and join
the democratic opposition. As long as the overwhelming majority of the oligarchy remain united around the goal of preserving the dictatorship at all costs,
the likelihood of peaceful transition is greatly diminished.

A major dilemma is that many members of the oligarchy, including many reformists, have committed crimes against humanity such as mass executions, sys-
tematic rape of young male and female political prisoners, and torture of chil-

dren and spouses of political prisoners.[376] How can one reconcile amnesty for those who have committed crimes against humanity with justice for the victims? How can one convince the population that in order to increase the likelihood for non-violent transition to democracy, the opposition has to offer amnesty to many members of the regime that have committed mass murder, assassinations, torture and the like? If the opposition is willing to offer amnesty for those who have committed crimes against humanity, what incentive members of the coercive apparatuses have for stopping repression? Should the opposition, set a particular date, after which those who commit crimes against humanity and other repressive actions would not be included for amnesty? There are no comfortable solutions for these dilemmas. Some of the crimes members of the fundamentalist oligarchy (including reformists) have committed, such as torture of children and spouses of political prisoners and rape of male and female political prisoners, make amnesty for them horribly offensive to the sense of justice of vast swaths of the population including member and the social base of the INF.

In April 2021, the INF publicly called for boycott of the June 2021 elections for presidency because it was an anti-democratic "election" that only fundamentalists were allowed to run. The INF argued that there were no freedoms of expression, of the press, of political parties, or of non-fundamentalists being allowed to run. The INF argued that such pseudo-elections were to deceive others to think that real elections are held in Iran and thus to provide popular legitimacy to a terribly unpopular and tyrannical regime.[377]

On June 2, 2021, the INF called upon the Iranian people who believe in democracy to organize and work with the INF in an organizational form.[378] On August 12, 2021, the INF called upon all major pro-democracy political forces to cooperate with the INF in establishing a broad-based coalition to create a democratic alternative to the fundamentalist dictatorship.[379]

---

376 For testimonies and sources see Masoud Kazemzadeh, *Islamic Fundamentalism, Feminism, and Gender Inequality in Iran Under Khomeini* (Lanham, Maryland: University Press of America, 2002).

377 Jebhe Melli Iran, "*Mellat Iran Az Entekhab Bein Bad Va Badtar Oboor Kardeh Ast*" [The Iranian Nation Has Moved on From Choosing Between Bad and Worse], (April 7, 2021), https://melliun.org/iran/257087.

378 Jebhe Melli Iran, "*Farakhan Jebhe Melli Iran, Cheh Bayad Kard?*" [Iran National Front's Call, What Should Be Done?], *Payam Jebhe Melli*, (June 2, 2021), http://jebhemeliiran.org/wp-content/uploads/2021/06/PayamJMI209.pdf.

379 Jebhe Melli Iran, "*Ettehad Melli Baray Tahaghogh Hakemiyat Melli*" [National Unity for the Realization of Popular Sovereignty], *Payam Jebhe Melli Iran*, (August 12, 2021), http://jebhemeliiran.org/wp-content/uploads/2021/08/PAYAM-JMI211.pdf.

Leadership

Members of the INF meet in conventions or plenums and elect members of the Central Committee, who in turn elect members of the Executive Committee and the Leadership Council. In late 2020, the INF changed its system and combined the role and membership of the Executive Committee and the Leadership Committee into one committee. Although the INF does not have the position of Secretary-General and most major decisions are made collectively, one person has usually been considered to be the number one leader of the organization at a particular period. Mossadegh was the number one leader while he was alive. Then, it was Allahyar Saleh, Karim Sanjabi, and Adib Boroumand.[380] Currently, Dr. Hussein Moussavian is the number one leader of the INF.

Moussavian was born in Tehran in 1941. He is a cardiologist. He has been a member of the INF since 1960. In 1960, he was a representative of the University of Tehran students at the INF. Because of his activities with the INF, he was arrested and sent to prison seven times during the Shah's regime. Moreover, SAVAK expelled him from the University of Tehran Medical School in 1963. He was allowed to return after three years of suspension. Again, SAVAK expelled him from his residency for cardiology, but was allowed to return after three years of suspension. About two months after the revolution, he became a member of the Central Committee and the Executive Committee. After Khomeini's infamous apostasy statement, he went underground for one year. He was arrested in December 2009, because the INF had supported the Green Movement and he was the Chairman of the Executive Committee. He spent about one month in solitary confinement in the Evin Prison.[381] He was the Chairman of the Executive Committee for about 12 years until 2017 (while Adib Boroumand was the Chairman of the Central Committee and the Leadership Council). On November 17, 2018, Moussavian was elected Chairman of the Central Committee and the Leadership Council.[382] In 2020, Leadership Council and the Executive Committee were combined. Dr. Moussavian has been elected as the Chair of the Lead-

380 Seyyed Morteza Moshir, *Khaterat Allahyar Saleh* [Memories of Allahyar Saleh], (Tehran: Vahid Publishers, 1985), https://hezbeiran.com/wp-content/uploads/2020/09/%D8%AE%D8%A7%D8%B7%D8%B1%D8%A7%D8%AA-%D8%A7%D9%84%D9%87%DB%8C%D8%A7%D8%B1-%D8%B5%D8%A7%D9%84%D8%AD.pdf.
381 Personal e-mail interview with Dr. Moussavian. For the full interview, please see Part III of this book.
382 Hussein Moussavian, *"Goftogo-e Doktor Hussein Moussavian, Rais Shora-y Jebhe Melli Iran, Ba BBC"* [Interview with Dr. Hussein Moussavian, Chairman of the Central Committee of the INF, with the BBC], (December 20, 2018), https://melliun.org/iran/191116.

ership-Executive Committee as well. The latest elections for the Central Committee and the Leadership-Executive Committee were held in November 2021. Moussavian was re-elected as the Chair of the Central Committee and a member of the Leadership-Executive Committee. Moussavian expresses his views on social media such as Tweeter and Instagram.[383]

The most well-known contemporary leader of the INF was Abbas Amir-Entezam, who was the longest-held political prisoner in the Islamic Republic of Iran.[384] He was in prison for 28 years and for another nine years he was given medical furlough. Many considered him, Iran's Nelson Mandela.[385] Amir-Entezam passed away on July 12, 2018 at age 85.

On the second anniversary of his passing, his chief interrogator, gave an interview.[386] The interrogator's real name is Mohammad Hussein Mottaghi, and his pseudonym is "Said Bagheri." According to Mottaghi, no evidence was found indicating that Amir-Entezam had committed espionage. But due to the anti-Bazargan and anti-American atmosphere, someone had to be victimized. Mottaghi says that as soon as Amir-Entezam came back from his mission from Sweden, he was arrested and taken to the former American embassy. The fundamentalist students who had invaded and occupied the U.S. embassy, had claimed that they found evidence of his spying for the U.S. Mottaghi says that Amir-Entezam was taken to a home belonging to an American embassy personnel that was behind the U.S. embassy. He interrogated Amir-Entezam for about one week in over 10 sessions. Mottaghi says that they finally reached the conclusion that none of the embassy documents showed any indication that Amir-Entezam had done any

---

383 See https://twitter.com/MoosavianHosein; and https://www.instagram.com/hoseinmoo savian/.

384 Fariba Amini, "Perseverance and Honor: Interview with Abbas Amir-Entezam," Iranian.com (February 22, 2006), https://iranian.com/2006/02/22/perseverance-and-honor/; Masoud Kazemzadeh, "Burning Candle: Honoring Abbas Amir-Entezam on the 25th Anniversary of His Arrest," Iranian.com (December 21, 2004), https://iranian.com/BTW/2004/December/Entezam/index.html?site=archive; and Abbas Amir-Entezam, "*Goftogo-e Hussein Dehbashi Ba Abbas Amir-Entezam*" [Hussein Dehbashi Interview with Abbas Amir-Entezam], Khasht Kham, No. 36 (2018), http://www.tarikhonline.ir/posts/main/subpage-single/id-217/ششم-و-سی-نوبت-–-خام-خشت-html.امیر انتظام-عباس-با-دهباشی-حسین-گفتگوی.

385 Roya Hakakian, "Abbas Amir-Entezam: Iranian Politician who went from deputy prime minister to longest-suffering political prisoner," *Independent*, (July 17, 2018), https://www.in dependent.co.uk/news/obituaries/abbas-amir-entezam-dead-cause-age-iran-jail-political-prison er-spy-deputy-prime-minister-a8451066.html.

386 Radio Farda, "*Bazjui Amir-Entezam: Jasosi Oo Esbat Nashod Va Ghorbani Maarekeh Amrika-Setizi Shod*" [Amir-Entezam's Interrogator: His Espionage was not Proven and Became a Victim of Anti-Americanism], (July 14, 2020), https://www.radiofarda.com/a/motaghi-on-amirentezam/30726246.html.

spying. The written result was sent to Ali Ghodosi, the Revolutionary Prosecutor General, stating that Amir-Entezam was innocent. Ghodosi wrote a letter to Ayatollah Khomeini, stating "never a reason was found pertaining to espionage by Amir-Entezam."[387] Mottaghi adds that "the revolutionary court hearings were held by Ayatollah Mohammad Mohammadi Gilani, which was more a political issue than a judicial issue."[388] Amir-Entezam was sent to solitary confinement for 454 days, and after that to the general prison population. He was furloughed in 1996 but was sent back to Evin Prison twice more. One, in 2000 when in an interview he called Assadollah Ladjevardi, the Chief Warden of Evin Prison, a *"jalad."*[389] Two, in 2003 when he wrote an article regarding two bills promoted by then-president Mohammad Khatami. In his article, Amir-Entezam wrote: "reforming the [fundamentalist] constitution will not solve any problem. The most civilized and democratic solution is to hold a referendum on the form of government in Iran under the supervision of international institution."[390] Amir-Entezam was a member of the INF Leadership Council.

Another prominent leader of the INF is Ms. Elaheh Mizani Amir-Entezam. She holds BA and MA degrees in political science from the School of Oriental and African Studies, University of London. She was pursuing her doctoral studies in 1979 when she returned to Iran.[391] Ms. Amir-Entezam is highly active and courageous, giving speeches on sensitive and dangerous occasions. For example, when the regime prevented the INF from holding its celebration for the 70th anniversary of its founding in October 2019, Ms. Amir-Entezam gave a public speech criticizing the regime's repression.[392] Ms. Elaheh Amir-Entezam was elect-

---

387 BBC Persian, *"Bazjoe Abbas Amir-Entezam: Eteham Jasosi Beh Oo Hargez Sabet Nashod"* [Abbas Amir-Entezam's Interrogator: The Accusation of Espionage Was Never Proven], (July 14, 2020), https://www.bbc.com/persian/iran-53404949.

388 Radio Farda, *"Bazjoe Amir-Entezam."*

389 The word *"jalad"* is a negative term in Persian and refers to an individual who is an extremely cruel executioner and torturer.

390 Radio Farda, *"Bazjoe Amir-Entezam."*

391 Maryam Dehkordi, *"Zanan Taasir-gozar Iran: Elaheh Mizani (Amir-Entezam)"* [Influential Women of Iran: Elaheh Mizani (Amir-Entezam)], Iran Wire, (May 20, 2020), https://iranwire.com/fa/features/38378.

392 Elaheh Amir-Entezam, *"Bakhshi Az Sokhanrani Elaheh Amir-Entezam Dar Sharayet Jologiri Az Aaeen 70 Salegi Jebeh Melli Iran"* [Part of the Speech of Elaheh Amir-Entezam When the Regime Prevented the Commemoration of the 70the Anniversary of the INF], (October 26, 2019), https://www.youtube.com/watch?v=EbkpfyX3l3I. For another example, see her speech at a private commemoration of the passing of Mr. Farzin Mokhber a long-time member of the Hezb Mellat Iran at Elaheh Amir-Entezam, *"Sokhanrani Khanum Elaheh Amir-Entezam Dar Salrooz Dargozasht Farzin Mokhber"* [Speech of Ms. Elaheh Amir-Entezam On the Anniversary of the Passing of Farzin Mokhber], (August 24, 2019), https://www.youtube.com/watch?v=JEsZBGr-k9A.

ed to the Leadership-Executive Committee and the Central Committee in November 2021. Another prominent leader is Dr. Ali Haj-Ghassemali. He is an anesthesiologist. He is a member of the Central Committee.

As of December 2021, there are 35 members of the Central Committee. Four of them are female: Elaheh Mizani Amir-Entezam; Parichehr Mobasheri, Dr. Azin Movahed, and Pourandokht Boroumand.[393] There are 9 members of the Leadership-Executive Committee. One is female: Elaheh Amir-Entezam.

The INF is banned in Iran. The fundamentalist regime has executed and assassinated many members of the INF.[394] In recent years, however, the regime has been less repressive. The INF leaders meet in private homes about once every two weeks. The leadership is under constant surveillance and are harassed by the Ministry of Intelligence and other coercive apparatuses.

The INF has a website, a Facebook account, a Twitter account, a You Tube Channel, and a Telegram account where one might find its official views on various subjects.[395] Between February 1979 and November 2021, the INF has published 212 issues of the *"Payam Jebhe Melli Iran,"* its official organ.[396] In the past several years, the INF has published the *"Payam Jebhe Melli Iran"* about once a month. This publication includes the INF's analyses of current events. The INF has also published a number of pamphlets. The INF publishes its views, analysis, and positions on various issues within hours or days after major events.[397]

---

393 Hussein Moussavian interview at Rangin-Kaman TV, *"Jame-e Shenasi Siasi Opposision Iran: Jebhe Melli Iran, Bakhsh 2"* [Political Sociology of the Opposition in Iran: Iran National Front, Part 2], You Tube, (July 9, 2020), https://www.youtube.com/watch?v=lLC4ypIeVYw.

394 Hamid-Reza Mosaiebian, *Mossadeghi-ha* [Supporters of Mossadegh], (Kermanshah, Iran: 2016), https://melliun.org/v/wp-content/uploads/2016/12/did-Mosadeghiha_960231_225.pdf.

395 The sites and accounts are http://jebhemeliiran.org/; https://www.facebook.com/jebhe melli/; https://twitter.com/jebhemeliiran/; https://www.youtube.com/channel/UCfqrNEkb_OP VOTjNOn0PSKQ/videos; and https://t.me/JMI_official/527.

396 Many of these are available at http://jebhemeliiran.org/?cat=13.

397 Examples of these *"elamieh"* [issue position statement, policy statement, proclamation, communique] are: INF's views on the war between Azerbaijan Republic and Armenia in October 2020; condemning the execution of Navid Afkari (Iran's national wrestling team champion who was executed with faulty due process perhaps to intimidate the people not to protest against the regime); support for Nasrin Sotoudeh (Iran's most famous human right rights lawyer jailed for defending political prisoners and dissidents); support for striking teachers and workers; and support for pro-democracy university students for organizing annual University Student Day.

Chapter 9
Iran National Front-Organizations Abroad

The Iran National Front-Organizations Abroad (INF-OA) has large numbers of members in Europe and the U.S. Officially, the INF and the INF-OA are independent from each other and are not responsible for the actions and policies of the other. In actuality, however, there are close relations between the two. For example, the leadership of the INF usually sends messages of solidarity and support to the conventions and meetings of the INF-OA and vice versa.[398] The members of the two organizations vociferously defend each other in public forums. Many members of the INF-OA were members of the INF when they resided in Iran. Both the INF-OA branches in the U.S. and Europe were established in the early 1960s. Dr. Mossadegh, who had been under house arrest, had smuggled a letter to his supporters outside and gave his permission and support for the establishment of INF branches outside Iran. The U.S. branch was established by Dr. Ali Shayegan and Dr. Mohsen Ghaemmagham in the 1960s.

The INF-OA holds its conventions once every two year. The delegates in the convention elect both members of the Central Committee (35 members) and the Executive Committee (3 members). The members of the Executive Committee are Dr. Homayoun Mehmaneche, Kambiz Ghaemmagham, and Bahman Mobasheri. There are two female members in the Central Committee: Ms. Behjat Mehrasa and Ms. Farideh Arabzadeh.[399]

Members hold online meetings about once a month. The INF-OA and the INF-OA (U.S. Section) have their own official websites and a Facebook account.[400] The membership is also highly active on Facebook, a common forum of political activity among Iranians inside and outside Iran. Some of the prominent and active members of the INF-OA are Kambiz Ghaemmagham, Dr. Mohsen Ghaemmagham, Dr. Ali Mehrassa, Dr. Homayoun Mehmaneche, Bahman Mobasheri, Hamid Sadr, Dara Nirui, Dr. Raymond Rakhshani, Dr. Mohammad Eghtedari, Dr. Bagher

---

398 For example, see https://iranazad.info/jebhehkharej/jkh16/12/19%20gozaresh%20payam ha.htm and https://iranazad.info/jebhehkharej/jkh18/11/26%20payam%20shoraye%20ali.htm.
399 Dr. Homayoun Mehmaneche interview at Rangin-Kaman TV, *"Jame-e Shenasi Siasi Opposision Iran: Jebhe Melli Iran, Bakhsh 2"* [Political Sociology of the Opposition in Iran: Iran National Front, Part 2], You Tube, (July 9, 2020), https://www.youtube.com/watch?v=lLC4ypIeVYw.
400 The sites are https://iranazad.info/ and http://jebhemelli.net/ and https://www.facebook. com/INFOA/?hc_ref=ARRdIGQdCJy1q-H2TkeMYsdi2StSodZLYzANMkdXyb87Fc97s98JXRK4yRJ8lY lehrU&fref=nf.

https://doi.org/10.1515/9783110782158-011

Samsami, Ms. Shahla Samsami, Mohammad Kassaeizadeh, Amir Reza Amir Bakhtiar, and Dr. Hadi Zamani. Dr. Mehmaneche is a physicist and has a doctorate in physics from the Technical University of Munich.[401] Dr. Ghaemmagham is a cardiologist. Dr. Ali Mehrasa is a pharmacologist. Dr. Samsami is a pediatrician. Ms. Samsami has a master's in psychology. Dr. Zamani is a professor of economics. Dr. Eghtedari is an economist. Dr. Rakhshani is a professor at the University of Southern California.

There are also many prominent personalities who are not (organizationally) members of the INF-OA but are considered by others and themselves to be INF members. This phenomenon is a weakness of the INF-OA, which it has not found a solution for.

There are several pro-democracy political parties and organizations operating outside Iran. One of the most active and influential was National Movement of Iranian Resistance (NMIR) under the leadership of Dr. Shapour Bakhtiar. Dr. Bakhtiar was assassinated by the agents of the Iranian government on August 6, 1991 in France. Although NMIR still exists as an organization, it is not very active. Several of its leaders have re-joined the INF-OA. For example, Dr. Mehmaneche is one of the top two leaders of the INF-OA. Others include Hamid Sadr and Amir Reza Amir Bakhtiar.

In 2003, a group of younger members of NMIR left that group and established the Iran Liberal Organization. They consider their political lineage to stem from the Constitutional Revolution of 1905, Dr. Mossadegh, the INF, and Dr. Bakhtiar. They are strong advocates of a secular liberal democratic republic. On economic policy, they are liberal in the European sense, which means they are center-right. They support liberal capitalist economic system.[402] In the Iranian context, this means that they oppose the crony capitalisms of the monarchists and the fundamentalists. Under both the monarchy and the fundamentalist regime, terribly repressive political systems have been combined with corrupt elites utilizing political connections to amass fantastic wealth through monopolistic import licenses, graft, illegal, and extra-legal means. The leaders of the Iran Liberal Organization are Dr. Ramin Kamran, Hassan Behgar, and Mahshid Amirshahi. All three are prolific sophisticated intellectuals.[403] The Iran Liberal

---

401 Dr. Mehmaneche is one of the top two leaders of the INF-OA. Dr. Mehmaneche's personal website is at https://homayoun.info/. His biography is at https://homayoun.info/?cat=1. For links to his articles and tv appearances see his website.
402 Iran Liberal Organization, "*Maram-Nameh Ma*" [Our Charter], (May 2020), https://iranlib eral.com/%d8%af%d8%b1-%d8%a8%d8%a7%d8%b1%d9%87-%d9%85%d8%a7/.
403 The group's site is https://iranliberal.com/.

Organization has a positive view on the INF and the INF-OA.[404] The INF-OA and the Iran Liberal Organization have established close and friendly relations.

The INF-OA has also been successful in establishing close cooperation with progressive republican organizations and political parties.[405] These include *Hambastegi Jomhurikahahn Iran* (Union for Secular Republic), *Etehad Jomhurikahan Iran* (United Republicans of Iran), and Left Party of Iran.[406]

From 2020, the INF-OA began close cooperation with a new center-left group called *"Hamsazi Melli Jomhurikhahan Social Democrat Va Laic Iran"* [National Covenant of the Social Democratic and Laic Republicans of Iran].[407] They produced a large number of videos of interviews with various political figures. In September 2021, they changed their name to *"Hezb Social Democrat Va Laic Iran"* [Social Democratic and Laic Party of Iran]. On November 10, 2021, the Social Democratic and Laic Party of Iran announced that it has officially asked to join the INF and that its request has been approved by the INF.[408]

From early 2021, another group called *"Jonbesh Jomhurikhahan Democrat Va Laic Iran"* [Movement of Democratic and Laic Republicans of Iran] joined the INF-OA and the Social Democratic and Liac Party of Iran, and they published a number of joint statements.[409]

---

404 Hassan Behgar, *"Jebhe Melli Bar Sar-e Do-Rahi"* [The National Front at a Fork on the Road] (January 3, 2021), https://iranliberal.com/%d8%a2%d8%b1%d8%b4%db%8c%d9%88-%d8%ad%d8%b3%d9%86-%d8%a8%d9%87%da%af%d8%b1/%d8%ac%d8%a8%d9%87%db%80-%d9%85%d9%84%db%8c-%d8%a8%d8%b1-%d8%b3%d8%b1-%d8%af%d9%88%d8%b1%d8%a7%d9%87%db%8c-%d8%ad%d8%b3%d9%86-%d8%a8%d9%87%da%af%d8%b1/.
405 For example, see https://iranazad.info/jebhehkharej/jkh18/12/10%20poshtibani%204%20sazeman.htm.
406 Their websites are https://iranian-republic.org/; http://jomhouri.com/jomhouri/; and https://bepish.org/.
407 The group's website is at https://rangin-kaman.net/hamsaazi/.
408 Social Democratic and Laic Party of Iran, *"Chera Hezb Ma Beh Jebhe Melli Iran Peyvast?"* [Why Our Party Joined the Iran National Front?], (November 10, 2021), https://melliun.org/iran/287089.
409 The group's website is at http://nedayeazady.org/.

Chapter 10
Criticisms of the INF

There are several criticisms of the INF. This chapter discusses seven of them.

The INF and Mossadegh Failed to Effectively Organize in Order to Defeat the 1953 Coup

This criticism is obviously true. In early 1953, Khalil Maleki and other INF members had asked Dr. Mossadegh to allow them to organize young INF members who had done their two-year national military service into an armed militia in order to defend the government and prevent a coup. Mossadegh opposed the proposal. He argued that if the INF organized an armed militia, then all other political parties would also organize armed militias, and then one could not have a democracy with all the political parties with armed militias. Between August 16 and 19, Dariush Forouhar and other leaders of the INF asked Mossadegh to distribute arms among his supporters. Mossadegh also opposed this. Forouhar had asked Mossadegh several months earlier to distribute arms among INF members, Mossadegh opposed that arguing that if they did that, that would send the signal that the INF government does not trust the armed forces.[410]

The INF and Mossadegh defeated the coup initially on August 16. But Kermit Roosevelt, the CIA's operations chief in Tehran, was both brilliant and persistent. On his second attempt on August 19, Roosevelt succeeded in overthrowing Mossadegh. There were large numbers of disturbances on August 17 and 18, most of them by members and supporters of the Tudeh Party. On the afternoon of August 18 Mossadegh ordered his supporters to leave the streets. The Tudeh Party also ordered its members and supporters to stay home and not to go to the streets on August 19. On the afternoon of August 18 and morning of August 19, Mossadegh ordered the police and security forces to establish order on the streets. Then, Roosevelt used that occasion to on the one hand, mobilize pro-Shah street mobs through his surrogates (Gen. Fazlollah Zahedi, Mozaffar Ba-

---

410 Parastu Forouhar, *"Kodeta-y 28 Mordad, Dariush Forouhar Va Meidan Baharestan"* [The August 19, 1953 Coup, Dariush Forouhar and Baharestan Field], Radio Zamaneh, (August 18, 2015), https://www.radiozamaneh.com/233101?fbclid=IwAR1CSYVEgD3U_K5VhNz4s-COeYmlYXkyP-jOw1_vbBuhsFSgRBSR_Q-AjZk. This contains segments of Dariush Forouhar's recollections on the coup.

https://doi.org/10.1515/9783110782158-012

ghaie, Ayatollah Kashani, Ayatollah Behbahani, Ayatollah Falsafi, and Fadaian Islam) and on the other hand to order his surrogates in the military to move towards Mossadegh's home and Tehran's radio station to carry out the coup.[411]

According to Stephen Kinzer, Roosevelt had an excellent psychological understanding of Mossadegh.[412] According to Kinzer, Roosevelt knew that Mossadegh was a gentleman, so he used that personality character to manipulate Mossadegh. He told the U.S. Ambassador to Iran, Loy Henderson, to tell Mossadegh that Iranian mobs were attacking American females and males on the streets. That Mossadegh was so upset to hear the story that in the presence of Henderson, he picked up the phone and ordered an announcement to all the people to go back home and empty the streets and ordered the police to come to the streets. This is also the view of Abrahamian, one of the foremost historians of Iran. In this view, Mossadegh was naïve and Roosevelt and Henderson were able to manipulate him.[413]

Recent declassified U.S. government documents, however, undermine this view. In 2017, the State Department's Office of Historian published a large number of documents. Henderson asked to see Mossadegh, and they talked for about one hour on the afternoon of August 18. Henderson wrote a long telegram to the State Department providing great detail about what they discussed. In this document, Henderson not only does not mention that Mossadegh was so manipulated, but rather, according to Henderson, Mossadegh was sarcastic and angry at the U.S. and believed that the U.S. was working with the British carrying out the coup.[414] Two days later, the U.S. Embassy in London gives the British Foreign Office a polished version of Henderson's telegram.[415] In both documents there is no mention of Mossadegh picking up the phone and ordering the police onto the streets. The latter report states:

---

411 Stephen Kinzer, *All the Shah's Men: An American Coup and the Roots of Middle East Terror* (Hoboken, New Jersey: Wiley, 2003).
412 Ibid.
413 Cosroe Chaqueri, *"Shalodeh-Shekani Yek Afsaneh"* [Debunking A Myth], Melliun, (August 19, 2013), https://melliun.org/iran/25870. In this article, Chaqueri makes good points about Mossadegh and Henderson that I have used here. Unfortunately, he makes personal attacks on Abrahamian that are not warranted and are in poor taste.
414 Loy Henderson, "Telegram From the Embassy in Iran to the Department of State," (August 18, 1953, 10 p.m.), https://history.state.gov/historicaldocuments/frus1951-54Iran/d280.
415 U.S. Government, Department of State, "Memorandum for the Record" https://history.state.gov/historicaldocuments/frus1951-54Iran/d281. This is a report from the U.S. State Department to the British Foreign Office.

Ambassador Henderson saw Prime Minister Mossedeq by appointment for an hour yesterday evening. He reported that Mossedeq was as usual courteous but the Ambassador detected in his attitude a certain amount of smoldering resentment.

The Ambassador told Mossedeq that he was particularly concerned at the laxity of the Iranian law enforcement agencies in permitting the increasing number of attacks on American citizens both in Tehran and other localities. Dr. Mossedeq replied that these attacks were almost inevitable as the Iranian people thought the Americans were disagreeing with them. The Ambassador replied that disagreements were no reason for attacks, and that if the Iranians really wanted the Americans out individual attacks were not necessary, as the Americans would go en masse. After stating that the law enforcement agencies were doing everything possible to give Americans protection, the Prime Minister assured Ambassador Henderson that he wanted the Aid Missions to remain in Iran. He thought they were performing valuable services and said he would look further into the matter of the protection of members of the Missions.....

Ambassador Henderson reported that Mossedeq appeared in a much better frame of mind at the end of the talk but that nevertheless, from his unusual reserve, the Ambassador was inclined to believe that Mossedeq was suspicious that the United States Government or at least United States officials were either implicated in the effort to oust him or were sympathetically aware of such an effort in advance. His remarks were interspersed with a number of little jibes which although semi-jocular in character were nonetheless barbed. In general the jibes hinted that the United States was conniving with the British to remove him as Prime Minister.[416]

According to my research, there is a more plausible explanation. In their recollections of the days between August 16 and 19, both Dariush Forouhar and Khosrow Seif say that on August 17, members and supporters of the Tudeh Party attacked the central headquarters of the Iran Nation Party at Baharestan Field and pretty much destroyed it.[417] Members and supporters of the INP arrive afterwards and there were fights between the supporters and members of the two parties. The police and security officials arrest many of them from both parties. When on August 18, Forouhar goes to Mossadegh's office, Mossadegh tells him to tell the members of his party to not worry, that he has ordered the police to arrest members of the Tudeh Party. And when Forouhar complains to the top security official present at Mossadegh's office, he tells him that it would take a day or two to release the members and supporters of his party as they were obviously innocent and only defending themselves from attacks from the Tudeh Party. It appears that Forouhar saw Mossadegh around noon, and Henderson saw Mossa-

---

416 Ibid.

417 Parastu Forouhar, "*Kodeta-y 28 Mordad, Dariush Forouhar Va Meidan Baharestan*" [The August 19, 1953 Coup, Dariush Forouhar and Baharestan Field], Radio Zamaneh, op. cit.; and Khosrow Seif, "*Tajdid Khatereh-e Az 28 Mordad Saal 1332*" [Retelling of Memories of August 19, 1953], Melliun, (August 18, 2020), https://melliun.org/iran/239253.

degh in the afternoon. All the documents that I have seen indicate that the reason that Mossadegh asked the people to leave the streets and ordered the police and security forces to establish order was due to the violence that the Tudeh Party was causing.

The CIA's official Secret History of the coup states that the CIA had *agents provocateurs* in the Tudeh Party and that it had ordered them to cause chaos.[418] The fact that for the Tudeh Party had been viciously attacking Mossadegh and the INF for years and that although the viciousness of these attacks had subsided somewhat in the previous several months, there had continued attacks in the various Tudeh Party publications. That history provided the opportunity for the CIA to use its *agents provocateurs* the way it did. Moreover, the Tudeh Party leadership failed to grasp the gravity of the situation and make clear public calls to its members and supporters. The recollections of both Forouhar and Seif indicate that the violent attacks were by members and supporters of the Tudeh Party. I have not seen any indication by the Tudeh Party that that attack was not carried out by its members.

Mossadegh made a number of mistakes. First and foremost, he should not have called upon his supporters to go home. The violent incidents were minor. Second, on the morning of August 19, Dr. Hussein Fatemi and others pleaded with Mossadegh to use the radio and call upon his supporters to come to the streets to defend his government as they had done in July 1952.[419] Mossadegh wanted to avoid bloodshed, so he refused the advice of his associates. Mossadegh clearly made a catastrophic mistake.

All the evidence indicates that the total number of violent mobs that Roosevelt had mobilized were less than 6,000. On previous days, tens of thousands of supporters of Mossadegh were on the streets. The CIA had sent to Washington, citations of Tehran newspapers and Radio Tehran putting the number of supporters of Mossadegh around 100,000.[420] Mossadegh's government fell not because there were people on the streets, who opposed him. Mossadegh's government fell because of the military attacks on his home/office, the Tehran Radio station, the Tehran Telegraph station, and the Offices of the Armed Forces Chief of Staff. About 27 tanks, many of the American Sherman tanks, attacked

---

418 U.S. Government, CIA Clandestine Service History, "Overthrow of Premier Mossadeq of Iran, November 1952-August 1953," March 1954, by Dr. Donald Wilber. https://nsarchive2.gwu.edu/NSAEBB/NSAEBB28/.
419 Zirakzadeh, "Interview," Harvard University, Iranian Oral History Project, op. cit.
420 Cosroe Chaqueri, "*Naghdi Bar Pareh-e Az Nazarat Piramoon Naghsh Hezb Tudeh*" [Critique on Some Views on the Role of the Tudeh Party], Melliun (August 30, 2013), https://melliun.org/iran/26615, endnote iv.

Mossadegh's house. Until late on August 19, tank shells, mortars, and machine gun fires were attacking Mossadegh's house/office. Col. Ezzatollah Momtaz, the chief of guards at Mossadegh's house, had only a handful of tanks (much smaller than Sherman tanks), but he was able to hold off the much superior force for hours through his superior tactics.[421] Similarly, it was the military and not civilians who took over the radio station as well as the telegraph station.

Mossadegh made another fatal mistake. On August 19, he appointed Gen. Mohammad Daftari as the Chief of Police. Gen. Daftari was Mossadegh's sister's son. Unknown to Mossadegh, Gen. Daftari had met with Zahedi earlier that day and was a supporter of the coup. Gen. Daftari went to Mossadegh and told him that he would stop the coup if Mossadegh appointed him the Chief of Police. Gen. Daftari then played a major role in carrying out the coup by convincing pro-Mossadegh officers not to support Mossadegh and switch sides to the pro-Zahedi side.[422]

Khosrow Qashqaee, the leader of the Qashqai tribe, told Mossadegh after the August 16 coup attempt that he has thousands of armed men in his tribal area that he can bring to Tehran to defend the government.[423] Mossadegh refused his offer. Even after the brutal murder of Gen. Afshartus and the exposure of plot for the use of violence by the monarchists against non-violent leaders of the INF, Mossadegh still believed in non-violent methods. Had Mossadegh listened to the advice of Fatemi and others, several hundred of his supporters would have died, but Iran would likely not have suffered more than 71 years of dictatorship since August 19, 1953.

In sum, in my opinion, this criticism of Mossadegh is valid.

---

421 Katouzian, *Musaddiq and the Struggle*, p. 192; Gholam-Hussein Sadighi, *"Kodeta-e 28 Mordad Beh Ravayat Gholam-Hussein Sadighi"* [The 1953 Coup According to Gholam-Hussein Sadighi], Tarikh Irani, (August 23, 2011), http://tarikhirani.ir/fa/news/1190/; and Ahmad Zirakzadeh, "Interview," Harvard University, Iranian Oral History Project, op. cit.

422 Katouzian, *Musaddiq and the Struggle*, pp. 191–192.

423 Khosrow Qashqaee and Mohammad Nasser Qashqaee were brothers, leaders of the powerful and armed Qashqaee tribe in the Fars province, strong supporters of Mossadegh, and members of the INF. See Mohammad Nasser Qashqaee, "Interview," Harvard University, Iranian Oral History Project, Las Vegas, Nevada, U.S., (January 1983), audio available at https://www.youtube.com/watch?v=wuLYQKUGIMO&list=PL-PRP1hqq8eLx_zqkyCtgKws5FpAU84j3.

Organizational Weaknesses in 1963–64

A major criticism of the INF is that it has had weak organization, particularly during 1963–1964. In 1963, Mossadegh told leaders of the Second National Front to dissolve it and re-organize the Third National Front. The Shah used that opportunity and arrested all the leaders of the INF and violently crushed them. The Shah had agreed to carry out the reforms demanded by the Kennedy administration in exchange for the U.S. support for his dictatorship. The Johnson administration fully supported the Shah's dictatorship and repressive policies.

This criticism is valid. Had Mossadegh not told the INF leaders to dissolve the Second INF and re-organize, then the INF would have had much better chance of resisting the Shah's repressive measures.

Lack of Activity between 1964 and 1977

The Shah had considered the INF as the primary threat to his dictatorship. Therefore, he had used SAVAK to violently repress their leaders and members. This is such a highly repressive period that even a teenage high school student writing a composition criticizing the Shah would be arrested and tortured by SAVAK. As an above-ground non-violent group, the INF became easy prey for the Shah's violent repression. The Shah also feared the left-wing guerrilla groups and violently repressed them, including extra-judicial assassinations of them by SAVAK. For example, before 1974, if a person was arrested for merely distributing leaflets for the INF or the leftist groups, he or she would get one or two years in prison. Between 1974 and January 1977 (when President Jimmy Carter assumed office) the punishment for merely distributing leaflets was ten years in prison. Whereas tortures before 1974 for distributing leaflets were mild torture, between 1974 and 1977, they would get the severe tortures that were given to members of the armed communist guerrillas.[424]

This criticism has some validity. However, one has to consider the possibilities of a non-violent above-ground moderate political party organizing under a highly repressive police state. The Shah's use of extreme torture and assassination was the primary cause of weakness of non-violent pro-democracy activities.

---

424 Mehdi Fatapour, "Interview," IRTV (August 2, 2020), https://www.youtube.com/watch?v= YLQu46N7rDg&feature. Fatapour was in Evin Prison and was an eyewitness to the Shah's policies. He has been a member of the Fadaian, then Fadaian-Majority. He is currently one of the top leaders of Left Party of Iran and United Republicans of Iran.

Under a regime that severely tortured teenage children for writing a composition, no one was safe to engage in any peaceful political activity.

The INF did have activities abroad. The members and supporters of the INF organized the Iranian students in the U.S. and Europe and were responsible for publicizing the Shah's gross violations of human rights. Much of the human rights activities in Europe and the U.S. were carried out by members and sympathizers of the INF. They had close contacts with groups such as Amnesty International. The INF members and sympathizers were involved in documenting and publicizing the Shah's gross violations of human rights.[425] It was such activities that pressured many governments in Europe and the U.S. to put pressure on the Shah in the 1970s to reduce repression.

INF Support for the 1977–1979 Revolution Paved the Path for Khomeini's Dictatorship

This is a common criticism by Iran's monarchists. They condemn the INF, all other opposition groups, and the people for opposing the Shah's rule. They argue that the Shah was modernizing Iran. That the INF and the people were ungrateful and traitors for opposing the Shah.[426] The fundamentalist regime has been so much more reactionary and repressive than the Shah's regime, that many people who are not monarchist are making this criticism as well. INF leaders have provided their answers.[427]

---

425 Kambiz Ghaemmagham, *"Khaterati Az Daneshjoyan Iran Dar Kharej Az Keshvar"* [Memoirs of the Iranian Students Outside the Country], Rangin-Kaman TV via You Tube, (May 12, 2020), https://www.youtube.com/watch?v=h3GZ8Z4i3sU.

426 The less extremist monarchists call themselves "constitutionalists." They are organized in the Constitutionalist Party of Iran. Foad Pashai has been the Secretary-General of the Constitutionalist Party of Iran. See his strong support for the dictatorship of the Pahlavi regime Rangin-Kaman TV, *"Jame-e Shenasi Siasi Opposision Iran: Gerayesh 'Saltanat-Talabi Va Mashrooteh-Khah', Bakhsh 1"* [Political Sociology of the Opposition in Iran: 'Monarchist And Constitutionalist' Tendency, Part 1], (August 28, 2020), https://www.youtube.com/watch?v=jTvIgeQ9_F0.

427 See the views of Dr. Moussavaian, Dr. Mehmaneche, and Dr. Ghassemi at Rangin-Kaman TV, *"Jame-e Shenasi Siasi Opposision Iran: Jebhe Melli Iran, Bakhsh 1"* [Political Sociology of the Opposition in Iran: Iran National Front, Part 1], You Tube, (July 2, 2020), https://www.you tube.com/watch?v=Td4STdpQYTU; and Rangin-Kaman TV, *"Jame-e Shenasi Siasi Opposision Iran: Jebhe Melli Iran, Bakhsh 2"* [Political Sociology of the Opposition in Iran: Iran National Front, Part 2], You Tube, (July 9, 2020), https://www.youtube.com/watch?v=lLC4ypIeVYw. Also see Hussein Moussavian, "Interview," Iran International TV, (May 2, 2020), https://melliun.org/iran/231112.

The INF makes a distinction between the struggle against the Shah and co-operating with Khomeini. The Shah, in the view of the INF, was both subservient to foreign powers and a dictator. The Iranian people since the Constitutional Revolution 1905–1911 have been struggling for independence and democracy. The INF was established in 1949 in order to achieve these objectives of the Constitutional Revolution.

The INF considers the fundamentalist regime to be far more dictatorial, reactionary, and brutal than the Shah's regime. The INF did work with Khomeini from late 1978 until early 1979. In hindsight, that was a mistake. In mid-1978, the INF did not know that Khomeini was dictatorial, reactionary, power-hungry, and extremely violent. Neither did other groups in Iran, various scholars, the U.S. government, or the British government. The INF (and others) should have known. Therefore, it is a valid criticism that INF should have known about Khomeini. This criticism is also valid for Iranian historians and intellectuals. The INF, like millions of Iranian people, made the mistake of believing Khomeini in Paris. In Paris, Khomeini, repeatedly promised democracy and freedom. He explicitly said that he would not accept any position of power and would go to Qom and engage in his work in the seminary. He further said that clerics would not become president. Khomeini obviously lied to the Iranian people. After establishing his dictatorship, Khomeini said that in Paris it was expedient to say what he said. He said that he did *"khod'eh"* [deception] and *"taghieh"* [lying], both of which are allowed in Shia Islam. His supporters boast that Khomeini fooled the Americans.

Although in hindsight it is easy to criticize the INF, one should not fall for "presentism" that is judging the past by what is known today. Although in 1963, Khomeini had issued fatwas against female franchise and land reform, it was possible that he had evolved by 1979. Although in his book (to be more precise a series of lectures he delivered in the early 1970s in Najaf at his seminary) he had advocated the concept of *velayat faghih*, in 1978 in Paris he condemned the Shah for repression and dictatorship and explicitly called for freedom and democracy. In mid-1978, it was obviously crystal clear that the Shah was a brutal tyrant. It was not clear what Khomeini would be. One of the main lessons that the Iranian people learned from the 1979 revolution is that one who is against a dictator, may not be against dictatorship.

The INF leaders argue that the Iranian people deserve independence, democracy, and human rights. Therefore, they have opposed both the Shah's regime and the fundamentalist regime. As democrats and nationalists, they had to oppose the Shah's regime that was subservient to foreign powers and a dictatorship. Had they known before 1978 what they learned in 1979, they would have done what Sadighi and Bakhtiar did.

By late September 1978, Khomeini had truly mass support. By then it was too late for a moderate non-violent political party to do much to change the course of history. The Shah's policies had created a revolutionary situation. By December 1978, there was virtually no chance to save the situation. The Shah appointed Bakhtiar prime minister on January 4, 1979. The monarchists blame the INF for not supporting Bakhtiar's efforts. According to Ahmad Zirakzadeh, by November, Khomeini had massive support among the people, and if the INF did not have support from Khomeini to accept the Shah's offer, then the INF government had to kill large numbers of the people and that was something many in the INF were not willing to do.[428] The split between the INF and Bakhtiar certainly weakened Bakhtiar, but the primary reason for the failure of Bakhtiar's efforts was not due to the INF opposition. It was the Shah's generals that went behind Bakhtiar's government and make secret agreements with Khomeini's camp, many of whom were summarily executed by Khomeini within days. For example, Gen. Hussein Fardoost, who had been the most powerful official after the Shah, had been secretly collaborating with Khomeini's group. The same is said of Gen. Abbas Gharabaghi, who was the Chairman of Joint Chiefs of Staff. The reason for the collapse of Bakhtiar's government is the decision made by the armed forces not to support Bakhtiar on February 12, 1979.[429] Large numbers of monarchists took their money and left the country in the months leading to February 11, 1979 rather than staying and resisting or assisting Bakhtiar. Finally, the Shah did not abdicate. This means that if Bakhtiar succeeded in calming the situation, the Shah would come back. And then the Shah could have dismissed Bakhtiar as he had done to other prime ministers and restore his dictatorship.

One may judge a ruler or his/her policies by the kind of results it produces. Iranian polity in the 1940s produced a vital and vigorous middle of the road liberal democratic political force. From 1953, and certainly from 1963, the Shah ruled Iran with iron fist and had absolute power over socioeconomic policies. It was the Shah's policies that produced Khomeini and his mass support by the late 1978 and early 1979. It was the Shah who violently suppressed the liberal democrats of the INF and the secular leftists while allowing conservative Islamic forces to propagate. In the words of Hussein Moussavian, if you have a garden with 10 plants and uproot 9 of them, but allow only one to exist, then that one plant would grow and capture the whole garden. The Shah crushed all other political forces but allowed the Islamic forces to grow. The Shah wanted

---

428 Zirakzadeh, "Interview," Harvard University, Iranian Oral History Project, op. cit.
429 Bakhtiar, *37 Rooz*, op. cit.

to use Islam to counter secular liberals and leftists. One of the charges against Dr. Mossadegh at his trial in 1953 was "apostacy."

The Shah repeatedly claimed that he was in contact with the hidden Shia Imams who would foretell him top secret information of the event that would soon transpire. Even in the following interview with Italian journalist Oriana Fallaci, he repeated his claims.[430]

Oriana Fallaci: My goodness, it must be a great nuisance! I mean, it must be pretty lonely being a king instead of a man.

Mohammad Reza Pahlavi: I don't deny I'm lonely. Deeply so. A king, when he doesn't have to account to anyone for what he says and does, is inevitably very much alone. But I'm not entirely alone because I'm accompanied by a force that others can't see. My mystical force. And I get messages. Religious messages. I'm very, very religious. I believe in God, and I've always said that if God didn't exist, it would be necessary to invent him. Oh, I feel so sorry for those poor souls who don't have God. You can't live without God. I've lived with God ever since the age of five. That is, since God gave me those visions.

OF: Visions, Majesty?

MRP: Yes, visions. Apparitions.

OF: Of what? Of whom?

MRP: Of prophets. Oh, I'm surprised you don't know about it. Everyone knows I've had visions. I even wrote it in my autobiography. As a child I had two visions. One when I was five and one when I was six. The first time, I saw our Prophet Ali, he who, according to our religion, disappeared to return on the day when he would save the world. I had an accident – I fell against a rock. And he saved me – he placed himself between me and the rock. I know because I saw him. And not in a dream – in reality. Material reality, if you see what I mean. I was the only one who saw him. The person who was with me didn't see him at all. But no one else was supposed to see him except me because... Oh, I'm afraid you don't understand me.

OF: Indeed I don't, Majesty. I don't understand at all. We had got off to such a good start, and instead now ... This business of visions, of apparitions.. It's not clear to me, that's all.

MRP: Because you don't believe. You don't believe in God, you don't believe me. Many people don't. Even my father didn't believe it. He never believed it, he always laughed about it. Anyway many people, albeit respectfully, ask if I didn't ever suspect it was a fantasy. My answer is no. No, because I believe in God, in fact of having been chosen by God to accomplish a mission. My visions were miracles that saved the country. My reign has saved the country and it's saved it because God was besides me. I mean, it's not fair for me to take all the credit for myself for the great things that I've done for Iran. Mind you, I could. But I don't want to, because I know that there was someone else behind me. It was God. Do you see what I mean?

OF: No, Majesty. Because.. well, did you have these visions only as a child, or have you also had them later as an adult?

---

430 Oriana Fallaci, *Interview with History* (Boston, MA: Houghton Mifflin Harcourt, 1977).

MRP: I told you, only as a child. Never as an adult – only dreams. At intervals of one or two years. Or even seven or eight years. For instance, I once had two dreams in the spans of fifteen years.

OF: What dreams, Majesty?

MRP: Religious dreams. Based on my mysticism. Dreams in which I saw what would happen in two or three months, and that happened just that way in two or three months. But what these dreams were about, I can't tell you. They didn't have to do with me personally; they had to do with domestic problems of the country and so should be considered as state secrets. But perhaps you'd understand better if instead of the word dreams I used the word presentiments. I believe in presentiments too. Some believe in reincarnation, I believe in presentiments. I have continuous presentiments, as strong as my instinct. Even the day they shot at me from a distance of six feet, it was my instinct that saved me. Because, instinctively, while the assassin was emptying his revolver at me, I did what in boxing is called shadow dancing. And a fraction of a second before he aimed at my heart, I moved aside in such a way that the bullet went into my shoulder. A miracle. I also believe in miracles. When you think I've been wounded by a good five bullets, one in my face, one in the shoulder, one in the head, two in the body, and that the last one stuck in the barrel because the trigger jammed... You have to believe in miracles. I've had so many air disasters, and yet I've always come out unscathed – thanks to a miracle while by God and the prophets.[431]

The Shah supported a massive Shia network. According to Dariush Homayoun, one of the Shah's top officials, the Shah was both a superstitious believer and wanted to use Islam against leftists.[432] Homayoun says that the Shah had given Islamists, many of whom became leaders of the post-revolution regime, influential positions from the Shah's court to the Ministry of Education. Until the last few weeks, the Shah's cabinet and the SAVAK considered the Islamic forces to be allies against leftists.[433] For example, as soon as INF or leftists would gather to organize the people, SAVAK would arrest them within a day or so. However, SAVAK left alone the Islamic forces even when they were organizing the people in 1978. The only groups that the Shah allowed room for political activities were Islamic groups such as the Hojatieh Society, an anti-communist and anti-Bahai organization. SAVAK actually encouraged religious persons to join the Hojatieh Society. After the revolution, many members of the Hojatieh joined Khomeini's movement and became its high officials. The Shah was very tolerant towards Is-

---

431 Ibid., pp. 267–269.

432 Dariush Homayoun, "*Mohammad Reza Pahlavi: Sargashteh Miyan Mazhab Va Farangi-Maabi*" [Mohammad Reza Pahlavi: Confused between Religion and Westernization], BBC Persian, (July 27, 2010), https://www.bbc.com/persian/iran/2010/07/100727_shah_annive30_homayoun_religion.shtml.

433 Ibid.

lamists and allowed them to preach in their mosques throughout Iran. As long as a cleric would not directly criticize the Shah, he was allowed to hold religious meetings.[434]

Moreover, the Shah gave huge financial assistance to build mosques and Islamic centers. Homayoun cites one source (Stanford University's Abbas Milani) that states that in 1941 when Mohammad Reza Pahlavi became king there were about 200 mosques in Iran, and when he was overthrown in 1979 there were over 50,000 mosques.[435]

The Shah criticized those Shia clerics that opposed him as not being true Muslims. In the struggle between the Shah and Grand Ayatollah Ruhollah Khomeini over which one was a true Muslim, the ayatollah won.[436]

In sum, INF leaders argue that it was the Shah's polices that gave rise to Khomeini and his social base. Had the Shah (and the U.S. and Britain) not carried out the coup in 1953, Iran's lukewarm democracy would have grown and consolidated. The INF was certainly able to establish democracy in 1951–53, in 1963, even in 1977. Perhaps as late as early 1978 the INF might have been able to bring stability and a modicum of democracy. But by November 1978, it was simply not possible for the INF to save the situation.

Non-Violent Methods of Struggle Against the Fundamentalist Regime Would Not Work

The INF strategy worked in 1951, July 1952, and 1977–1979. Some argue that this strategy had a chance to work against the Shah's regime because the Shah's regime was a mild authoritarian regime (in comparison with the fundamentalist regime) and the characteristics of the Shah's patrons the U.K. and the U.S. Because of the liberal democratic nature of the British and American polities, there were limits to how much violence and brutalities their client states could use against their own populations. These critics argue that the fundamentalist regime is an ultra- right-wing totalitarian regime similar to European fascism. That the fundamentalists are not going to accept the wishes of the Iranian people and are willing to mass slaughter the non-violent protesters. These critics

---

434 Mehdi Fatapour, "Interview," IRTV, (August 2, 2020), https://www.youtube.com/watch?v=YLQu46N7rDg&feature.
435 Ibid.
436 Hassan Yousofi-Eshkevari, *"Akharin Shah Shii Jahan Aya Mazhabi Bood?"* [Was the Last Shia King in the World Religious?], BBC Persian, (July 27, 2010), https://www.bbc.com/persian/iran/2010/07/100727_shah_anniv30_eshkevari_religion.shtml.

argue that such regimes (e. g., Nazi Germany, fascist Italy, ISIS, al Qaeda, and the fundamentalist regime ruling Iran) will use massive violence against the un-armed people. The critics argue that one has to look at how the fundamentalist regime and its proxy, the Lebanese Hezbollah, have used massive violence to keep their ally Bashar al-Assad in power in Syria. These critics argue that the only way to overthrow the fundamentalist regime is to use armed struggle. More-over, the fundamentalist regime's allies such as China, Russia, Syria (under Assad family), and Venezuela (under Hugo Chavez and Nicolás Maduro) are themselves brutal dictatorships. This means that not only they would not be con-cerned with dictatorship, repression, and human rights violations, but actually would themselves be threatened by the spread of democracy.

The INF believes that the situation in Iran is similar to those in the former USSR, Eastern European communist regimes, apartheid South Africa, and Chile under Pinochet. In other words, the fundamentalist regime is in a slow-mo-tion collapse. The INF strategy is to present a democratic alternative to the ruling dictatorship. The INF believes that by creating a powerful democratic opposition, they may be able to assist in the transition to democracy and prevent anarchy or another dictatorship. Future will show whether this criticism is valid or not.

Why Is the INF Not Willing to Cooperate with the Monarchists?

The Iranian monarchists want to restore the Pahlavi monarchy and install Reza Pahlavi as king.[437] Both the INF and INF-OA oppose cooperating with the mon-archists.[438] They argue that most political groups in Iran have evolved a great deal since 1979, gradually becoming more and more democratic. The bulk of the monarchists, however, have become even more authoritarian than they were in 1979. The less authoritarian monarchists call themselves "constitutional-ists." The non-monarchists refer to the more extreme monarchists as *"Shaholla-his,"* which is a derogatory term. They use this term because these monarchists openly talk about using violence to establish their dictatorship and use vulgar

---

437 Mr. Pahlavi's official site is http://rezapahlavi.org/. The English language page is http://en. rezapahlavi.org/.
438 Personal e-mail interview with Dr. Hussein Moussavian, February 5, 2019. See the full inter-view in Part III in this book. Hussein Moussavian, "Interview" Iran International TV, (May 2, 2020), https://melliun.org/iran/231112; and Homayoun Mehmaneche, *"'Demokrat-hae' Keh Ol-goyeshan Dictatorha Hastand"* ['Democrats' Whose Models are Dictators], Melliun, (June 25, 2020), https://melliun.org/iran/235285.

words in attacking others.[439] Many monarchists (including the bulk of the "constitutionalists") do not even consider the fact that the Shah was a dictator. Rather than admitting their mistakes (dictatorship, repression, torture, assassinations, executions of political prisoners), many monarchists have told me that the Shah should have killed more of the opponents and dissidents. The monarchists praise Reza Shah and Mohammad Reza Shah and hoist their portraits at their rallies and meetings.[440]

The monarchists have not apologized for the terrible dictatorship that they had inflicted on the Iranian people. Moreover, they blame the opponents of the Shah including the pro-democracy forces for resisting their dictatorship and blame the current fundamentalist dictatorship on those who opposed the Pahlavi rule.[441] The monarchists usually call the 1979 revolution *"Shoresh 57"* [Rebellion of 1979], and the opponents of the Shah *"Shoreshian"* [rebels].[442] Both the less authoritarian monarchist groups (e. g., the Constitutionalist Party of Iran and Farashgard), and the more extremist monarchists strongly support and profusely praise the rule of Reza Shah Pahlavi and Mohammad Reza Shah Pahlavi and condemn the pro-democracy forces and the INF.

For the INF (as well as other non-monarchists), the two Pahlavi kings were tyrants who did not allow freedoms of expression, the press, political parties, and elections. For the INF, the monarchists are unrepentant revanchists, who want to re-impose their dictatorship. The very fact that the pro-democracy forces such as the INF consider the Pahlavi regime to have been a brutal dictatorship and the monarchist strongly support the policies of the Pahlavis, make any cooperation between the two groups very difficult although both strongly oppose the fundamentalist regime.

In addition, many monarchists also believe that the 1979 revolution was a conspiracy by the U.S. and the U.K. to overthrow the Shah (who they say was making Iran strong) and put in power Khomeini so that Iran would be their colony.[443] These conspiracy theories are advocated not only by the extreme monar-

---

439 In this book, I use the term "more extreme monarchists" to refer to this faction of the monarchists.

440 See the views of top two less extremist monarchists at: Rangin-Kaman TV, *"Jame-e Shenasi Siasi Opposision Iran: Gerayesh 'Saltanat-Talabi Va Mashrooteh-Khah', Bakhsh 1"* [Political Sociology of the Opposition in Iran: 'Monarchist And Constitutionalist' Tendency, Part 1], (August 28, 2020), https://www.youtube.com/watch?v=jTvIgeQ9_FO.

441 Ibid.

442 Ibid. Also see another monarchist group called *"Farashgard"* at its website: https://iran revival.com/. In Persian, these terms have strong negative connotations.

443 Rangin-Kaman TV, *"Jame-e Shenasi Siasi Opposision Iran: Gerayesh 'Saltanat-Talabi Va Mashrooteh-Khah', Bakhsh 1"* [Political Sociology of the Opposition in Iran: 'Monarchist And

chists, but also by the least authoritarian monarchist leaders. For example, the least authoritarian monarchists are those who had been working with Dr. Shapour Bakhtiar. In recent interviews (September 2020), two high-level monarchists who served as cabinet ministers in Bakhtiar's government expressed such conspiracy views. Mr. Sirus Amouzegar served as Bakhtiar's Minister of Information (responsible for propaganda but not intelligence) and Dr. Manuchehr Razmara (Minister of Health).[444] Amouzegar said that two and half years before the revolution, the Shah criticized the "Jews in American mass media" for problems in the U.S. and did not renew Iran's oil concessions to the West, therefore, they began the plot to overthrow him. Dr. Razmara said that the Carter administration gave $150 million to Khomeini (to overthrow the Shah).[445] These conspiracy theories seem strange to scholars and many non-Iranians, but they are common among Iranian monarchists. Such differences over the basic facts of Iranian history and politics make conversation between the two groups, much less cooperation, very difficult.

All available evidence and scholarship confirm President Carter's statement in his memoirs that his policy was the continuation of past American policies toward Iran. In President Carter's words: "I continued, as other Presidents had before me, to consider the Shah a strong ally."[446] Considering Iran to be of strategic significance, the Carter administration had exempted the Shah from the President's human rights policy.[447]

Reza Pahlavi, the last crown prince of Iran, claims that he supports democracy and has asked all the opposition groups to accept him as the leader of all

Constitutionalist' Tendency, Part 1], (August 28, 2020), https://www.youtube.com/watch?v=jTvI geQ9_FO.

444 Rangin-Kaman TV, "*Jame-e Shenasi Siasi Opposision Iran: Gerayesh 'Dr. Shapour Bakhtiar', Bakhsh 1*" [Political Sociology of the Opposition in Iran: The Tendency of 'Dr. Shapour Bakhtiar, Part 1], (September 12, 2020), https://www.youtube.com/watch?v=EK1RodoZcbY; and Rangin-Kaman TV, "*Jame-e Shenasi Siasi Opposision Iran: Gerayesh 'Dr. Shapour Bakhtiar', Bakhsh 2*" [Political Sociology of the Opposition in Iran: The Tendency of 'Dr. Shapour Bakhtiar, Part 2], (September 18, 2020), https://www.youtube.com/watch?v=1GhsIal_nAE. The supporters of Dr. Bakhtiar includes both monarchists and non-monarchists. It is necessary to emphasize that the non-monarchist supporters of Dr. Bakhtiar usually do not express conspiracy views. They usually express rational explanations of the roots of the revolution such as the Shah's dictatorship and lack of legitimacy.

445 Ibid.

446 Jimmy Carter, *Keeping Faith: Memoirs of a President* (New York: Bantam Books, 1983), p. 435.

447 Carter, ibid., pp. 433–458; and Alexander Moens, "President Carter's Advisers and the Fall of the Shah," *Political Science Quarterly*, Vol. 106, No. 2 (Summer 1991), pp. 211–237.

the opposition.[448] Monarchists, including the three monarchist groups mentioned above, are even more explicit that all others should accept Reza Pahlavi as the leader of all the opposition.[449] This condition is unacceptable to the INF. Mr. Pahlavi claims that he supports democracy, a claim that leaders of the INF do not find very credible. The reason is that Mr. Pahlavi has proudly displayed the portraits of his father and grandfather and has praised their rule. Mr. Pahlavi has merely conceded that mistakes were made. But he has not condemned the brutal dictatorship of his father and grandfather, or their stealing vast wealth from the Iranian people. Therefore, INF leaders do not trust Mr. Pahlavi.[450] Dr. Moussavian has rejected any cooperation with Mr. Pahlavi. Moussavian has argued that Mr. Pahlavi took a public oath and declared himself king. Pahlavi has not abdicated or repudiated his claim to be king. The INF believes that the most appropriate form of democracy for Iran is a republican system. Moussavian argues that Mr. Pahlavi should first repudiate his claim to be king, and then he may make calls for cooperation with pro-democracy forces, and then those democratic forces who want to may cooperate with him.[451] Obviously, after the establishment of democracy in Iran, all groups (including monarchists) have the right to participate in politics. In other words, all parties (including monarchists) have the right to have their organizations, headquarters, publications, and participate in elections.

In his interviews, Mr. Pahlavi has stated many positions which have made it very difficult for pro-democracy forces to trust him as a genuine pro-democracy activist. For example, in his interview with Michel Taubmann, a French journalist, which has been published as a pamphlet, Mr. Pahlavi calls the 1953 coup "myth" and adds that before 1953, his father was a constitutional monarch

---

448 Reza Pahlavi, "*Peyman Novin*" [New Pact], (September 28, 2020), https://www.youtube.com/watch?v=pON_QVdAnoU.

449 Rangin-Kaman TV, "*Jame-e Shenasi Siasi Opposision Iran: Gerayesh 'Saltanat-Talabi Va Mashrooteh-Khah', Bakhsh 1*" [Political Sociology of the Opposition in Iran: 'Monarchist And Constitutionalist' Tendency, Part 1], (August 28, 2020), https://www.youtube.com/watch?v=jTvIgeQ9_FO.

450 Homayoun Mehmaneche, "Interview," Kalameh TV, (October 1, 2020), https://melliun.org/iran/243083; and Mohsen Ghaemmagham, "*Dar Peyman Aghay Reza Pahlavi, Chera Sohbati Az Dictatori Shah Nist?*" [Why There is No Talk of the Shah's Dictatorship in Mr. Reza Pahalvi's New Pact?], Melliun, (September 29, 2020), https://melliun.org/iran/243161.

451 Hussein Moussavian, "Interview with Radio Asr Jadid," (October 9, 2020), https://melliun.org/iran/243845.

and respected the 1906 Constitution.[452] Mr. Pahlavi says: "It is true that my father had the support of America. But talking about a coup is myth making. Mossadegh's government had lost its support, otherwise how can one speak of its collapse in less than three days? No center of conspiracy, no foreign government, even with the largest resources, create such a miracle."[453] Pahlavi's interview was published in 2018. By the time of this interview, CIA's own documents on the coup have been published. Moreover, American officials, such as Secretary of State Madeline Albright, President Bill Clinton, President Barrack Obama, and Secretary of State Hillary Clinton had publicly acknowledged the American role in the coup and had expressed regret in the U.S. role in undermining democracy in Iran.[454] On March 17, 2000, then-Secretary of State Madeleine Albright said:

> In 1953 the United States played a significant role in orchestrating the overthrow of Iran's popular Prime Minister, Mohammed Mossadegh. The Eisenhower Administration believed its actions were justified for strategic reasons; but the coup was clearly a setback for

---

452 Reza Pahlavi, *Zaman Entekhab* [Time for Choosing], (2018), https://downloadeketab.files. wordpress.com/2013/11/d8afd8a7d986d984d988d8af-daa9d8aad8a7d8a8-d8b2d985d8a7d986. pdf. Interview with Michel Taubmann.
453 Ibid., p. 18.
454 I am citing the words of these American officials to show that although American officials have finally admitted American role in the 1953 coup, Mr. Pahlavi and monarchists still refuse that reality. As an aside, it is politically significant to emphasize that American officials' admittance did not have the effect they thought such acknowledgments would have on either the fundamentalist regime or on the pro-democracy opposition. American officials from President Clinton to President Obama had a fundamentally flawed understanding of Iranian politics. Khomeini opposed and hated the U.S. not because of the 1953 coup but because of the 1963 reforms. Right-wing Islamic forces had collaborated with the U.S. and the Shah in the 1953 coup. Fundamentalist officials have publicly and privately used the CIA coup as propaganda attacks on the U.S. American officials' admission of the CIA role also had little effect on Iranian pro-democracy groups. The reason is that such admission was not an announcement that the U.S. would henceforth oppose dictatorship and support democracy in Iran. On the contrary, American officials made explicit that they were making such admission in order to appease the fundamentalist regime and to begin rapprochement with the ruling theocratic dictatorship. At the very same time that President Obama was criticizing Eisenhower's support for the Shah's dictatorship and against Mossadegh's pro-democracy side, Obama himself was engaging Ayatollah Khamenei's dictatorship and undermining pro-democracy Iranians. The fundamentalist regime has been far more dictatorial and repressive than the Shah's regime. If one should criticize Eisenhower for his support of the Shah's dictatorship, shouldn't one also criticize Obama for his appeasement of the far more reactionary and tyrannical fundamentalist regime? For an analysis of these see Masoud Kazemzadeh, *U.S.-Iran Confrontation: Alternative Scenarios and Consequences* (forthcoming), chapter 2.

Iran's political development. And it is easy to see now why many Iranians continue to resent this intervention by America in their internal affairs.

Moreover, during the next quarter century, the United States and the West gave sustained backing to the Shah's regime. Although it did much to develop the country economically, the Shah's government also brutally repressed political dissent.[455]

Former President Bill Clinton, in an interview with American journalist Charlie Rose during the 2005 World Economic Forum in Davos, Switzerland, said the following:

> ...Iran's a whole different kettle of fish—but it's a sad story that really began in the 1950s when the United States deposed Mr. Mossadegh, who was an elected parliamentary democrat, and brought the Shah back in...
>
> ...Iran was what it was [in the 1980s under the fundamentalist regime] because we got rid of the parliamentary democracy back in the '50s; at least, that is my belief.
>
> ...I publicly acknowledged that the United States had actively overthrown Mossadegh and I apologized for it...[456]

On June 4, 2009, in his major address in Cairo, then-President Barack Obama said: "In the middle of the Cold War, the United States played a role in the overthrow of a democratically elected Iranian government."[457] In October 2011, then-Secretary of State Hillary Clinton, in an interview with the BBC Persian, said: "And so we have regretted what happened in 1953."[458]

Between August 19, 1953 and 1978, it was illegal in Iran to say or publish on the role of the CIA and MI6 in the coup. The Shah's regime would arrest, torture, and probably kill the person who expressed that. The denial of the role of the CIA and the MI6 in the overthrow of Mossadegh has become a major partisan belief for the monarchists who deny the veracity of declassified U.S. government documents, U.S. officials, and scholarly research. For the INF, Mr. Pahlavi's denial of the coup and the CIA role in it, indicates that either he is ignorant of the basic facts of Iranian history or he is well aware of them but lies about them.

---

455 Secretary of State Madeleine K. Albright, "Remarks," U.S. Department of State, (March 17, 2000), https://1997-2001.state.gov/statements/2000/000317.html. For the video of the segment see https://www.youtube.com/watch?v=Q5HYUtYa3wI.

456 Bill Clinton, "Interview with Charlie Rose," (January 2005), https://larouchepub.com/other/interviews/2005/3206clinton_rose.html.

457 Barack Obama, "Remarks by the President at Cairo University," (June 4, 2009), https://obamawhitehouse.archives.gov/the-press-office/remarks-president-cairo-university-6-04-09.

458 Hillary Clinton, "Interview with the BBC Persian," (October 26, 2011), https://www.youtube.com/watch?v=ED0iU-sMaGA&t=1410s.

In the same interview, Mr. Pahlavi repeats that his father ruled constitutionally before 1953. This assertion is also false. Declassified U.S. government documents show that from the very beginning, Mohammad Reza Shah wanted to become an absolutist dictator like his father. Many powerful prime ministers, such as Gen. Razmara, pleaded with the U.S. embassy to tell the Shah not to interfere in the affairs of the government and tell his family members to respect the 1906 constitution and not interfere in government activities.[459] The following is from a CIA classified report of August 30, 1950:

> 1. ... in line with his attitudes toward previous Iranian governments, the Shah is anxious to retain control of the present government. Likewise, the Shah's sisters want to continue their personal influence in affairs of state.

> 2. ... Prime Minister Razmara is resisting this interference from the Court and informant states that, as a result, serious conflict is developing between the Court and the Prime Minister with the Shah and his sisters intriguing with certain Majlis factions to weaken the Prime Minister's authority.

> 3. ... it is Razmara's belief that, if the United States and British Governments were jointly to point out to the Shah the dangers of such intervention, the Shah would listen and would probably alter his attitude. Informant stressed the fact that Razmara would not want legal opposition curbed, but needs assistance only to restrain what he considers to be the Shah's unconstitutional and behind-the-scenes interference.[460]

For the INF, because Mr. Pahlavi is not willing to acknowledge and condemn the anti-constitutional and dictatorial actions of his father, then he is not a democrat. For the INF, between 1941 and 1953, Iran was a lukewarm constitutional democracy not because of the actions of Mohammad Reza Shah Pahlavi, but despite them. That period witnessed a struggle between the Shah who wanted to re-establish absolute dictatorship and various forces such as the INF that wanted to promote democracy. The August 1953 coup was a victory for the anti-democratic forces.

The INF wants to create a broad coalition in order to establish democracy. The INF does not believe that the monarchists are a pro-democracy force in Iran today. For the INF, the bulk of the monarchists in Iran are more a threat to democracy than a force for it. Therefore, it would not make much sense to cooperate with them. In 1978, the pro-democracy forces did not know much about Khomeini, his supporters, and his political project. That is not the case with the

---

459 U.S. Government, CIA, "Court Interference in Government Activity," (August 30, 1950), https://www.enghelabe-eslami.com/component/content/article/21-didgagha/tarikhi/31232-2018-11-17-14-50-28.html?Itemid=0
460 Ibid.

Pahlavi monarchists. There exists an actual history of dictatorial rule from 1925 to 1979. It is necessary to add that the overwhelming majority of republican groups and activists hold strong antipathies towards the monarchists and do not accept Mr. Pahlavi as their leader.[461]

Why Is the INF-OA Willing to Cooperate with the Left Party of Iran?

It is true that the main force behind the Left Party of Iran (LPI) is the Fadaian-Majority, and that the Fadaian-Majority has had a terrible history of dictatorial ideology, collaboration with the Tudeh Party (fully subservient to the Soviet Union), collaboration with the fundamentalist regime, and working with the KGB.

First, the Soviet Union collapsed in 1991, therefore, one does not have to worry about Soviet Union's nefarious influence in Iran. Second, although the LPI considers itself a Marxist party, it is explicitly against dictatorship. Third, those who founded the LPI explicitly condemned and criticized their own past dictatorship and support for the fundamentalist regime. Fourth, Fadaian-Majority has explicitly, publicly, and privately apologized to Iranian liberal democrats for its slanderous and vicious attacks in 1979 – 1983. Fifth, the LPI has been moving away from its support for the reformist faction of the fundamentalist oligarchy to working with pro-democracy forces. This development is positive for the prospects of democratization. The LPI has a social base inside Iran and outside Iran. The Fadaian-Majority had been strongly supporting voting for reformist fundamentalists in all the elections since 1997. The LPI called for a boycott is the 2020 Majles elections. The INF and INF-OA have been strongly calling for boycott of elections since 2002.

Would the LPI continue to work with the pro-democracy forces or would it go back to supporting the reformist faction of the fundamentalist regime? Would the LPI continue to uphold democracy and freedom, or would it go back to embracing dictatorship and Leninist policies? It is not clear how the LPI would evolve. The pro-fundamentalist regime collaborationist forces (e.g., Farrokh Negahdar, Maliheh Mohammadi) are still highly influential among the

---

461 BBC Persian, "*Payman Novin: Naghsh Reza Pahalvi Dar Mobarezeh Bah Jomhuri Islami Chist?*" [New Pact: What is the Role of Reza Pahlavi in the Struggle Against the Islamic Republic?], (October 1, 2020), https://www.youtube.com/watch?v=jyrpKcCG_i8; and Mehrdad Darwishpour, "Interview," Iran International TV, (September 29, 2020), https://www.youtube.com/watch?v=MELUjl4YiCU.

LPI. Anti-democratic and authoritarian heritage still influences many LPI leaders and members. The LPI is the largest Iranian leftist party. The continuation of working with the pro-democracy forces by the LPI would be good for the prospects of democracy and harmful for the fundamentalist regime. In all likelihood, working with pro-democracy forces, enhances the power of the pro-democratic faction within the LPI. If that is the case, then the INF-OA working with the LPI is positive for the prospects of democratization in Iran. By April 2021, however, it appears that the faction under the leadership of Negahdar has the upper hand again.

Chapter 11
Political Situation in Iran Today

The fundamentalist regime is suffering from serious crises. These include a severe crisis of legitimacy, crisis of succession to the Supreme Leader, economic crisis, intra-elite factionalism, and confrontation with powerful foreign opponents. These crises have made the regime more unstable than before.

Crisis of Legitimacy

There is no reliable way to measure the support or opposition to the regime. There are no free and democratic elections in Iran. Only members of the fundamentalist oligarchy are allowed to run in the elections. The data the regime presents on elections are not even accepted by members of the oligarchy. For example, in the 2009 presidential election, two top members of the fundamentalist oligarchy (Mir-Hussein Moussavi and Mehdi Karoobi) refused to accept the results the regime announced. Opinion surveys using phone interviews or door to door interviews are not credible in a country that is highly repressive and dictatorial.[462] Therefore, we can only guess the support base of the regime and the opposition.

According to Sadegh Zibakalam, only 10 to 20 percent of the population supports the regime.[463] Zibakalam is the most famous political science professor at the University of Tehran. What makes Zibakalam's estimate significant is not his faculty position, but because he is regarded as one of the top intellectuals of the reformist and expedient factions of the fundamentalist regime. Zibakalam has been close to President Hassan Rouhani and Ayatollah Akbar Rafsanjani. Rafsanjani was one of the most powerful members of the ruling oligarchy, a two-

---

462 Several scholars have attempted to conduct surveys and other ways to measure the attitudes of the Iranian people using various methods such as online surveys. For the best example, see Pooyan Tamimi Arab and Ammar Maleki, "Iran's secular shift: new survey reveals huge change in religious beliefs," The Conversation, (September 10, 2020), https://theconversation.com/irans-secular-shift-new-survey-reveals-huge-changes-in-religious-beliefs-145253. For other examples of various observers who have attempted to measure indications of the attitudes of the Iranian people, see Masoud Kazemzadeh, "The Perils and Costs of a Grand Bargain with the Islamic Republic of Iran," op. cit.

463 Sadegh Zibakalam, "If a referendum is held today, over 70% would say no to an Islamic republic," Deutsche Welle, (January 5, 2018), https://www.youtube.com/watch?v=GuXyEtMgAOI.

https://doi.org/10.1515/9783110782158-013

term president, the head of the Assembly of Experts that chose Khamenei for the position of Supreme Leader, and the Head of the Expediency Council (which allowed him access to the true vote counts). Zibakalam, himself, was one of the top fundamentalists who was responsible for the purge of universities from professors and students who were liberal, secular, or Marxist during the "Islamic Cultural Revolution" in the early 1980s. In an interview with the Persian language program of the German state news agency Deutsche Welle, Zibakalam said: "If there was a referendum on the Islamic Republic ... over 70 percent of the people would vote no to the Islamic Republic, and the officials of the regime know this as well."[464] Many observers believe that the regime's base of support is less than 20 percent of the population.[465]

Iranians have been voting with their feet. According to the International Monetary Fund, Iran has had the largest "brain drain" in the world since the 1990s, with about 150,000 to 180,000 leaving the country annually.[466] An article in the *Los Angeles Times*, places the number of Iranians leaving annually at 180,000.[467] According to the Medical Council of Iran, about 3,000 physicians emigrated from Iran in 2020.[468] One physician tells the *Los Angeles Times* correspondent in Tehran that about 30% of his colleagues have left Iran for Western Europe and North America since 2009.[469] According to Ali-Reza Monadi, Chairman of the Education and Research Committee of the Majles, in the Iranian calendar year 1398 (March 21, 2019 to March 19, 2020), about 900 university professors emigrated from Iran.[470] According to one official at Tehran Nurses Organization, during the past year, about 500 nurses officially filed papers to leave

---

464 Ibid.

465 For indications on the social base of the regime see Masoud Kazemzadeh, "The Perils and Costs of a Grand Bargain with the Islamic Republic of Iran," *American Foreign Policy Interests*, Vol. 29, No. 5 (2007), pp. 301–327; and Masoud Kazemzadeh, "Five Possible Outcomes Following the Mass Protests in Iran," Radio Farda, (February 6, 2018), https://en.radiofarda.com/a/iran-unrest-scenarios-war-revolution-uprising/29023446.html.

466 Golnaz Esfandiari, "Iran: Coping With The World's Highest Rate of Brain Drain," Radio Farda, (March 8, 2004), https://www.rferl.org/a/1051803.html; Financial Tribune, "Brian Drain Continues in Iran," (November 9, 2016), https://financialtribune.com/articles/people/53254/brain-drain-continues.

467 Omid Khazani, "Just when they're needed most, Iran's doctors are leaving in droves," *The Los Angeles Times*, (May 23, 2021), https://www.latimes.com/world-nation/story/2021-05-23/iran-brain-drain-doctors-exodus-covid-pandemic.

468 Ibid.

469 Ibid.

470 ISNA, "*Monadi: 900 Ostad Dar Sal 98 Az Iran Kharej Shodand*" [Mondai: 900 Professors Left Iran in the Year 2019–2020], (March 6, 2021), https://www.isna.ir/news/99121612250.

Iran each month.[471] The official added that many nurses leave without filing officially.[472]

Many who have left Iran cite oppressive political and social policies of the fundamentalist regime for their decision to leave.[473] More recently, many cite the economic conditions after the sanctions were imposed by the Trump administration.[474]

Crisis of Succession to the Supreme Leader

The fundamentalist system has concentrated enormous powers in the hands of the position of Supreme Leader. Khamenei has been Supreme Leader since 1989. Khamenei was born in 1939. In 2021, at age 82, he has been the Supreme Leader for 32 years. It is not clear who will be the next Supreme Leader. It is safe to assume that he and his supporters want someone who belongs to their hardline faction to be the next Supreme Leader. It is also safe to assume that members of the other fundamentalist factions (i.e., reformist and expedient) want someone from their faction to be the next Supreme Leader. This has further exacerbated the intra-elite struggles for power. Khamenei has allowed members of reformist and expedient factions to run for presidency, Majles, Assembly of Experts, and other positions. Many members of the hardline faction are not as inclusive as Khamenei and may use the powers of the office of Supreme Leader to purge

---

471 Iran International, *"Nezam Parastari Tehran: Mahaneh 500 Parastar Be Dalil Hoghogh Paeen Az Iran Mohajerat Mikonand"* [Tehran Nurses Organization: Every Month 500 Nurses Emigrate From Iran Due to Low Wages], (April 11, 2021), https://iranintl.com/%D8%AA%D8%A7%D8%B2%D9%87-%DA%86%D9%87-%D8%AE%D8%A8%D8%B1/%D9%86%D8%B8%D8%A7%D9%85-%D9%BE%D8%B1%D8%B3%D8%AA%D8%A7%D8%B1%DB%8C-%D8%AA%D9%87%D8%B1%D8%A7%D9%86-%D9%85%D8%A7%D9%87%D8%A7%D9%86%D9%87-%DB%B5%DB%B0%DB%B0-%D9%BE%D8%B1%D8%B3%D8%AA%D8%A7%D8%B1-%D8%A8%D9%87-%D8%AF%D9%84%DB%8C%D9%84-%D8%AD%D9%82%D9%88%D9%82-%D9%BE%D8%A7%DB%8C%DB%8C%D9%86-%D8%A7%D8%B2-%D8%A7%DB%8C%D8%B1%D8%A7%D9%86-%D9%85%D9%87%D8%A7%D8%AC%D8%B1%D8%AA-%D9%85%DB%8C%E2%80%8C%DA%A9%D9%86%D9%86%D8%AF, also available at https://melliun.org/iran/257437.
472 Ibid.
473 Esfandiari, op. cit.
474 Khazani, op. cit.

other factions. There is a high likelihood that there would be violence among fundamentalists after Khamenei's death.[475]

One of the few hard-liners who had support among reformist and expedient members of the fundamentalist oligarchy was Gen. Qassem Soleimani.[476] Gen. Soleimani was, perhaps, the only hard-liner, who could have appealed to expedient and reformist fundamentalists to give a new hardline Supreme Leader a chance. The U.S. killing of Gen. Soleimani on January 3, 2020 eliminated the one major figure that might have been able to bring some calm and reassurance to various members of the ruling fundamentalist oligarchy.

The regime in general, and the IRGC in particular, had spent massive efforts in creating a political persona for Soleimani in the previous 15 years. Soleimani was portrayed as the "superman" who protected Iran's national interests and expanded Iran's power over neighboring countries. Since the early 2000s, he was kept assiduously out of Iran's domestic repressive policies and its intra-elite factional fights.[477] Soleimani was portrayed as above politics and factions and as protector of Iran. But why did the regime do that? In my opinion, the IRGC had done this in order to create a person who could save the regime in its time of existential crisis. For example, if there was to be a war with the U.S., or in case of upheaval due to the passing of the Supreme Leader, Soleimani could play the role of the "savior" of the country. There is no one within the fundamentalist oligarchy that could play that role today. The regime's efforts were partially successful. Virtually all the supporters of the fundamentalist regime (reformists, expedients, and hard-liners) as well as some on-fundamentalists supported Soleimani as was demonstrated by the large-scale mourning of his death. However, the lack of success of the propaganda was demonstrated by the protesters during the protests in January 2020. During the protests since January 11, the protesters have burned and tore down Soleimani's banners that the

---

475 Masoud Kazemzadeh, "Post-Khamenei Iran and American National Interests," *The Hill*, (July 11, 2016), http://thehill.com/blogs/pundits-blog/foreign-policy/287175-post-khamenei-iran-and-american-national-interests.

476 Mohsen Ghaemmagham, "*Ghassem Soleimani – Dar Khedmat Nezam Estebdad Mazhabi Va Vali Faghih*" [Ghassem Soleimani – In Service of the System of Religious Dictatorship and Fundamentalist Regime], (January 19, 2020), Melliun, https://melliun.org/iran/223359.

477 In 1999, Soleimani was among a group of 24 high-ranking IRGC generals who wrote a confidential letter to then-president Mohammad Khatami threatening that if he did not crush the student protests, they would intervene themselves. The letter was leaked to the press and published to further embarrass Khatami. Supreme Leader Khamenei promoted these signatories in subsequent years. The letter was considered to be a veiled threat to carry out a coup by hardline IRGC generals. A translation of the letter is available at https://web.archive.org/web/20121012133424/http://www.iranian.com/News/1999/July/irgc.html.

regime had placed in various places.[478] Slogans chanted were not only against the Supreme Leader and the IRGC but also called Soleimani a murderer.[479] Many protesters chanted that the IRGC and Basij are the equivalent of ISIS.[480] Moreover, many of the slogans were against all forms of dictatorship whether fundamentalist or monarchist.[481]

Economic Crisis

The more financial resources and political legitimacy are provided to the fundamentalist regime, the higher the likelihood that the fundamentalist regime may continue to muddle through. The more economic and political sanctions are imposed on the fundamentalist regime, the higher the likelihood of regime collapse.

The pressures from the Trump administration, particularly the economic sanctions, have greatly undermined the regime's economic stability.[482] The nuclear accord, known as the Joint Comprehensive Plan of Action (JCPOA), was

---

478 VOA, *"Moatarezan Dar Tehran Bilbord Qassem Soleimani Ra Atesh Zadand"* [Protesters in Tehran Set Ablaze Qassem Soleimani's Billboards], (January 12, 2020), https://ir.voanews.com/episode/mtrdan-dr-thran-bylbwrd-qasm-slymany-ra-atsh-zdnd-235040; and VOA, *"Pareh Kardan Bannerhay Tablighati Qassem Soleimani Tavasot Mardom Dar Tehran"* [Tearing Down of Propaganda Banners for Qassem Soleimani by the People, of Tehran], (January 12, 2020), https://ir.voanews.com/episode/iran-235050.

479 VOA, *"Koshteh Nadadim Keh Sazesh Konim, Rahbar Ghatel Ro Setayesh Konim"* [We Did Not Have Deaths in order to Compromise, And Praise the Murderer Supreme Leader], (January 13, 2020), https://ir.voanews.com/episode/kshth-ndadym-kh-sazsh-knym-rhbr-qatl-rw-staysh-knym-shar-hzaran-mtrd-nfr-dr-thran-235018; and VOA, *"Soleimani Ghatel-e Rahbaresh Ham Ghatel-e"* [Soleimani is a Murder, His Leader is a Murderer], You Tube, (January 11, 2020), https://www.youtube.com/watch?v=1bl6ITEoStQ&app=desktop.

480 VOA, *"Basiji Sepahi, Daesh Ma Shomae"* [Basij and IRGC You are Our ISIS], (January 13, 2020), https://ir.voanews.com/episode/bsyjy-spahy-dash-ma-shmayy-shar-mrdm-mtrd-dr-mshhd-235013.

481 VOA, *"Marg Bar Setamgar Cheh Shah Basheh Cheh Rahbar"* [Death to the Oppressor, Whether Shah or Supreme Leader], (January 13, 2020), https://ir.voanews.com/episode/iran-protest-sunday-235014. The slogans against monarchy were due to chats in favor of monarchists in other demonstrations. Monarchists usually chant *"Reza Shah Roohat Shad"* [Reza Shah, Your Soul Be Happy]. The pro-democracy protesters like the slogans *"Esteghlal, Azadi, Jomhuri Irani"* [Independence, Freedom, Iranian Republic] and *"Na Sharghi, Na Gharbi, Jomhuri Irani"* [Neither East, Nor West, Iranian Republic].

482 Behrang Tajdin, *"Eghtesad Iran Beh Ravayat Panj Nemoodar Dar Panjomin Salgard Barjam"* [Iran's Economy According to Five Charts In the Fifth Anniversary of the JCPOA], BBC Persian, (July 13, 2020), https://www.bbc.com/persian/business-53381573.

reached between the fundamentalist regime and P5+1 (5 permanent members of the UN Security Council and Germany) on July 14, 2015. President Donald Trump withdrew from the JCPOA on May 8, 2018.

According to President Rouhani, the sanctions have cost the government about $214 billion in revenues between May 2018 and August 2020.[483] According to Rouhani, Iran received about $120 billion from the sale of oil in 2011. Due to U.S. sanctions, Rouhani says that Iran only received about $20 billion in 2019.[484] According to Eshagh Jahangiri, First Deputy President, Iran's income from the sale of oil declined from about $100 billion (the year is not clear) to about $8 billion in the previous Iranian calendar year (March 20, 2019 to March 20, 2020).[485] Both Rouhani and Jahangiri are referring to Iran's sale of oil in 2019, but provide different figures.[486] Probably, Jahangiri is referring to the "legal" sale of Iran's oil, whereas Rouhani might be referring to both "legal" and "secret" sales of Iran's oil.[487] According to Majid Reza Hariri, the Chairman of the Iran-China Chamber of Commerce, before sanctions Iran used to sell about $120 billion dollars of oil annually during the good years. Iran's non-oil exports in 2018 brought about $40 billion. Because of the sanctions, the non-oil exports brought about $30 billion the current year. Hariri attributes the declines to the U.S. sanctions and Covid-19.[488]

---

483 Ibid.

484 Radio Farda, "Iran's Oil Revenue Dropped to Less Than $20 Billion, Rouhani Says," (September 14, 2020), https://en.radiofarda.com/a/30838504.html.

485 Radio Farda, "Rouhani Says Sanctions Cost Government 900 Trillian Rials in Revenues," (August 26, 2020), https://en.radiofarda.com/a/rouhani-says-sanctions-cost-government-900-trillion-rials-in-revenues/30803859.html.

486 The Iranian government does not always provide official figures. And when they do, different government entities provide contradictory data. For example, both the Central Bank of Iran and the Statistical Center of Iran are part of the president's administration and the president appoints their chairmen. These two entities (whose chairmen are appointed by president Rouhani and work for him) have provided different figures for Iran's GDP. Therefore, scholars and other observers usually rely upon the speeches and interviews of officials for various data. See Fereydoon Khavand, "Interview," Radio Farda, (October 6, 2020), https://www.radiofarda.com/a/30876747.html.

487 In order to avoid U.S. sanctions, Iran has developed extensive secret trade networks whereby Iranian oil tankers secretly download their oil at night to other oil tankers which then sell it usually to Chinese companies. Iran provides huge discounts, and the Chinese government ignores such trades. The interlocuters (Iranians and non-Iranians) make many millions of dollars by providing such services.

488 ILNA, "*Rais Otagh Bazargani Iran Va Chin Dar Goftego Ba ILNA*" [Interview with the Chairman of the Iran-China Chamber of Commerce], (October 4, 2020), https://www.ilna.news/fa/tiny/news-977917.

For the following two years after the JCPOA, Iran's GDP went up by about 17%. Since Trump's election, Iran's GDP has shrunk by about 20%.[489] In 2019, Iran's GDP declined by over 8%.[490] This was the third year in a row (2017, 2018, and 2019) that Iran's GDP declined. According to official regime data, the per capita annual income declined by about 35% from 2011 to 2019.[491]

According to the IMF, by 2018, Iran's net debt was less than $118 billion. The IMF projects that this figure will rise to about $258 billion by the end of 2020. This figure is about 44% of Iran's GDP, according to the IMF. According to the IMF report, the annual state budget deficit for 2020 would be around $58 billion. Moreover, large amounts of Iran's foreign reserves are not accessible due to the U.S. sanctions. According to the IMF, in 2018, Iran had access to about $122 billion of its foreign reserves. By October 2020, about $8.8 billion was accessible to the Iranian government from its money outside Iran.[492]

According to the Iranian government, the inflation rate which had gone down to less than 10% by 2015 has gone up again to over 40%.[493] The Statistical Center of Iran which works directly under the government has officially announced that the inflation rate is around 26 percent.[494] Even the official state news agency ILNA that is close to President Rouhani, casts doubt on the accuracy of the data. According to an economist that ILNA has interviewed the real inflation rate is over 60 percent in September 2020.[495]

Looking at the market exchange rate of Iran's national currency, the rial, would be a better way to capture the decline of Iran's economy. The rial has been in gradual decline since the fundamentalists came to power in 1979. Since Trump's withdrawal from the JCPOA, the rial has suffered historical declines, usually right after the U.S. announced more pressures. In 1978, one

---

489 Behrang Tajdin, *"Eghtesad Iran Beh Ravayat Panj Nemoodar Dar Panjomin Salgard Barjam,"* op. cit.

490 Jamshid Asadi and Mehdi Jamali, *"Gozar Az Eghtesad Nezam Valaee Beh Eghtesad Bazzar Bonyad: Naghsh 'Bazzar Azad',"* [Transition from the Fundamentalist Regime Economy to Market Orientated Economy: The Role of 'Free Markets'], Iran-Emrooz, (July 22, 2020), http://www.iran-emrooz.net/index.php/politic/more/85222/.

491 Ibid.

492 All the figures in this paragraph are from a report by the IMF released on October 19, 2020. See Radio Farda, "Iran's Net Debt, 44% of its GDP, IMF Says," (October 20, 2020), https://en.radiofarda.com/a/iran-s-net-debt-44-of-its-gdp-imf-says/30903332.html.

493 Ibid.

494 ILNA, *"Ehsan Soltani Dar Goftogo Ba ILNA: Tavarom Vaghe-e Balay 60 Darsad Ast"* [Interview with Ehsan Soltani: Real Inflation is Over 60 Percent], (September 20, 2020), www.ilna.news/fa/tiny/news-970141.

495 Ibid.

U.S. dollar was about 70 rials. In 2015, after the JCPOA, rial was stable at around 30,000 rials to one dollar. After Trump's withdrawal from the JCPOA, on May 8, 2018, one dollar reached 70,000 rials.[496] On May 10, 2018, one dollar reached about 80,000 rials. With the Trump administration's policy of "Maximum Pressure," restricting the fundamentalist regime's access to world markets, on July 19, 2020, one U.S. dollar was about 260,000 rials.[497] This was the lowest value for the rial in history until then. The Central Bank of Iran (CBI) injected about one billion dollars into the currency exchange market during July and August in order to prop up the value of the rial, which brought the exchange rate to 210,000 rials to one dollar. However, the rial fluctuated thereafter reaching a major decline on September 9, trading for over 250,000 rials to one dollar.[498] On September 14, 2020, the rial reached another historic low at 269,500 rials to a dollar. On September 20, 2020 on the eve of the U.S. announcing that it would carry out the UN sanctions that the JCPOA had suspended (although U.S. allies the U.K., France, and Germany officially stated that the suspension of the UN sanctions would continue), the rial dropped to its then lowest level against dollar trading at around 273,000.[499] Right after Trump's speech at the UN General Assembly, the rial dropped to its lowest level again on September 23, 2020 trading at about 281,000 rials to one dollar.[500] By September 26, the rial dropped trading around 293,000 rials to a dollar.[501] On October 1, 2020, the rial again establish another low record. One dollar was traded for 300,000 rials.[502] According to Radio Farda, between February 1979 and October 1, 2020,

---

496 Radio Farda, "Iranian Currency Roils As Trump Decision Looms," (May 8, 2018), https://en.radiofarda.com/a/iran-currency-drops-ahead-of-trump-nuclear-announcement/29214907.html.

497 Radio Farda, "Iran's Rial Hits New Historic Low Against US Dollar, Other Currencies," (July 5, 2020), https://en.radiofarda.com/a/iran-rial-hits-new-historic-low-against-us-dollar-other-curren cies/30706985.html; and Radio Farda, "Devaluation of Iran's Currency Accelerates With Dollar Hitting 260,000 Rials," (July 19, 2020), https://en.radiofarda.com/a/devaluation-of-iran-s-currency-accelerates-with-dollar-hitting-260-000-rials/30735734.html.

498 Radio Farda, "Dollar Soars to Near Record Level in Iran," (September 9, 2020), https://en.radiofarda.com/a/dollar-soars-to-near-record-level-in-iran-/30829462.html.

499 Radio Farda, "*Nerkh Dollar Va Tala Dar Iran Record Dobareh Zad*" [The Price of Dollar and Gold in Iran Hit Another Record], (September 20, 2020), https://www.radiofarda.com/a/30848568.html.

500 Radio Zamaneh, "*Dollar Az Marz 28 Hezar Tooman Oboor Kard*" [Dollar Crossed the 28,000 Toman Border], (September 23, 2020), https://www.radiozamaneh.com/539959.

501 Radio Farda, "*Dollar Beh Kanal 30 Hezar Toman Nazdiktar Shod*" [Dollar Got Closer to 30,000 Toman], (September 26, 2020), https://www.radiofarda.com/a/30859135.html.

502 Radio Farda, "*Sekkeh Az Marz 15 Million Gozasht; Dollar 30 Hezar Toman Shod*" [Gold Coin Crossed the 15 Million Rial Border; Dollar Became 30,000 Toman], (October 1, 2020), https://www.radiofarda.com/a/30868839.html.

the value of the dollar went up by 4,285 times to the rial.[503] On October 8, 2020, the U.S. Secretary of Treasury, Steven Mnuchin, announced sanctions on 18 financial institutions in Iran.[504] On October 11, 2020, the rial dropped exchanging for 317,000 rials to one dollar. On October 12, the Chairman of the CBI, Abdol-Nasser Hemmati, announced that in order to support the value of the rial, the CBI would inject $50 million daily.[505] On October 14, one dollar was sold for 318,500 rials.[506] On October 15, one dollar was sold for 322,000 rials.[507] On October 20, 2020, however, the value of the dollar all of the sudden dropped by more than 30,000 rials.[508] One of the main financial daily in Tehran, *Donya-e Eghtesad*, gave the reason as "many foreign exchange and gold coin traders were worried about the U.S. election and were afraid to hold onto their dollars and thus there were many sellers in the market."[509] Dr. Fereydoon Khavand, one of the most prominent Iranian economists, explained that although the primary reason for the reduction of the value of the rial is the structural maladies of the economy and the U.S. sanctions and particularly the Trump administration's "Maximum Pressure" campaign, but there is also a short-term psychological element as well. Only two weeks before the November 3 elections in the U.S., many thought that Joe Biden might win and he might ease on the sanctions on the fundamentalist regime. In that case, the fundamentalist regime would be able to sell oil and the regime's foreign exchange would drastically rise, thus the value of the rial would also rise. That concern, according to many observers, was the primary reason for selling off dollars and the rise in the rial's value on October 19 and 20.[510] With Biden's victory, the price of the dollar and gold declined by about

---

503 Ibid.

504 Radio Farda, "Washington Blacklists Iran's Entire Financial Sector," (October 8, 2020), https://en.radiofarda.com/a/washington-blacklists-iran-s-entire-financial-sector/30883130.html.

505 Radio Farda, "*Gheymat Dollar Az 32 Hezar Toman Gozasht*" [The Price of Dollar Crossed 32 Thousand Toman], (October 15, 2020), https://www.radiofarda.com/a/dollar-Iran/30894913.html.

506 My monitoring of the prices at the website https://bonbast.com/ on October 14, 2020. This is one of the most reliable sites on exchange rates for rial.

507 Radio Farda, "*Gheymat Dollar Az 32 Hezar Toman Gozasht*" [The Price of Dollar Crossed 32 Thousand Toman], (October 15, 2020), https://www.radiofarda.com/a/dollar-Iran/30894913.html.

508 Radio Farda, "*Kahesh Bish-Az 3 Hezar Tomani Gheymat Dollar Dar Bazaar Arz Tehran*" [Reduction of More Than 3,000 Toman of Dollar's Value at Tehran's Foreign Exchange Market], (October 20, 2020), https://www.radiofarda.com/a/30902739.html.

509 Ibid.

510 Fereydoon Khavand, "*Bazaar Arz Iran Taht-e Taasir Entekhabat Amrika*" [Iran's Foreign Exchange Market Under the Impact of the American Elections], Radio Farda, (October 19, 2020), https://www.radiofarda.com/a/30901565.html. Some believe that due to pressure from President

20% in a matter of days. By November 7, the dollar was exchanged for less than 230,000 rials.[511] On November 8, the U.S. Secretary of State Mike Pompeo announced that the U.S. would impose a flood of new sanctions on Iran (until the Trump administration would leave the White House). It was said that Israel and several Arab countries would cooperate closely to make these sanctions more effective. Within hours, the value of rial declined again and was exchanged at round 270,000 rials by November 9, 2020.[512] By mid-December 2020, the value of the rial remained more or less the same. President Biden drastically changed the U.S. policy toward the fundamentalist regime. Due to the Biden policy, the fundamentalist regime oil exports increased, thus providing the economy with dollars. The value of the rial rose and remained stable at around 200,000 rials to a dollar between January and October 2021.

It has been the policy of the CBI to inject dollars into the marker in order to stem the decline of the rial's value. With drastic decline of the amount of dollars in the hands of the regime (from sale of oil, petrochemicals, and other exports), the CBI is less and less able to support the value of the rial. This has greatly contributed to the hyper-inflation since 2018.

The decline in the sale of oil (and other exports) causes budget deficits. The government then has had to borrow from the CBI. The CBI has pursued three policies to provide money to the government. First, it has printed rials to finance the budget deficit. Second, it has made what the CBI calls "*naghdinegi shebha pool sepordeh modat-dar*" [semi-liquidity "demand deposits" or "time deposits"] in various banks. Third, it has borrowed from banks.

In February 2021, after years of printing money, finally the Chairman of the CBI publicly admitted that the CBI had been doing precisely what the critical economists had been saying for years. Abdol-Nasser Hemmati made the public admission that the regime had no other way to make the payments but to

---

Rouhani, the CBI had to inject about $50 million daily and that might have also had some influence on the market.

511 Deutsche Welle, "*Piroozi Biden Va Taasir An Bar Kahesh Bahayeh Dollar Va Talla Dar Iran*" [Biden's Victory and Its Effect on the Reduction of Prices of Dollar and Gold], (November 8, 2020), https://www.dw.com/fa-ir/%D9%BE%DB%8C%D8%B1%D9%88%D8%B2%DB%8C-%D8%A8%D8%A7%DB%8C%D8%AF%D9%86-%D9%88-%D8%AA%D8%A7%D8%AB%DB%8C%D8%B1-%D8%A2%D9%86-%D8%A8%D8%B1-%DA%A9%D8%A7%D9%87%D8%B4-%D8%A8%D9%87%D8%A7%DB%8C-%D8%AF%D9%84%D8%A7%D8%B1-%D9%88-%D8%B7%D9%84%D8%A7-%D8%AF%D8%B1-%D8%A7%DB%8C%D8%B1%D8%A7%D9%86/a-55535683.

512 Radio Farda, "*Navasan-e Gheymat Dollar Dar Ashofteh Bazaar Iran*" [The Fluctuations of the Price of Dollar in Iran's Chaotic Market], (November 9, 2020), https://www.radiofarda.com/a/30938959.html.

print money.[513] According to a report by the CBI in February 2021, due to printing money, the rials in circulation in November 2020, was 70% higher than the amount of rials in circulation in November 2019.[514] And the amount of rials in circulation in November 2020 was 2.5 times that of the amount of rails in circulation in November 2018.[515] The same CBI report states that the government's debt to domestic banks rose by 36% over the previous year (November 2019) and by 74% over November 2018. According to the International Monetary Fund (IMF), the total debt of the Iranian government in 2020 is around $260 billion which is about 40% of Iran's GDP. The IMF states that the Iranian government's total debt more than doubled over the previous two years. The foreign debt of the Iranian government is a little more than $9 billion.[516] The CBI report puts the annual inflation rate at 30.5% in November 2020.[517] According to the IMF, Iran's annual inflation rate in 2020 was the sixth highest in the world; the highest being Venezuela, Zimbabwe, Sudan, Lebanon, and Suriname.[518]

The injection of massive amounts of liquidity into the market without proportionate increase in production and services produces inflation. The injection of massive amounts of rials into the market has produced inflation in Iran. As the value of the rial declines and the value of the dollar increases, the price of imports increase, which further increases inflation. In order to protect the value of their savings and income, the people convert their rials to dollars and gold (coins, jewelry, bullion). Thus, the prices of food, autos, rents, homes, and land increase while incomes and savings decline in real purchasing power. The prices of the dollar and gold as well as anecdotal evidence seem to indicate that the data the regime announces on inflation and unemployment rates are false and underestimate the real decline in Iran's economy.

The Covid-19 pandemic in 2020, made the economic situation worse. Also the decline in the price of oil due to the global economic decline, further reduced the regime's oil income by October 2020.

---

513 Radio Farda, "*Rais Kol-e Bank Markazi: Baray Taamin Manabeh Rahi Joz Chaap Eskenas Nadarim*" [Chairman of the Central Bank: We Have No Other Way But to Print Money to Make Payouts], (February 3, 2021), https://www.radiofarda.com/a/31083483.html.

514 Radio Farda, "*Owjgiri Naghdinegi Va Bedehi Dowlat Iran Beh Bank-ha Dar 9 Mah Aval 99*" [Rise of Liquidity and Iran's Government Debt to the Banks In the First 9 Months of the Year 1399], (February 6, 2021), https://www.radiofarda.com/a/31089592.html.

515 Ibid.

516 Ibid.

517 Ibid.

518 Ibid.

It is necessary to add that the economy under the fundamentalist regime has not been a "normal" economic system. There is very little true private sector.[519] Since capturing power in 1979, much of the economy has been owned and controlled by fundamentalist Shia clerics and fundamentalist lay. Initially through outright expropriation, they accumulated vast wealth. Then through utilizing extra legal means, force, and political connections, the top officials get the coveted monopolistic licenses to import various products, get around custom duties and the like. Peter Waldman of the *Wall Street Journal* has called the system "clergy capitalism" in a front-page article in 1992.[520] Paul Klebnikov of *Forbes* magazine has called the regime's rulers "millionaire mullahs."[521] Elaine Sciliano of the *New York Times* has referred to the elites as like the "Mafia families." [522]

The bulk of the economy is under the control of fundamentalist entities such as the "*Setad Farman Ejraee Imam*" [Headquarter for the Execution of Imam Khomeini's Order], "*Bonyad*" [foundations], the IRGC, and religious shrines (as well as the state). According to a study by Reuters, Ayatollah Khamenei directly controls the *Setad*, which has assets worth over $94 billion.[523] *Bonyads* are also under the control of the Supreme Leader. According to one source, *bonyads* control somewhere between 10% and 20% of Iran's GDP.[524] One such *bonyad*, is the "*Bonyad Moztazafin*" (the Foundation of the Deprived), which has assets worth over $10 billion.[525] The IRGC is believed to control over 40% of the economy. IRGC's biggest economic holding is *Khatam al-Anbia*. To these, one might add religious shrines that after the revolution came under the direct control of the regime. The biggest such shrine is "*Astan Qods Razavi*" [Eight Shia Imam Reza Holy Shrine] in Mashhad. The *Astan Qods Razavi* is one of Iran's largest economic conglomerates. Its real estate assets alone are estimated to be worth between $15 billion and $20 bil-

---

519 Asadi and Jamali, "*Gozar Az Eghtesad Nezam Valaee Beh Eghtesad Bazzar Bonyad: Naghsh 'Bazzar Azad'*," op. cit.

520 Peter Waldman, "Clergy Capitalism: Mullahs Keep Control of Iran's Economy with an Iron Hand," *The Wall Street Journal*, (May 8, 1992), pp. 1, 16.

521 Paul Klebnikov, "Millionaire Mullahs," *Forbes* (July 20, 2003), https://www.forbes.com/global/2003/0721/024.html#54378f504108.

522 Elaine Sciliano, "Interview," PBS, (April 17, 2002), https://www.pbs.org/wgbh/pages/frontline/shows/tehran/interviews/sciolino.html.

523 Steve Stecklow, Babak Dehghanpisheh, and Yeganeh Torbati, "Reuters Investigates: Assets of the Ayatollah," Reuters, (November 11, 2013), https://www.reuters.com/investigates/iran/#article/part1.

524 Klebnikov, "Millionaire Mullahs."

525 Ibid.; and Waldman, "Clergy Capitalism," op. cit.

lion.[526] It is believed (although hard to verify) that four entities Setad, IRGC's Khatam al-Anbia, Bonyad Mostazafin, and the *Astan Qods Razavi* own about 60% of Iran's economy. These entities do not pay taxes, and the Majles and the government have no oversight rights of them. They operate at the pleasure of the Supreme Leader. These businesses hire those who prove loyalty to the regime. For lack of a better term, I call this group, fundamentalist *nomenklatura*. In addition to these fundamentalist businesses, the state apparatus itself (before and after the revolution) owns vast economic entities including oil and natural gas.

Iran possesses enormous oil and natural gas reserves, which provide the regime with vast amounts of resources. Iran contains the fourth largest known crude oil reserves and the second largest natural gas reserves in the world. Iran is number one in the world in terms of total value of its crude oil and natural gas reserves (known reserves at current prices). The income from the sale of oil, and natural gas goes directly to the hands of the government. This vast income makes the regime in Iran highly autonomous from the social classes in society. Therefore, those countries and companies that purchase oil and gas from the regime ruling Iran, provide the fundamentalist regime the resources that enable it to dominate the Iranian people. In other words, by purchasing oil from the Islamic Republic, these countries and companies are interfering in the internal political struggles in Iran in favor of the fundamentalists and against the people who oppose them. The vast oil and gas income allows the regime to pay for its vast coercive apparatuses, keep the fundamentalist *nomenklatura* happy, fund the state apparatuses, coopt non-fundamentalists, and provide subsidies for some goods and services (e. g., fuel, electricity, and bread) to buy social submission.

The income from the sale of oil and gas ranging between $40 billion to about $120 billion annually has kept the "clerical capitalist system" afloat despite the many structural flaws and weaknesses of the fundamentalist economic system.[527] The economic sanctions simply took out the annual injection of billions of dollars that kept the system muddling through.

---

526 Abdolreza Ahmadi, *"Astan Qods Razavi: Dowlat Penhan Tofangdar"* [Imam Reza Holy Shrine: Government in the Shadow with Guns], Independent Persian, (December 15, 2019), https://www.independentpersian.com/node/32851 provides the figure of $20 billion. Jamshid Asadi, *"Astan Qods Razavi: Daraeehay Pichideh, Hesabrasi Naroshan"* [Imam Reza Holy Shrine: Complex Assets, Unclear Transparency], Radio Farda, (February 24, 2019), https://www.radio farda.com/a/commentary-on-Iran-powerful-religious-institute-astan-qods-razavi/29787445.html provides the figure of $15 billion.

527 Iran's annual income from oil, natural gas, and petrochemical depend on the global prices and how much Iran is able to export. In 2011, under President Mahmoud Ahmadinejad, the government's income from sale of oil reached the record level of around $120 billion.

The fundamentalist regime's ideological foreign policy of spending billions of dollars for its wars in Iraq, Syria, Yemen, Lebanon and elsewhere not only take money from investments in Iran, but also creates tensions with regional and world powers depriving the people of normal and prosperous lives like others in the region.[528] For example, in 2019, the GDP per capita in Iran was $5,219. Corresponding figures for the following countries were: Lebanon $8,257; Turkey $10,862; Oman $14,982; Saudi Arabia $20,028; Bahrain $22,579; Kuwait $27,359; UAE $37,622; and Qatar $59,324.[529] The opposition to the fundamentalist regime's regional policies is often expressed by large segments of the population. For example, one of the most common slogans of the protesters in recent years has been *"Na Ghazeh, Na Lobnan, Janam Fadayh Iran"* [Neither Gaza, Nor Lebanon, My Life for Iran]. Another slogan is *"Sorieh ra raha kon, fekri be hale ma kon"* [Leave Syria alone, do something for us].

The fundamentalist regime has suffered great setbacks in its policy in Syria since 2018 due to successful Israeli military operations.[530] Saudi Arabia has waged a successful diplomatic campaign condemning and isolating the fundamentalist regime in both the Arab League and the Organization of Islamic Cooperation.[531] In August and September 2020, the United Arab Emirate and Bahrain established normal relations with Israel under the auspices of the United States. Soon, Sudan and Morocco established normal relations with Israel. Common security concerns over the fundamentalist regime ruling Iran motivated these Arab regimes and Israel to establish friendly relations. The fundamentalist regime has made public threats against the leadership of both the UAE and Bahrain.[532]

---

528 Mansour Farhang, *"Malikholiah Sodor Enghelab Va Chalesh 'Gheire Khodiha'"* [Melancholy of the Export of the Revolution and "non-fundamentalists"], Iran Emrooz, (September 12, 2020), http://www.iran-emrooz.net/index.php/politic/more/85845/.

529 World Bank, "National Accounts Data, GDP Per Capita," (2019), https://data.worldbank.org/indicator/NY.GDP.PCAP.CD.

530 Reuters, "Israel's outgoing defence minister says Iran starting to withdraw from Syria," (May 18, 2020), https://www.reuters.com/article/us-israel-iran-syria/israels-outgoing-defence-minister-says-iran-starting-to-withdraw-from-syria-idUSKBN22U2MU.

531 Reuters, "Arab League labels Hezbollah terrorist organization," (March 11, 2016), https://www.reuters.com/article/us-mideast-crisis-arabs/arab-league-labels-hezbollah-terrorist-organization-idUSKCN0WD239; and Middle East Monitor, "Saudi Arabia blocked Iran from participating in OIC meeting, says ministry," (February 3, 2020), https://www.middleeastmonitor.com/20200203-saudi-arabia-blocked-iran-from-participating-in-oic-meeting-says-ministry/.

532 Radio Farda, "Iran's Khamenei Says U.A.E. 'Betrayed' Islamic World With Israel Normalization Deal," (September 1, 2020), https://en.radiofarda.com/a/iran-s-khamenei-says-u-a-e-betrayed-islamic-world-with-israel-normalization-deal/30814699.html; Radio Farda, "Iran Condemns Bahrain Deal With Israel," (September 12, 2020), https://en.radiofarda.com/a/iran-condemns-bah

The Biden Presidency: Respite or Reprieve

If the economic, military, and diplomatic pressures continue, there is a high likelihood of regime collapse in Iran as occurred in Eastern Europe, the Soviet Union, and the apartheid regime in South Africa.

The Obama policy of rapprochement with the fundamentalist regime provided the regime great deal of legitimacy and financial benefits (from the sale of oil). Obama's policy thus prolonged the fundamentalist dictatorship's rule. The Trump policy of "Maximum Pressure" imposed strong sanctions on the fundamentalist regime and greatly undermined the regime's economic situation and political stability. Trump's policy began when it left the JCPOA in May 2018. The pressure policy was in effect only between May 2018 and January 2021. When the Biden administration took office in January 2021, the fundamentalist regime was on highly precarious economic and political situation. The regime's economy was in shambles, its influence in Iraq and Syria reduced greatly, and politically under great pressure. Biden's election has been a huge psychological boost to the fundamentalist regime.

The U.S. policy towards the fundamentalism regime would have great influence on the prolongation of dictatorship or the emergence of democracy in Iran. If the Biden administration were to continue Trump's pressure policy on the fundamentalist regime, the likelihood of regime survival would be very low and the likelihood of regime collapse and transition to democracy high. If the Biden administration were to return to Obama policies of appeasement, the likelihood of the fundamentalist regime survival would be high, and the likelihood of transition to democracy would be much lower.

Between January and late November 2021, the fundamentalist regime witnessed huge reductions of pressure from the United States. During this period, the Biden administration was pursuing a policy of enticing the fundamentalist regime to return to the JCPOA via suspending many sanctions and lax enforcing of many others. Therefore, the fundamentalist regime was able to export more oil (and other goods and services) and the economic situation became more stable between January 2021 and late November 2021. It is believed that the fundamentalist regime was able to export over 1 million barrels of oil per day, bulk of it illegally to China at huge discounts via smugglers and secret third parties. At the height of Trump's pressures, such oil exports had declined to about 100,000 barrels per day. Due to Biden's policies, the value of the rial rose against the dollar

rain-deal-with-israel/30834978.html; and Radio Farda, "IRGC Threatens Bahrain with Tough Revenge," (September 14, 2020), https://en.radiofarda.com/a/30838530.html.

until late October 2021. For this period the value of rial was stable at around 200,000 rials to a dollar.

Despite the Biden administration's appeasement policies, the fundamentalist regime since Raisi's inauguration has pursued more aggressive policies towards the U.S. and in the negotiations on the return to JCPOA restrictions on its nuclear policies. Several Biden administration officials made threats that the U.S. would increase sanctions again if the fundamentalist regime would continue its aggressive policies. These threats were not taken seriously by fundamentalist officials. Biden administration's withdrawal from Afghanistan and handing over it to the Taliban indicated to the fundamentalist regime that the Biden administration was leaving the Middle East and was afraid to pay the price of opposing fundamentalist forces.

The JCPOA negotiations between November 29 and December 3, 2021 failed because of the unrealistic positions of the fundamentalist regime. On December 5, the value of rial plunged. On December 5, 2021 one dollar was traded at 304,500 rials.[533] On December 6, the rial dropped for the third day in a row, exchanging for 310,400 rials to a dollar.[534] It remains to be seen whether the Biden administration would continue its appeasement policies or would the administration change to a confrontational posture toward the fundamentalist regime.

China, Russia, and the EU

China and Russia consider democracy an ideological threat to their authoritarian systems. A transition to democracy in Iran would not benefit China and Russia. Not surprisingly, therefore, they have provided support to the fundamentalist regime. European democracies have pursued friendly economic, diplomatic, and political relations with the ruling fundamentalist dictatorship in Iran as they did with the Pahlavi dictatorship. This is (perhaps) surprising considering that the fundamentalist regime has conducted terrorist activities on European soil (U.K., Germany, France, Austria, Italy, Bulgaria, Poland, the Netherlands, Bel-

---

533 VOA, "*Paslarzehay Binatijeh Mandan Mozakerat Vean, Arzesh Rial Iran Beh 'Paentarin Had Dar Tarikh' Resid*" [The Aftershocks of Failure of the Vienna Talks, The Value of the Iranian Rial Reached "Its Lowest Point in History"], (December 5, 2021), https://ir.voanews.com/a/iran-rials-jcpoa-talks/6340254.html.

534 Radio Farda, "*Nerkh Dollar Az 31 Hezar Tooman Obor Kard; Sooghot 25 Darsadi Arzesh Rial Dar 100 Rooz Dowlat Raisi*" [Price of Dollar Crossed the 31 Thousand Tooman; 25 Percent Fall of the Value of Rial During the 100 Days of Raisi's Government], (December 6, 2021), https://www.radiofarda.com/a/iran-dollar-rise-raeisi/31596216.html. One tooman is 10 rials.

gium, Sweden, Spain, and Switzerland) numerous times.[535] These terrorist activities include bombings, assassinations, and kidnapping. Several of the agents of the regime have been arrested, convicted, and jailed. Some assassins have been simply let go; for example, in Austria for the assassinations of Dr. Qassemlou and two of his lieutenants. Some were exchanged for European citizens jailed in Iran; for example, by France for the assassination of Dr. Bakhtiar. Many terrorist activities have been foiled by their intelligence and security agencies such as the attempt to bomb the annual meeting of the PMOI in France in 2018.[536] The fundamentalist regime uses terrorism as a major tool of statecraft in its foreign policy.[537]

Before 2012, many believed that the European governments' friendly relations with the fundamentalist regime were due to lucrative trade relations. After 2012, many believe that these friendly relations have been due to Europeans' fears about massive refugees pouring into their countries that revolution or regime change might produce. Or perhaps, foreign policies of European governments are formulated on Realist grounds and their pronouncements about democracy and human rights have been little more than window dressings.

It appears that in the United States, public discussion on foreign policy pays far more attention to concerns for democracy and human right than it does in Europe. It is true that human rights and democracy have been used as expedient and applied selectively. However, it may also be true that under certain conditions and for some administrations in the United States concerns for democracy and human rights play a role in the formulation of foreign policy.[538] We have observed major changes in American foreign policy towards the fundamentalist regime.[539] Ebrahim Raisi's presidency would have no effect on the foreign policies of China and Russia. The effects of Raisi's presidency on the U.S. and Europeans are not clear.

---

535 U.S. Government, Department of State, *Outlaw Regime: A Chronicle of Iran's Destructive Activities*, (Washington, DC: 2018), https://www.state.gov/wp-content/uploads/2018/12/Iran-Report.pdf, p. 15; Radio Farda, *"Gozaresh Jadid: Jomhuri Islami 'Dast Kam 540 Irani' Ra Dar Kharej Az Keshvar Koshteh Ya Rebodeh Ast"* [New Report: The Islamic Republic Has Murdered or Kidnapped "At Least 540 Iranians" Outside the Country], (July 28, 2021), https://www.radiofarda.com/a/boroumand-foundation-we-has-identified-more-than-540-iranians-whose-murder-or-kidnapping-is-attributed-to-the-islamic-republic-of-iran/31380796.html; and Iran International, *"Emrooz"* [Today], (July 28, 2021), https://www.youtube.com/watch?v=eVj_ajlNSW4.
536 Ibid.
537 Masoud Kazemzadeh, *The Grand Strategy of the Islamic Republic of Iran* (Forthcoming).
538 Kazemzadeh, *Iran's Foreign Policy*, op. cit.
539 Masoud Kazemzadeh, *U.S.-Iran Confrontation: Alternative Scenarios and Consequences* (Forthcoming).

Chapter 12
Conclusion

The study of various opposition groups in Iran is fortuitous because if the fundamentalist regime were to collapse, it would be beneficial to scholars and policy makers to have a better understanding of Iran's main opposition groups. The precarious situation of the fundamentalist regime makes the study of the INF of great interest if the post-fundamentalist regime is going to be a democratic political system.

Democracy in post-fundamentalist Iran is not inevitable. None of the other major opposition groups has a democratic past.[540] If Iran's post-fundamentalist system is going to be democratic, the INF would have to play a major role. Mossadegh's call for the rally in October 1949 and the INF letter to the Shah in June 1977 were turning points in Iranian history. The INF has been Iran's main pro-democracy political party.[541] It remains so today.

In order to increase the likelihood of democracy in Iran, a number of factors have to occur. First, the leaders of the INF and INF-OA have to increase their activities. Second, the INF and INF-OA have to make coalitions with other pro-democracy parties and groups. Third, the more other pro-democracy groups and individuals join or make coalitions with the INF and INF-OA, the higher the likelihood of democracy. Fourth, the larger the number of Iranian people join and support the INF, the higher the likelihood of democracy in Iran. It remains to be seen whether they are able and willing to make the necessary compromises and adjustments to be the feasible alternative to the fundamentalist regime. Their failure to do so will pave the path for the anti-democratic forces to become the main alternatives to the fundamentalist regime.

A major component of Iranian political culture has been the lack of ability to work together in large organizations. This is true for right-wing monarchists, ultra-right fundamentalists, and ultra-left communists as well as center-left and center-right pro-democracy organizations. This element of Iranian political culture has usually made it easy for the ruling dictatorships (both monarchy and the fundamentalist regime) to continue to rule despotically despite enjoying small base of support. However, when the ruling dictatorship has been weak, all of the sudden many disparate groups have coalesced in order to confront and or

---

540 Masoud Kazemzadeh, "Opposition Groups," in Mehran Kamrava and Manochehr Dorraj, eds. *Iran Today: An Encyclopedia of Life in the Islamic Republic*, Vol. II. (Westport, Connecticut: Greenwood Press, 2008), pp. 363–367.
541 See Figure 1 in chapter 8.

https://doi.org/10.1515/9783110782158-014

to overthrow the ruling regime. For example, cooperation occurred during the Constitutional Revolution 1905–1911, the oil nationalization movement 1951–1953, and the Iranian Revolution 1977–1979.

Since the 1980s, there have been several major attempts to form broad coalitions among various opposition groups. When it appeared that the fundamentalist regime was about to collapse, all of the sudden these attempts became more serious with partial success. And when the regime was able to weather the crisis, various groups went their own way. If Iran's history is a guide, when it would appear that the fundamentalist regime is going to collapse, we should observe formation of broad coalitions among opposition groups. The current low-key efforts to cooperate with each other are positive indications of the abilities of the various pro-democracy groups to cooperate and form formidable political coalitions.

This book has described the political history of Iran's main pro-democracy political party as well as the party's analysis, platform, leadership, ideology, and strategy. This research has also analyzed the INF's mistakes, shortcomings, and achievements. Due to the INF's struggles in the past 72 years, the Iranian people have a democratic option. Those countries that lack such a party and such a history of struggles have a much lower likelihood of transition to democracy.

Iran has all the main ingredients for transition to democracy.[542] The simple fact that the Iranian people have produced phenomena such as the constitutional revolution 1905–1911, a democratic constitution in 1906, lukewarm democratic governments during 1906–1925 and 1941–1953, the INF, and large numbers of truly democratic activists and leaders indicate that the Iranian people are capable of establishing a democratic form of government today.

However, neither transition to democracy nor democratic consolidation is inevitable. Human agency matters, as do the international conditions, the ideological milieu, as well as the balance of power among various social classes and forces. This book has described the defeat of democracy in Iran in the past 72 years. It has also described its challenges and successes.

This book has described the strengths and weaknesses of Iran's largest pro-democracy political party. It has shown that the INF has been a "real political party." The founding, history, and continued activities of the INF demonstrate that the establishment of democracy in Iran is a serious possibility. This study should assist the readers in understanding democracy's likelihood as an option and possibility in Iran today.

---

542 Parsa, *Democracy in Iran*, op. cit.

Appendix 1: INF Documents

(1) The INF Position Statement on the Land Reform (January 23, 1963)

On January 23, 1963, the INF issued the following statement on the land reform. Much of the land reforms had already been carried out in the previous two years under the cabinet of Dr. Ali Amini and pressure from the Kennedy administration. The Shah had dismissed Amini and was holding a referendum on January 26, 1963 on a number of reforms, the primary being land reform. The INF statement became known as "Reform Yes, Dictatorship No." The following is my translation.[543]

With:
Abolition of the [feudalistic] system of landlord and peasants
Land and water for farmer
Fruit of labor for worker
Rule of the people and freedom for all the people
Abolition of colonialism and exploitation

Yes, I Agree

With:
Authoritarian rule and interference by the Shah in government, regime of fear, and terror by the SAVAK [secret police], imposition of imperialist rule on the country, transgression of the police, the gendarmerie, and government officials in cities and villages

No, I Oppose

---

[543] The text in Persian is available at Jebhe Melli Iran, "*Bayanieh Jebhe Melli Iran Dar Bareh Enqelab Sefid Va Hameh-Porsi Enqelab Sefid 6 Bahman 1341*" [Statement of the Iran National Front on the White Revolution and the Referendum on January 26, 1963], (January 23, 1963), https://melliun.org/iran/195488.

https://doi.org/10.1515/9783110782158-015

(2) Excerpts from INF Statement on the Land Reform (January 26, 1963)

The following contains brief excerpts from a 5-page document. The primary author of the analysis was Dr. Mohammad Ali Khonji, an economist, a major thinker, one of the theoreticians of the Socialist Party of Iran, and one of the leaders of the INF. Like all other major documents, it was modified and ratified by members of the Executive Committee and Central Committee. Beginning on January 20, 1963, the Shah's regime began arresting leaders of the INF. After the publication of the January 23 statement and this statement on January 26, the regime began the wholesale arrest of INF leaders and members. By early February, more than 150 leaders and prominent members of the INF were arrested by the Shah's secret police SAVAK. The following is my translation.[544]

Iran National Front
Establishment of Legal Government is the Goal of the Iran National Front

The Honorable People of Iran
You know well that the peasants and workers of our country live under harsh and terrible conditions and their [feudal] landowners with the assistance of the power of the ruling regime and the repression of gendarmerie and security forces pillage the fruit of their labor and tale all their basic human rights.

The ruling regime with the use of police and SAVAK has created an atmosphere of fear and terror among the population and has completely violated the rights and liberties of the people....

In order to put an end to all these injustices and for the purpose of abolishing oppression and repression, the Iran National Front, has made its objective to struggle against this corrupt regime which has been imposed on our nation by the assistance and approval of foreign powers and is the sources of all these corruption and oppression.

The Iran National Front believes that creating a prosperous life for the farmers can only be possible by the abolition of the [feudal] system of landlord and peasantry, and land and water be given to the farmers of Iran would be able to have their destiny in their own hands free from all sorts of deceptions and manipulations.

---

544 Jebhe Melli Iran, *"Bayanieh Jebhe Melli Iran Dar Bareh Enqelab Sefid Va Hameh-Porsi Enqelab Sefid 6 Bahman 1341"* [Statement of the Iran National Front on the White Revolution and the Referendum on January 26, 1963], (January 26, 1963), https://melliun.org/iran/195488.

The Iran National Front believes that the corrupt ruling regime is the primary cause of the regime of repression, oppression in cities and villages...

A regime which has destroyed all the legal liberties from the people and with thousands of atrocities and oppressive measures has pulverized human rights of our country, and has undermined the most basic rights of the people that is to elect their representatives and a government based on elections, is now going to hold a referendum as an excuse to destroy constitutionalism and the rights of the nation.

... referendum or any other kind of popular will can only occur under conditions of freedom. In a country which all the principles of democracy and liberties are wiped out, and extremely harsh censorship of the press have been instituted, and there exist no freedoms of the thought, expression, and association, and the police and SAVAK prevent the publication of any nationalist newspapers, publications, and papers, how can popular will be expressed?

It [Iran] is a country that no one has the right to express his view and the newspapers do not even have the right to publish political opinion as advertisement... In such a country, ... such a referendum is for ... deception.

A referendum can only represent the public opinion which has been taken under legal conditions and respecting various individual and social freedoms.

... A king who for 10 years has been ruling tyrannically against the basic constitutional laws of the country and with disregard of the rights of the people, and has appointed and dismissed any cabinet at will and without any regard for the opinion of the people and has held elections for the Majles under an environment of terror and fear and without any kind of freedoms and has sent hand-picked and fake representatives to the parliament and all the laws and economic and judicial rules and polices are by his own personal approval, is now officially interferes in all the legislative and executive aspects of the country and has not left any aspect of the constitution.

... The Iranian people, we are issuing a warning that our country is at the precipice of being officially transformed from a constitutional and democratic system to a system of tyranny and reactionary regime.

(3) Excerpts from the Open Letter by Dr. Karim Sanjabi, Dr. Shapour Bakhtiar, and Dariush Forouhar to the Shah (June 12, 1977)

The years between 1973 and 1976 were, arguably, the most repressive years under the Shah. In March 1975, the Shah abolished his sham two-party system and replaced it with a one-party system. The members of the Majles were literally hand-picked by the Shah and SAVAK before the elections. The Shah announced the creation of his Rastakhiz [Resurrection] Party. In a chilling speech, the Shah ordered all Iranians to join his party. He added that those who did not join his sole party "are traitors who must either go to prison or leave the country."[545]

Before 1973, the most severe tortures were reserved only for members of armed guerrilla groups. Between 1973 and 1976, even high school children who were arrested for writing a composition critical of the regime were subject to similar severe tortures. Some of these tortures included putting the political prisoners on a metal bedframe through which electricity was running making it a grilling device. The political prisoners were literally burnt on these toasters. Due to the activities of INF activists abroad and others, human rights organizations were made aware of these gross human rights violations. Amnesty International declared the Shah's regime the worst violator of human rights in the world for the year 1975. In April 1975, SAVAK murdered nine prominent leftist political prisoners outside the Evin Prison saying they were escaping.

The Shah also did a number of things without any regard for the sentiments of the population. For example, in 1976, the Shah changed the Iranian calendar's origin from the Prophet Mohammad's hejra [migration from Mecca to Medina] to the founding of the rule of Cyrus the Great of the Achaemenian dynasty. So, overnight Iran's calendar went from the year 1355 to 2535. The Shah's own economic policies after the fourfold rise in oil prices in 1974, had caused major inflation and monumental waste. For example, many cargo ships had to wait for up to six months to unload their cargo due to lack of port facilities and those with perishable items had to throw away their cargo. Due to lack of storage facilities, equipment were stored outside and many were thus ruined. Rather than correcting his economic mistakes, the Shah's policy of fighting inflation became jailing small shopkeepers and closing their stores.

The election of Jimmy Carter in November 1976 changed the political atmosphere in Iran. During his campaign, Carter had promised placing human rights concerns, including those of America's right-wing allies, on his agenda. He specifically mentioned the human rights violations of the Shah twice during his campaign. However, after he became president, Carter exempted the Shah's regime from his human rights campaign due to Iran's strategic significance. The perception of both the Shah and the opposition was that the Carter administration would order the Shah to respect human rights.

---

545 Misagh Parsa, *Social Origins of the Iranian Revolution* (New Brunswick: Rutgers University Press, 1989), 183.

The very first public expression of criticism of the Shah was by Dr. Ali Asghar Haj Seyyed Javadi, who published a long essay, which did not receive much publicity. Then, on June 12, 1977, a letter signed by three prominent leaders of the INF was published and was widely distributed in much of the country. This letter is considered by many scholars to be the beginning of the Iranian Revolution. The full text in Persian is available at http://jebhemeliiran.org/?p=2101. The following is my translation of excerpts of the letter.

Your Majesty,

... We are writing this letter when the country is on the verge of collapse, all paths have reached a dead-end, public necessities such as foodstuffs and housing with extreme inflation are becoming scare, agriculture and ranching are being destroyed, infant industries and human capital are in crises and deterioration, trade balance and the terms of imports and exports have reached dangerous levels, oil this God-given resource is being wasted, the announced programs of reforms and revolution have failed, and worst of all the violations of human rights and individual and social liberties, and violations of the principles of the Constitution, along with [secret] police violence have reached a maximum. Proliferation of corruption, prostitution, and sycophancy have corrupted human dignity and national ethics.

... One has no choice but to consider all these calamities in the national life attributable to the management of the country, a management that is against the explicit text of the Constitution, and the Universal Declaration of Human Rights, and has become dictatorial and personal in the person in the form of the monarchical system. The "monarchical system"...after the Constitutional Revolution [of 1905], gained a legal definition and in the Constitution [of 1906] and its Amendments have clearly delineated that "power of the country reside in the people" and "the person of the king has no responsibility [of governing]."

... Therefore, the only path is to...desist from dictatorial rule, submit absolutely to the constitutional principles, restore the rights of the people, respect the Constitution and the Universal Declaration of Human Rights, abandon the one-party rule, permit freedom of the press, freedom for political prisoners and allow the return of political exiles, and the establishment of a government that is based on the majority of [the parliament's] representatives that have been freely elected by the people and considers itself responsible for governing the country based on the Constitution.

Dr. Karim Sanjabi, Dr. Shapour Bakhtiar, Dariush Forouhar
June 12, 1977

(4) "INF Proclamation: Peaceful Revision of the Power Structure is the Necessity of Iran Today" (February 1, 2020)

Iran National Front
Peaceful Revision of the Power Structure is the Necessity of Iran Today

In the early morning hours of Wednesday January 8, 2020, the Islamic Revolutionary Guards Corps, fired two missiles at the Ukrainian passenger airplane killing all 176 people on board, 148 of them Iranians. Many of the Iranians were among the most educated and included university students, scientists, and physicians. This event was not only a human error but a humanitarian catastrophe. This painful occurrence caused sadness in the global community and grief and mourning among the Iranian nation. The sadness and grief were greatly increased because the ruling regime lied to the people for three days and declared the cause of the event to have been the airplane's mechanical failure. And, only after persistence and pressure from other countries, the regime had to confess the truth and accept responsibility.

In the middle of the night on November 15, 2019, the Islamic Republic regime, all of the sudden and without any preparation and without discussing the matter with the people, or passage in its own so-called parliament declared the up to tripling of gasoline prices. This strange way of announcing the gasoline price rise, caused massive protests of the Iranian nation in about 200 large and small cities and towns, who saw that would increase the price of other necessities. The people's protests were harshly repressed and drowned in blood. Hundreds of people were killed, thousands were injured, and thousands have been jailed.

The grave mistakes and horrible wrongdoings of the Islamic Republic regime do not end with only these two events. In the past 41 years, the regime has committed numerous horrendous crimes. The first and the most significant mistake of the rulers after the revolution was undermining of the goals of the Iranian nation for carrying out the revolution such as freedom, independence, and justice. The rulers even undermined the goal of establishing an independent and non-aligned foreign policy, the expression of which was enshrined in the slogan "Neither East, Nor West." Ten months after the victory of the revolution, the invasion and occupation of the U.S. Embassy and taking its employees hostage, were the cause of conflict and unnecessary enmity of the Islamic Republic with the United States. This enmity has continued to the present day and caused incalculable costs for our country. The 8-year war between Iraq and Iran with all the material damages and the loss of hundreds of thousands young Iranians were among the consequences of the hostage taking. Rather than accepting the cease-fire in 1982, the regime postponed accepting the U.N. cease-fire resolution 598 until 1988, prolonging the war by six more years, years in which the bulk of the material and human costs were incurred.

Other regime crimes include: the illegal massacre of thousands of political prisoners during August and September 1988; the disgusting Chain Murders in 1998; violent attacks of university students in 1999; harsh repression of protesters after the disputed 2009 election resulting in killing of protesters on the streets, and the tragedies at Kahrizak prison [torture and rape of male and female political prisoners and their deaths under torture]; and the violent repression of the protests of the people in over 100 cities and towns during December 2017-January 2018, resulting in many deaths and thousands in jails. The extensive corruption and rampant graft of astronomical figures of thousands of billions [of Iranian currency], have destroyed the country's economic capacities. Wrong foreign policies, which have caused conflicts with our neighboring countries have wasted huge amounts of the country's finances and resulted in confrontations with the international community and have isolated our country. The above policies are causing our country to enter a situation like that of North Korea.

As the result of these wrong policies and actions, today the Islamic Republic regime is in a condition that can no longer continue these methods and has left no future for itself. The Iranian society is burning in great anger and the country is on the verge of explosion.

About a year and half ago, on July 27, 2018, the Iran National Front released its three-article proposals for the solution of the accelerating crises to the Islamic Republic regime. First, all political prisoners and prisoners of conscious in the country have to be released. Second, all the basic and fundamental liberties of the Iranian people, such as freedoms of expression, speech, political parties, assemblies, and free elections have to be respected. And third, there has to be a free and fair election for a Constituent Assembly to be held under the supervision of a popular committee which enjoys acceptance among all forces, in order to revise the structure of power.

The Iran National Front, as the political home of Dr. Mossadegh and as the organization which has given rise to many pro-democracy parties and groups, now and under the present dangerous conditions declares that it is ready, with the assistance of all political groups and civil society organizations – such as those of workers, teachers, university students, women, retirees, lawyers, human rights activists, university professors, bazaar merchants, and shop keepers – to manage this change and peaceful transition to build Iran and bring it to a successful end.

The insistence of the regime to continue its failed path and the continuation of the present situation will have disastrous and catastrophic consequences for our country.

Iran National Front, Tehran
Saturday February 1, 2020

Appendix 2: INF-OA Documents

(1) "We Do Not Want Enriched Uranium, We Want Iran" (November 25, 2011)

"Until the time that we have freedom, democratic control, and transparency in Iran, even peaceful use of nuclear energy could lead to dangerous consequences including catastrophes for the health of the people. Only when democratic controls and freedom exist in Iran and dangers and advantages of nuclear energy have been made clear for the public, then the people could decide on this issue."

Declaration of the First Congress of the Iran National Front-Organizations Abroad, February 1– 3, 2008.[546]

The Honorable People of Iran,
The spread of sanctions to the Central Bank and the export of oil products, indicates that world powers are serious about targeting the economy. Not only the Islamic Republic has not been able to clear doubts and concerns of the world community on the Nuclear weapons dimensions of the nuclear program, but the IRI has pursued policies that increase such worries, which have created a standoff and the end result of which could bring conflict and war for our country.

The catastrophe is that it is not clear the advantages for our country's national interest for having nuclear energy. For about three decades the ruling elite of the Islamic Republic have politicized "nuclear energy" not only in regards to the nuclear power plant but also in the cat and mouse game in regards to nuclear weapons in their own megalomania. The rulers of the Islamic Republic have not explained for the people what are the advantages and disadvantages for Iran of developing nuclear energy. They have not explained for the people what role nuclear weapons development could play for the defense of Iran. Rather, they keep beating the drums of "Nuclear energy is our definite right." The regime's policies are leading our country to economic collapse and even war and destruction.

Many have asked the question that why Iran, which possess large crude oil and natural gas reserves that it could exploit cheaply and easily, has devoted so much resources needs to develop nuclear energy, which is not economical given the huge costs Iran has encountered. The Iranian government has not been able to provide convincible answer for many domestic and international

---

546 https://iranazad.info/jebhehkharej/jkh11/11/25enrichment.htm

https://doi.org/10.1515/9783110782158-016

observers. Many international observers have come to believe that the real objective of the Islamic Republic is not to have nuclear energy, rather to have nuclear bombs in order to preserve their regime and be able to bully their neighbors.

The Islamic Republic has wasted astronomical resources for the "Bushehr Nuclear Power Plant", and untold amounts for the uranium enrichment activities. The great costs associated with economic sanctions by themselves have greatly harmed Iran's economic development. One could compare Iran with our neighbors who do not have oil to see how far behind Iran is in term of economic prosperity. If we take into account the costs of treasonous treaties that have been signed with Russia and China, one could see how this regime is leading Iran towards a catastrophe.

Our concerns are not limited only to the costs to the economy and the grave threats to the environment. The ramifications of the policies pursued by Khamenei and his cronies in stubbornly insisting in uranium enrichment, which have increased worries and enmity of other countries against Iran, are far graver than the financial losses.

The world community whose negotiations with the corrupt authorities who rule Iran have not borne fruit is gradually reaching the conclusion that with the lack of success with sanctions and political isolation, it has no other choice but to resort to military option. The leaders of the Western countries ask themselves, which policy option is more dangerous for the West? They ask themselves is an Iran with nuclear weapons which would bring about a nuclear arms race in the region is safer or conducting a military attacks on the nuclear facilities in Iran is worthwhile? The Western countries are worried that if the Islamic Republic gains nuclear weapons, then there are other countries in the Middle East who would consider "their own inalienable right" to also get nuclear weapons, which would lead to a situation that could easily get out of control in a sensitive region in the world which contains vast energy reserves.

The world asks us: Where do the Iranian people stand on this conflict, and what solutions do they propose to assuage the concerns and worries around the globe? How we, who have consistently condemned warmongers around the world and could, not provide any guarantees to the world that the use of nuclear energy in Iran will not lead to nuclear weapons program? Could we convince the world that this regime's sole objective and purpose for the nuclear program is for peaceful purposes, a regime we know full well is a terribly tyrannical regime which has been lying to us for the past 33 years?

Dear compatriots,

We are of the opinion that using our rights could be best being achieved under freedom and democratic rule by the people. As long as the purpose of the uranium enrichment has not become clear for the people of Iran and the world and the Iranian people are not allowed to make their own decisions on this issue freely and the world community feels that it has to react against the regime's ambitions, the continuation of the enrichment process only strengthens warmongers inside and outside Iran. When uranium enrichment leads to such grave economic and political results and takes Iran to the brink of a catastrophic war, we should force Khamenei and his regime to stop their adventurism and constant crisis by halting the enrichment and stop taking Iran toward a catastrophe planned by international warmongers.

Executive Committee of the Iran National Front- Organizations Abroad
Kambiz Ghaemmagham, Bahman Mobasheri, Dr. Houmayun Mehmaneche
November 25, 2011

(2) "December 7: Today Like Yesterday"

December 7 is the "University Student Day" in Iran. Several days before December 7, 1953, pro-INF students at the University of Tehran had a made a call to hold a rally by the students on the campus to condemn the trial of Dr. Mossadegh for treason in the military court. Afterwards, it was announced that there would be an official visit by then-Vice President Richard Nixon to Tehran to express the U.S. support for the Shah's rule. Until that day, the university campus was regarded a safe zone that the military would not enter.

After holding their peaceful rally, the students were returning to their classrooms, when all-of-the sudden, the Shah's military invaded the campus and began shooting directly at the students. Three students were killed by the regime that day: Ahmad Ghandchi and Mehdi Shariat-Razavi, who were supporters of the INF, and Mostafa Bozorgnia, who was a supporter of the Tudeh Party. Since, then, students hold rallies at universities to commemorate that day. It has become a rallying point for pro-democracy and progressive students who gather and express their opposition to the dictatorships of the Shah and the fundamentalist regime.

Usually, the INF and the INF-OA issue proclamations for this day supporting the students and their democratic demands. Usually, the fundamentalist regime respects the tradition of the coercive apparatuses not entering the university campus. However, on a number of occasions, the fundamentalist regime (like the Shah's regime) has violated that tradition and has sent in their coercive apparatuses to campuses to arrest and repress the students.

In this proclamation, the INF-OA compares the repression and dictatorship of the fundamentalist regime with that of the Shah's regime. The following is my translation of excerpts of the proclamation.[547]

From the next day after the infamous coup against the popular government of Dr. Mossadegh on August 19, 1953, which imposed the Shah's dictatorship on the country, and popular resistance sprang up in various parts of the society, the University of Tehran was one of the main strongholds of resistance. The coup regime undermined the independence of the university and militarily occupied the campus. Armed military personnel went inside campus buildings, to classrooms, and offices of professors and administration officials. However, the students not only did not retreat, but also increased their resistance. The opposition to the coup and demands for the return of the popular government of Dr. Mossadegh despite the military occupation and imposed silence, had undeniably stronger and stronger echoes at the university. The coup regime which had not been able to intimidate the students, carried out the plan to massacre the defenseless students. On December 7, 1953, three students from the technical college of the University of Tehran, Ahmad Ghandchi, Mehdi Shariat-Razavi, and Mostafa Bozorgnia, were targeted by the soldiers' bullets and killed on the university campus.

Thus, December 7th was named the "Student Day," and ever since, every year, in addition to Iranian students and the supporters of the nationalist movement, some other political groups also commemorate the memory of this day. What did those students want and for what did they struggle for? Their main opposition was to the British-American orchestrated coup of August 19, which brought to power the dictatorship of Mohammad Reza Shah Pahlavi as well as to struggle to achieve independence, freedom, and democracy that the government of Mossadegh was the symbol of that national demand.

The Shah's regime had for many years had deprived the students from any above-ground political activities and develop contacts with the population, had therefore prevented the transition of ideas on liberty and democracy to the broader society. On the contrary, the Shia clerics had all the freedom to have their mosques and Koranic reading classes which enabled them to propagate and spread extremely reactionary and anti-nationalist ideas among vast swats of the population. The end result was that during the sensitive period of the revolution, this segment of the population came to regard Ayatollah Khomeini as

---

547 INF-OA, "*16 Azar, Emrooz Niz, Manand Dirooz*" [December 7, Today Like Yesterday], (December 6, 2015), https://iranazad.info/jebhehkharej/jkh15/12/06%2016%20azar%2094.htm.

the symbol of their anti-dictatorial struggles. Ayatollah Khomeini used this opportunity and gradually changed the nature of the people's movement from the freedom-seeking and nationalist movement to the anti-nationalist Islamic revolution and instead of establishing "Independence, Freedom, and Social Justice,", began establishing Islamic government. Thus, a system came to rule Iran that its main objective was to transform the Iranian nation to Islamic ummah and to privilege Shia among the world's Muslims.

The repression of the fundamentalist regime had brought much harm to Iran; however, it energized the students to continue their struggles for nationalist and popular objectives that had been left unfulfilled. For example, we can clearly observe at the peek of the student movement during July 9, 1999 and protests of millions during 2009 protests when they said "Where is my vote?" the demands for democracy.

(3) "The Military Intervention of the Islamic Republic of Iran in Middle Eastern Countries is Against the National Interests of Iran"

The fundamentalist regime has spent a great amount of resources on exporting its fundamentalist revolution abroad. The INF and INF-OA oppose the fundamentalist regime's jingoistic and expansionist foreign policy as motivated by its fundamentalist ideology and against the national interest of Iran. The following is the full text.

INF-OA, "The Military Intervention of the Islamic Republic of Iran in Middle Eastern Countries is Against the National Interests of Iran," (December 19, 2015).

There have been many reports coming from Syria that the Islamic Republic of Iran (IRI) has been increasing its military role in that country until a report that the regime has reduced the number of the Islamic Revolutionary Guards Corps personnel from around 8,000 to about 700. Although the regime claims that the IRGC's personnel are mere advisers, the facts illustrate the opposite.

The Qods Force, the foreign force branch of the IRGC, under the leadership of Gen. Ghassem Soleimani, has been organizing many forces including irregular Shia militia and Afghan Shias in a paramilitary force called "Fatemiyn Corps" and sending them to Syria. At least 50 members of the Qods Force have been reported killed in Syria in the past few months. In news outlets in Iran, those dead are referred to as "the martyrs of defense of the Shrine [of Zeinab]", and when a newspaper used the term "killed" instead of "martyred" for a Qods Force general, the paper was closed and the editor was sent to the court. There are also reports that those IRGC personnel who have refused to go to Syria or have asked for retirement have been court marshalled.

Assad's dictatorship has led to about 250,000 dead, one million injured, and millions of refugees. The anti-Sunni discriminatory chauvinist policies of Assad, like similar policies by the Nouri al-Maliki government in Iraq, have caused large segments of the Sunni community to embrace Sunni fundamentalist groups.

Due to the fact that the IRGC is regarded as a foreign Shia occupying force by many in Syria, the presence of the IRGC is not only not a solution, but is part of the problem, and their continued presence only prolongs and increases bloodshed and violence. The lives and treasure of Iran are being wasted in a war that has no positive connection to Iran's national interests and are pursued in ideological adventurism of the fundamentalist regime ruling Iran in order to preserve its illegitimate regime.

The ruling Shia fundamentalist regime by such policies has placed itself against the large majority of the population in the region who are Sunni Moslems. We can observe that despite providing huge support to many dictatorial regimes and extremist fundamentalist groups, many of them oppose many policies and interests of Iran. For example, the Assad regime opposes Iran's ownership of the three islands in the Persian Gulf, and as Iran's financial aid was decreased Hamas has sided with Saudi Arabia taking its financial aid.

The Iran National Front-Abroad opposes the Islamic Republic's military interventions in Iraq, Syria, and other countries in the Middle East. As we have stated in the past, such policies by the fundamentalist regime ruling Iran drag our people to unnecessary wars and are against the interests of the Iranian people.

The Islamic Republic's military interventions in the countries of the Middle East, under the banner of defense of the power of Shia religion, have increased sectarian tensions and will cause the targeting of Iran for retaliation by extremist Sunni fundamentalist groups. The deaths of Iranian people for adventurisms of the Shia fundamentalist dictatorial regime should not be tolerated.

In our opinion, the Iranian people and all the freedom-loving peoples of the region, who struggle for peace, friendship, democracy, and against the forces of destruction, share similar interests and should act in solidarity. The continuation of such wars which help fundamentalist groups (Shia and Sunni) and dictatorial regimes, harm all the peoples of the region.

Victory to the pro-democracy forces of the Middle East in the struggle to liberate themselves from the clutches of dictatorial regimes and fundamentalist forces, which is the pre-condition for the achievement of freedom, prosperity and ending the presence of global powers in the region.

Iran National Front Organizations-Abroad
December 19, 2015
info@iranazad.info
http://www.iranazad.info

(4) INF-OA, *"Ean Namayesh Maskhareh Entekhabat Nist"* [This Farce Is Not Elections] (November 11, 2019)

Dear compatriots,[548]
The freedom-loving people of the world,

The absolutist clerical regime has shown that it does not tolerate political freedoms, social freedoms, free political parties, and free elections. The right to be elected and to elect has no real meaning under this regime. The Office of the Supreme Leader, various security entities, the Ministry of Intelligence, the Ministry of the Interior, and the Council of Guardians deprive individuals in various stages from participating in elections under various pretexts. Free press, free political parties, and free tribunes do not exist for elections. The prisons are full of freedom-seeking activists and dissidents. No political party or political group that opposes the fundamentalist regime has the opportunity to engage in activities. The absolutist clerical regime not only does not allow any political, party, or social activities, it does not even a simple gathering of the members of the INF to commemorate the 70th anniversary of its establishment. Any newspaper that publishes a criticism is closed down and the journalists who publish criticisms are jailed, lashed, and tortured. Under such conditions, the regime chooses a handful of its candidates and allows them to participate in these election shows. The political, economic, and financial corruption has reached such levels that even members of the oligarchy have begum to complain about them.

In the past 70 years, the Iran National Front has always defended popular sovereignty, rights and liberties of the people, freedom of political parties, freedom of the press and mass media, and free elections. The INF been struggling for realizing the legitimate rights of the Iranian people. We demand real and free

---

548 https://iranazad.info/jebhehkharej/jkh19/11/11%20entekhabat.htm

elections under the supervision of the representatives of all the social classes and strata in Iran.

The Iran National Front-Organizations Abroad, considers the lack of free elections in the country as an insult to the great people of Iran. We do not accept as election this ridiculous show and will not participate in such a spectacle. We except the honorable and democratic people of Iran and all of our supporters to actively condemn this farce that the regime calls elections. We demand free elections under the complete supervision of reputable people.

Iran National Front, Organizations Abroad
November 11, 2019

(5) "The 25 Year Strategic Agreement Between the Islamic Republic and China and Similar Agreements Do Not have Legitimacy for the Nation of Iran" (July 10, 2020)

The INF and INF-OA believe that in pursuing its ideological foreign policy of exporting the fundamentalist revolution, fighting against the U.S., Israel, Saudi Arabia, and challenging the liberal international order, the fundamentalist regime has had to give far reaching concessions to Russia and China that have gravely undermined Iran's national interests and the security and prosperity of the Iranian people. The INF and the INF-OA have consistently criticized and condemned the fundamentalist regime's sacrificing of Iran's national interests for the adventurist and dangerous foreign policy of the regime. In July 2020, it was revealed that the regime was secretly negotiating a secret agreement with China that included major economic and military concessions to China. The following is my translation of excerpts of the statement.[549]

The big danger of the regimes that have been weakened, like the Islamic Republic, is that in order to get out of the whirlpool that they themselves have created, is that they grasp for any branch no mater how small. Granting huge proportions of the Caspian Sea to Russia is one example. Proving fishing permits to the [gi-

---

549 INF, *"Gharar-dad 25 Saleh Rahbordi Jumhuri Islami Ba Chin Va Gharar-dad-hay Moshabeh An Baray Mellat Iran Rasmiyat Nadarad"* [The 25 Year Strategic Agreement Between the Islamic Republic and China and Similar Agreements Do Not have Legitimacy for the Nation of Iran], (July 10, 2020), https://iranazad.info/jebhehkharej/jkh20/07/10%20gharardad%2025%20saleh. htm.

gantic] Chinese fishing vessels which have caused unemployment and poverty for Iranian fishermen and harming the marine environment and destroying the fishing stocks of the Persian Gulf, are but a few other examples of the agreements that the Islamic republic has granted China in order to gain its "support" in "international bodies."

... This agreement is being signed at a time when the Islamic Republic, due to sanctions and enmity with the West, lacks the opportunity to choose, and is at a disadvantaged situation against China.

... These days, the world is witnessing the destruction of democracy in Hong Kong and the establishment of dictatorship of the Communist Party of China there. When many advanced countries, fearful of the intervention by the Chinese in their telecommunication and internet and the abuse of the government of China of their communications, have been withdrawing services such as 5G from Chinese companies such as Huawei, the Islamic Republic has granted the development of 5G in Iran to China.

... This agreement not only undermines the achievements of the Iranian people in the past 150 years against colonial domination and imposes on Iran a colonial domination today that is much worse than before, but also ignores the Islamic Republic's own earlier slogan of "Neither East, Nor West."

... The rulers of the Islamic Republic, consider Iran their own property to do as they wish, consider the Iranian people to be minors, and consider themselves to be their guardians. The 25-year agreement with China demonstrates that the Islamic Republic, in order to continue it rule, is even willing to put the country in the hands of imperialist countries, so that it may continue to rule a few more days. ...

The Iran national Front-Organizations Abroad, warns China and all other countries that partake in this agreement, that the Iranian people demonstrated the successful boycott of the pseudo-elections in March 2020 that this regime lacks legitimacy and lacks the right to be regarded as the legitimate representatives of the Iranian people. This agreement and similar [imperialist] agreements such as the agreement on the Caspian Sea, and fishing in the Persian Gulf, were granted without informing the Iranian people and gaining their votes; therefore, the Iranian people do not recognize these imperialist agreements as legitimate.

Iran National Front-Organizations Abroad
July 10, 2020
http://www.iranazad.info

Appendix 3: Interview with the INF Leader

The following interview was conducted in Persian via e-mail with Dr. Hussein Moussavian. Dr. Moussavian sent back his responses on February 5, 2019. Dr. Moussavian is the Chairman of the INF Central Committee and the Chairman of the Leadership Council. The INF does not have a secretary-general, but one person is usually regarded to be its number one leader. Since November 17, 2018, Dr. Moussavian has been the number one leader of the INF. Before then, he was the Chairman of the Executive Committee for about 12 years.

Masoud Kazemzadeh: During the Shah's era, how many times were you arrested and for how long were you a political prisoner? What were the reasons for your arrests?

Dr. Hussein Moussavian: During the Shah's era, I was arrested and jailed about 7 or 8 times. Fortunately, the arrests occurred in periods that the arrests did not last long. The longest time in prison was about two months and in total I was in prison for about 6 months. The first time I was arrested was on January 11, 1960 when I was a student in 11th grade in high school. On that day, students at high schools throughout Tehran went on protest and strike. The pretext for the protest was the new rules for examinations, but in reality they were to protest and oppose the coup regime. I was arrested for organizing and participating in that protest. I was sent to solitary confinement for about one month at the Ghezel Ghaleh Prison. At that time, Dr. Manuchehr Eghbal was Prime Minister and announced at the Majles that the protests were carried out by orange sellers on the streets. In reality, hundreds of high school students were sent to prisons.

After 1961, my arrests were due to my activities in the Iran National Front, which had begun its open activities again. On the afternoon of December 7, 1961, after participating in the commemoration of the ceremonies at the graves of the martyrs of December 7 (1953), at the Imamzadeh Abdollah, while returning back to Tehran, I was arrested close to my home and sent to Ghezel Ghaleh Prison. The next time was in 1962. I had gone to a photography studio and had placed an order for printing of 100 copies of photos of Dr. Mossadegh and 100 copies of photo of Dr. Fatemi on a street that on those days was called Shahbaz Street. When I went back to the photography studio to pick up the photos, I was arrested by SAVAK agents, who in all likelihood had been informed by the owner of the photography store. On another occasion, I was arrested in front of the Takht-e Jamshid Cinema on Takht-e Jamshid Street while distributing a press release by the Iran National Front among those leaving the cinema. During the summer of 1963 I was arrested and sent to prison for two months along

https://doi.org/10.1515/9783110782158-017

with many other members of the Iran National Front, because the INF had opposed the fake elections for the Majles.

My expulsion from the university and banning of continuing my education were longer. In 1964, fourteen student members of the Iran National Front at the University of Tehran were expelled (merely due to being members of the INF). I was attending the Medical School at the University of Tehran. While I was taking my exams in Serology in August 1964, I was called out of the classroom and told that I was expelled from the university. I was banned from continuing my university attendance for three years until 1967.

In 1971, I was attending the Medical School at the University of Tehran for my Specialty. My Specialty program was in its sixth month, when I was expelled from the Medical School again. One year after being expelled from the University of Tehran Medical School, I participated for the exams for residency at the National University Medical School. I was ranked first (among all the applicants) and was admitted to its program. After being at the National University Medical School for about six months, SAVAK opposed my continuing work that and thus the university had to ask me to leave. This expulsion also lasted three years. In 1975, I was able to re-enter the residency program at the National University Medical School. I completed my residency in 1978.

Kazemzadeh: After the revolution, how many times were you arrested and for how long were you a political prisoner? What were the reasons for your arrests?

Dr. Moussavian: After the revolution in Dey 1359 [December 22, 1980 to January 20, 1981], I was arrested at the publication distribution center because I was a member of the INF Executive Committee and editor-in-chief of the *Payam Jebhe Melli Iran*. I was taken to the Revolutionary Court at Chahar-rah Ghasr. I was under arrest for only one day and after several hours of interrogations, I was released. Apparently, the ruling group had not made the decision to begin confrontation with the Iran National Front then. After June 15, 1981, and the declaration of apostasy of the Iran National Front by Ayatollah Khomeini, I had to go underground and did not go to my home or place of employment for one year. I was a member of the Executive Committee of the INF and was the INF official responsible for organizing the meeting and rally on June 15. During this period, Dr. [Karim] Sanjabi, Chairman of the Leadership Council, Dr. [Mehdi] Azar, Chairman of the Executive Committee, and Hajj Ghassem Lebaschi, member of the Executive Committee, secretly left the country, and other members of the Leadership Council and Executive Committee went into hiding. After [the protests of] the Green Movement and December 2009 protests, I was arrested at my home and sent to solitary confinement for about one month at Evin Prison, because I was chairman of the Executive Committee of the Iran National Front.

Kazemzadeh: Please write a few sentences about yourself that should be in this publication.

Dr. Moussavian: I was born in 1941 in Tehran. At the beginning of Dr. Mossadegh's nationalist government, I was 10 years old, and when the coup occurred on August 19, 1953, I was 12 years old. From my youth I was a supporter of Dr. Mossadegh and the Iran National Front. From then until now, which 65 years has passed since the coup, despite all the difficulties and deprivations, I am and I have always been an activist in the path of Mossadegh and the Iran National Front which means in the path of freedom, independence, and social justice.

Kazemzadeh: The goal of the Iran National Front is the "Establishment of National Sovereignty." Does the Iran National Front consider "National Sovereignty" to be the same thing as democracy or the meaning of these words are something else?

Dr. Moussavian: When there exists democracy, there are free elections and real parliament is established, and the government that is thus based on real parliament and real representatives is national sovereignty; therefore, we can consider democracy and national sovereignty to be the same thing, the establishment of which is the goal of the Iran National Front.

Kazemzadeh: What is the INF's strategy for achieving its goal of establishing democracy?

Dr. Moussavian: The strategy of the Iran National Front for achieving its goal of establishing democracy is exclusively political struggles, exposing the mistakes of the rulers, and suggesting constructive proposals to the people of Iran. The three-element proposal [see Chapter 6] to the regime is actually a roadmap for the struggles of the Iranian people as well, meaning that the Iranian people can use these demands as their main and primary demands. Freedom of all political prisoners, establishment of political freedoms for the Iranian people such as freedoms of the express and publications, freedoms of political parties and assembly, freed elections, and finally the establishment of a real Constituent Assembly for planning for the future of Iran.

Kazemzadeh: In the INF's strategy, does the INF want to achieve its goal by itself, or does it want to cooperate with other political parties and groups? If the answer is to have cooperation and coalitions with other political parties and groups, in the view of the INF, with which parties and groups one may cooperate, with which parties and groups at this juncture one may not cooperate but depending on the situation that the national interests demand one has to cooperate, and with which parties and groups, one should never cooperate?

Dr. Moussavian: In order to achieve its goals, the Iran National Front is prepared to cooperate and make coalitions with other political parties and groups that accept its principles. These principles include: freedom; independence; social justice; a parliamentary republican system; separation of religion and the state; support for territorial integrity and unity of the country; and emphasis on the preservation of the Persian language while respecting all the languages of Iran's ethnic groups. Obviously making a coalition with those who do not accept these principles would be meaningless.

Select Bibliography

Abd-Khodaee, Mohammad Mehdi. *"Goftogo-e Hussein Dehbashi Ba Mohammad Mehdi Abd-Khodaee"* [Hussein Dehbashi Interview with Mohammad Mehdi Abd-Khodaee], Khesht Kham, No. 42 (2018), https://www.aparat.com/v/LxJpW/خشت_خام_%2F_نوبت_چهل_و_دوم_%. حسین_گفتگوی_2F.

Abrahamian, Ervand. *Iran Between Two Revolutions.* Princeton: Princeton University Press, 1982.

Abrahamian, Ervand. *The Iranian Mojahedin.* New Haven: Yale University Press, 1989.

Abrahamian, Ervand. *Khomeinism: Essays on the Islamic Republic.* Berkeley: University of California Press, 1993.

Abrahamian, Ervand. "The 1953 Coup in Iran," *Science & Society*, Vol. 65, No. 2 (Summer 2001), pp. 182 – 215.

Ahmadi, Abdolreza. *"Astan Qods Razavi: Dowlat Penhan Tofangdar"* [Imam Reza Holy Shrine: Government in the Shadow with Guns], Independent Persian, (December 15, 2019), https://www.independentpersian.com/node/32851.

Akhavi, Shahrough. "Iran," in Frank Tachau, editor. *Political Parties of the Middle East and North Africa.* Westport, Connecticut: Greenwood Press, 1994, pp. 133 – 173.

Albright, Madeleine K. "Remarks," U.S. Department of State, (March 17, 2000), https://1997-2001.state.gov/statements/2000/000317.html. For the video of the segment see https://www.youtube.com/watch?v=Q5HYUtYa3wI.

Aldrich, John H. "Political Parties in and Out of Legislatures," in Rhodes, R. A. W., Sarah A. Binder, and Bert A. Rockman, editors, *The Oxford Handbook of Political Institutions.* Oxford: Oxford University Press, 2006, pp. 555 – 576.

Amini, Fariba. "Perseverance and Honor: Interview with Abbas Amir-Entezam," Iranian.com (February 22, 2006), https://iranian.com/2006/02/22/perseverance-and-honor/.

Amir-Entezam, Abbas. *"Goftogo-e Hussein Dehbashi Ba Abbas Amir-Entezam"* [Hussein Dehbashi Interview with Abbas Amir-Entezam], Khasht Kham, No. 36 (2018), http://www.tarikhonline.ir/posts/main/subpage-single/id-217/خشت-خام--نوبت-سی-و-ششم--گفتگوی-حسین-امیرانتظام-عباس-با-دهباشی.html.

Amir-Entezam, Elaheh. *"Sokhanrani Khanum Elaheh Amir-Entezam Dar Salrooz Dargozasht Farzin Mokhber"* [Speech of Ms. Elaheh Amir-Entezam On the Anniversary of the Passing of Farzin Mokhber], (August 24, 2019), https://www.youtube.com/watch?v=JEsZBGr-k9A.

Amir-Entezam, Elaheh. *"Bakhshi Az Sokhanrani Elaheh Amir-Entezam Dar Sharayet Jologiri Az Aaeen 70 Salegi Jebeh Melli Iran"* [Part of the Speech of Elaheh Amir-Entezam When the Regime Prevented the Commemoration of the 70the Anniversary of the INF], (October 26, 2019), https://www.youtube.com/watch?v=EbkpfyX3l3I.

Amir-Khosravi, Babak. *Nazar Az Doroon Beh Naghsh Hezb Tudeh Iran* [Inside Perspective on the Role of the Tudeh Party], Tehran: Etellaat, 1996. https://www.iran-archive.com/start/230.

Amir-Khosravi, Babak. *Hasel Yek Omr: Zendeginameh Siasi Babak Amir-Khosravi* [Results of a Life: Political Memoirs of Babak Amir-Khosravi], Sweden, 2020.

Amir-Khosravi, Babak. *"Goftogo"* [Interview], (no date), http://www.rezafani.com/index.php?/site/comments/amirkhosravi/.

https://doi.org/10.1515/9783110782158-018

Amnesty International, *Blood-soaked Secrets: Why Iran's 1988 Prison Massacres Are Ongoing Crimes Against Humanity*. London: 2017. https://www.amnesty.org/download/Docu ments/MDE1394212018ENGLISH.PDF.

Amnesty International, "Iran: Top government officials distorted the truth about 1988 prison massacres," (December 12, 2018), https://www.amnesty.org/en/latest/press-release/ 2018/12/iran-top-government-officials-distorted-the-truth-about-1988-prison-massacres/.

Anvari, Abdul-Karim. *Talash Baray Esteghlal: Khaterat Siasi* [Struggle for Independence: Political Memoirs]. London: Self-Publication, 2015. https://melliun.org/v/wp-content/up loads/2020/08/talash-baraye-esteghlal.pdf.

Arani, Sharif. "Iran: From the Shah's Dictatorship to Khomeini's Demagogic Theocracy," *Dissent*, No. 27 (Winter 1980), pp. 9 – 26.

Arjomand, Said Amir. *The Turban for the Crown: The Islamic Revolution in Iran*. Oxford and New York: Oxford University Pres, 1988.

Asadi, Jamshid. *"Astan Qods Razavi: Daraeehay Pichideh, Hesabrasi Naroshan"* [Imam Reza Holy Shrine: Complex Assets, Unclear Transparency], Radio Farda, (February 24, 2019), https://www.radiofarda.com/a/commentary-on-Iran-powerful-religious-institute-astan-qods-razavi/29787445.html.

Asadi, Jamshid, and Mehdi Jamali. *"Gozar Az Eghtesad Nezam Valaee Beh Eghtesad Bazzar Bonyad: Naghsh 'Bazzar Azad',"* [Transition from the Fundamentalist Regime Economy to Market Orientated Economy: The Role of 'Free Markets'], Iran-Emrooz, (July 22, 2020), http://www.iran-emrooz.net/index.php/politic/more/85222/.

Ashoori, Dariush. "Interview," with Ali Limonadi, IRTV, (June 25, 2021), https://www.youtube. com/watch?v=UeXIOEqFyLU.

Ashraf, Ahmad and Ali Banuazizi, "The State, Classes and Modes of Mobilization in the Iranian Revolution," in *State, Culture and Society*, Vol. 1, No. 3 (1985), pp. 3 – 40.

Assoudeh, Eliot. "Shia Phoenix: Is Iran's Islamic Republic a Variety of Political Religion?" *The Journal for Interdisciplinary Middle Eastern Studies*, Vol. 4 (2019), pp. 57 – 95, https:// www.ariel.ac.il/wp/jimes/shia-phoenix-is-irans-islamic-republic-a-variety-of-political-reli gion/.

Azar, Mehdi. "Interview," Harvard University, Iranian Oral History Project, Norfolk, Virginia, U.S., (March 31, 1983), https://curiosity.lib.harvard.edu/iranian-oral-history-project/cata log/32-azar__mehdi01, audio available at https://www.youtube.com/watch?v=fb9bY0Cd zAo; https://www.youtube.com/watch?v=NbTa4inBEQo; and https://www.youtube.com/ watch?v=2P4SlfyoZiQ.

Azarang, Abdol Hussein. *"Jebhe Melli Iran, Bozorgtarain Eatelaf Nirohayeh Siasi Iran Dat Tarikh Moaser Iran Ta Pish Az Enghelab Islami 1357"* [Iran National Front, the Largest Coalition of Political Forces in Iran's Contemporary History Until the Islamic Revolution of 1979], *Encyclopaedia Islamica* (no date). https://web.archive.org/web/ 20150318064343/http:/www.encyclopaediaislamica.com/madkhal2.php?sid=4503.

Azimi, Fakhreddin. "On Shaky Ground: Concerning the Absence or Weakness of Political Parties in Iran." *Iranian Studies*, Vol. 30, Nos. 1–2 (1997), pp. 53–75.

Azimi, Fakhreddin. "Unseating Mosaddeq: The Configuration and Role of Domestic Forces," in Gasiorowski, Mark J., and Malcolm Byrne, eds. *Mohammad Mosaddeq and the 1953 Coup in Iran*. Syracuse: Syracuse University Press, 2005, pp. 27–101.

Azimi, Fakhreddin. *The Quest for Democracy in Iran: A Century of Struggle Against Authoritarian Rule*. Cambridge, MA: Harvard University Press, 2010.

Azin, H. *"Beh Bahaneh Dargozasht Ali Khavari"* [On the Occasion of the Passing Away of Ali Khavari], Gooya News, (March 24, 2021), https://news.gooya.com/2021/03/post-49972. php.

Azizi, Arash. *"Ali Khavari, Rahbar Hezb Tudeh Iran Keh Bood Va Chegoneh Beh Rahbari Resid?"* [Ali Khavari, Who Was the Leader of the Tudeh Party of Iran and How Did He Become Its Leader?], Iran Wire, (March 23, 2021), https://iranwire.com/fa/features/ 47298.

Baghaie-Kermani, Mozaffar. "Interview," Harvard University, Iranian Oral History Project, Franklin Lake, New Jersey, U.S., (April 11, 1986), https://curiosity.lib.harvard.edu/iranian-oral-history-project/catalog?f%5Binterviewee_ssim%5D%5B%5D=Baghaie-Kermani%2C +Mozaffar, audio available at https://www.youtube.com/watch?v=oUJy80mMap0&list=PL-PRP1hqq8eK6WhFOLGa3MQyO9fL5v70q.

Bakhtiar, Shapour. *37 Rooz Paas Az 37 Saal* [37 Days after 37 Years] Los Angeles: Radio Iran Press, 1982. https://melliun.org/nehzat/n05/37rouz.htm.

Bakhtiar, Shapour. "Interview," Harvard University, Iranian Oral History Project, Paris, (March 7, 1984), audio available at https://www.youtube.com/watch?v=t47-vBeVsdo& list=PL-PRP1hqq8eK17Y8j0Gfzpb_f7KVS-lrX.

Bakhtiar, Shapour. "Speeches." https://www.facebook.com/ShapourBakhtiar/.

Barzegar, Jamshid. *"Hagh Ray Zanan: Az Fohasha ta Hefz Islam"* [Female Franchise: From Prostitution to Protection of Islam], BBC Persian, (July 15, 2014), https://www.bbc.com/ persian/iran/2014/07/140715_l10_jb_women_vote.

Batou, Jean. "Maxime Rodinson Was a Revolutionary Historian of the Muslim World," Jacobin, (January 31, 2021), https://www.jacobinmag.com/2021/01/maxime-rodinson-islam-mid dle-east.

BBC Persian, *"Taasis Bonyad Jahani Holocast Dar Tehran"* [Establishment of the Global Foundation of the Holocaust in Tehran], (December 14, 2006), www.bbc.co.uk/persian/ iran/story/2006/12/061214_mf_holocaust.shtml.

BBC Persian, *"Karnameh Fadian Khalq, Aksariyat"* [History of Fadaian, Majority], (February 16, 2011), https://www.youtube.com/watch?v=RLwMFzWZMmg.

BBC Persian, *"Hezb Tudeh"* [Tudeh Party], (January 31, 2012), https://www.youtube.com/ watch?v=m5rJtrrRlks.

BBC Persian, *"Ahzab Irani"* [Iranian Political Parties] (February 7, 2012), https://www.youtube. com/watch?v=v6JYeBkvwos.

BBC Persian, *"Aya Khalil Maleki 1 Estesna Ast?"* [Is Khalil Maleki One Exception?], (May 10, 2018), https://www.youtube.com/watch?v=ACQ2EBXHwX0.

BBC Persian, *"Bohtan Barayeh Hefz Nezam"* [Defamation for Preserving the Regime], (December 18, 2018), with English subtitles, https://www.youtube.com/watch?v= qIwgrSnxwLI.

BBC Persian, *"Mostenad Farzand Enghelab: Dastan Zendegi Va Marg Sadegh Ghotbzadeh Ghesmat 1"* [Documentary Child of the Revolution: Story of Life and Death of Sadegh Ghotbzadeh Part 1], (February 9, 2020), https://www.youtube.com/watch?v=PWB0lM8-cQo.

BBC Persian, *"Mostenad Farzand Enghelab: Dastan Zendegi Va Marg Sadegh Ghotbzadeh Ghesmat 2"* [Documentary Child of the Revolution: Story of Life and Death of Sadegh Ghotbzadeh Part 2], (February 10, 2020), https://www.youtube.com/watch?v=vpyLiEUtT_ o.

BBC Persian, "*Mostenad Farzand Enghelab: Dastan Zendegi Va Marg Sadegh Ghotbzadeh Ghesmat 3*" [Documentary Child of the Revolution: Story of Life and Death of Sadegh Ghotbzadeh Part 3], (February 10, 2020), https://www.youtube.com/watch?v=HiyOu4fk R2I.

BBC Persian, "*Bazjoe Abbas Amir-Entezam: Eteham Jasosi Beh Oo Hargez Sabet Nashod*" [Abbas Amir-Entezam's Interrogator: The Accusation of Espionage Was Never Proven], (July 14, 2020), https://www.bbc.com/persian/iran-53404949.

BBC Persian, "*Payman Novin: Naghsh Reza Pahalvi Dar Mobarezeh Bah Jomhuri Islami Chist?*" [New Pact: What is the Role of Reza Pahlavi in the Struggle Against the Islamic Republic?], (October 1, 2020), https://www.youtube.com/watch?v=jyrpKcCG_i8.

Beheshti, Vahid. "Interview," Iran International, (March 5, 2021), https://www.youtube.com/watch?v=M-eWP9AUmiY.

Behgar, Hassan. "*Jojeh Fashistha Sar Az Tokhm Dar Miavarand!*" [Fascist Chicks Are Hatching], (July 3, 2005), www.iranliberal.com/Maghaleh-ha/Hassan_Behgar/jojeh.htm.

Behgar, Hassan. "*Jebhe Melli Bar Sar-e Do-Rahi*" [The National Front at a Fork on the Road], (January 3, 2021), https://iranliberal.com/%d8%a2%d8%b1%db%8c%d9%88-%d8%ad%d8%b3%d9%86-%d8%a8%d9%87%da%af%d8%b1/%d8%ac%d8%a8%d9%87%db%80-%d9%85%d9%84%db%8c-%d8%a8%d8%b1-%d8%b3%d8%b1-%d8%af%d9%88%d8%b1%d8%a7%d9%87%db%8c-%d8%ad%d8%b3%d9%86-%d8%a8%d9%87%da%af%d8%b1/.

Behrooz, Maziar. *Rebels with A Cause: The Failure of the Left in Iran*. London: I.B. Tauris, 1999.

Behrooz, Maziar. "The 1953 Coup in Iran and the Legacy of the Tudeh," in Mark Gasiorowski and Malcolm Byrne, eds. *Mohammad Mosaddeq and the 1953 Coup in Iran*. (Syracuse: Syracuse University Press, 2005), pp. 102–125.

Belen Soage, Ana. "Hasan al-Banna or the Politicisation of Islam," *Totalitarian Movements and Political Religions*, Vol. 9, No. 1 (March 2008), pp. 21–42. https://www.researchgate.net/publication/233003241_Hasan_al-Banna_or_the_Politicisation_of_Islam.

Bill, James A. *The Eagle and the Lion: The Tragedy of American-Iranian Relations*. New Haven and London: Yale University Press, 1988.

Bill, James A. and Wm. Roger Louis, eds. *Musaddiq, Iranian Nationalism and Oil*. Austin: University of Texas Press, 1988.

Borger, Julian. "British spy's account sheds light on role in 1953 Iranian coup," *The Guardian*, (August 17, 2020), https://www.theguardian.com/world/2020/aug/17/british-spys-account-sheds-light-on-role-in-1953-iranian-coup.

Bowcott, Owen. "Secret CIA study reveals British role in Iran coup," *The Guardian*, (April 16, 2000), https://www.theguardian.com/world/2000/apr/17/iran.

Bozorgmehr, Jalil. *Mossadegh Dar Mahkameh Nezami* [Mossadegh at the Military Trial], Vol. 1, Entesharat Nehzat Moghavemat Melli Iran, no date. http://jebhemeliiran.org/wp-content/uploads/2015/09/Mosadegh_Dar_Mahkameh_1.pdf.

Bozorgmehr, Jalil. *Mossadegh Dar Mahkameh Nezami* [Mossadegh at the Military Trial], Vol. 2, Entesharat Nehzat Moghavemat Melli Iran, no date. http://jebhemeliiran.org/wp-content/uploads/2015/09/Mosadegh_Dar_Mahkameh_2.pdf.

Carter, Jimmy. *Keeping Faith: Memoirs of a President*. New York: Bantam Books, 1983.

Chaqueri, Cosroe. "Did the Soviets play a role in founding the Tudeh party in Iran?," *Cahiers du Monde russe*, Vol. 40, No. 3 (1999), pp. 497–528.

Chaqueri, Cosroe. *"Shalodeh-Shekani Yek Afsaneh"* [Debunking A Myth], Melliun, (August 19, 2013), https://melliun.org/iran/25870.

Chaqueri, Cosroe. *"Naghdi Bar Pareh-e Az Nazarat Piramoon Naghsh Hezb Tudeh"* [Critique on Some Views on the Role of the Tudeh Party], Melliun (August 30, 2013), https://melliun.org/iran/26615.

Chaqueri, Cosroe. *"53 Nafar Beh Ravayat Kambakhsh: Gozaresh Serri Beh Rofaghay Ruus"* [Group of 53 According to Kambakhsh: The Secret Report to Russian Comrades], Melliun (January 2, 2014), https://melliun.org/iran/33964.

Chehabi, Houchange. *Iranian Politics and Religious Modernism: The Liberation Movement of Iran Under the Shah and Khomeini.* Ithaca, NY: Cornell University Press, 1990.

Clinton, Bill. "Interview with Charlie Rose," (January 2005), https://larouchepub.com/other/interviews/2005/3206clinton_rose.html.

Clinton, Hillary. "Interview with the BBC Persian," (October 26, 2011), https://www.youtube.com/watch?v=ED0iU-sMaGA&t=1410s.

Cottam, Richard. *Nationalism in Iran.* Pittsburgh: University of Pittsburgh Press, 1964.

Cottam, Richard. *Iran and the United States: A Cold War Case Study.* Pittsburgh: University of Pittsburgh Press, 1988.

Darbyshire, Norman. "Transcript of Interview with Norman Darbyshire for End of Empire," (1985), National Security Archives, (August 2020), https://nsarchive.gwu.edu/dc.html?doc=7033886-National-Security-Archive.

Darwishpour, Mehrdad. "Interview," Iran International TV, (September 29, 2020), https://www.youtube.com/watch?v=MELUjl4YiCU.

Davarpanah, Parviz. *"Takhrib Maghbareh Sargord Mahmoud Sakhaee Afsar Shaheed Jebhe Melli Iran"* [Destruction of the Tomb of Captain Mahmoud Sakhaee the Martyred Officer of the Iran National Front], Iran Liberal, (October 5, 2008), http://www.iranliberal.com/Maghaleh-ha/EXtra/Davar_Sakhaie.htm.

Dehkordi, Maryam. *"Zanan Taasir-gozar Iran: Elaheh Mizani (Amir-Entezam)"* [Influential Women of Iran: Elaheh Mizani (Amir-Entezam)], Iran Wire, (May 20, 2020), https://iranwire.com/fa/features/38378.

Deutsche Welle, *"Piroozi Biden Va Taasir An Bar Kahesh Bahayeh Dollar Va Talla Dar Iran"* [Biden's Victory and Its Effect on the Reduction of Prices of Dollar and Gold], (November 8, 2020), https://www.dw.com/fa-ir/%D9%BE%DB%8C%D8%B1%D9%88%D8%B2%DB%8C-%D8%A8%D8%A7%DB%8C%D8%AF%D9%86-%D9%88-%D8%AA%D8%A7%D8%AB%DB%8C%D8%B1-%D8%A2%D9%86-%D8%A8%D8%B1-%DA%A9%D8%A7%D9%87%D8%B4-%D8%A8%D9%87%D8%A7%DB%8C-%D8%AF%D9%84%D8%A7%D8%B1-%D9%88-%D8%B7%D9%84%D8%A7-%D8%AF%D8%B1-%D8%A7%DB%8C%D8%B1%D8%A7%D9%86/a-55535683.

Diba, Farhad. *Dr. Mohammad Mossadegh: A Political Biography.* London: Croom Helm, 1986.

Esfandiari, Golnaz. "Iran: Coping With The World's Highest Rate of Brain Drain," Radio Farda, (March 8, 2004), https://www.rferl.org/a/1051803.html.

Etemadi, Nasser. *"Chera Mardom Iran Ebrahim Raisi Va Ozaeh Keshvareshan Ra Shabih Eichmann Va Alman Nazi Midanand?"* [Why the Iranian People Consider Ebrahim Raisi and the Condition of Their Country to Be Similar to Eichmann and Nazi Germany?], Radio France International, (August 6, 2021), https://www.rfi.fr/fa/%D8%A7%DB%8C%D8%B1%D8%A7%D9%86/20210806-%DA%86%D8%B1%D8%A7-%D9%85%D8%B1%D8%AF%D9%85-%D8%A7%DB%8C%D8%B1%D8%A7%D9%86-%D8%A7%D8%A8%D8%B1%

D8%A7%D9%87%DB%8C%D9%85-%D8%B1%D8%A6%DB%8C%D8%B3%DB%8C-%D9%
88-%D8%A7%D9%88%D8%B6%D8%A7%D8%B9-%DA%A9%D8%B4%D9%88%D8%B1%
D8%B4%D8%A7%D9%86-%D8%B1%D8%A7-%D8%B4%D8%A8%DB%8C%D9%87-%
D8%A2%DB%8C%D8%B4%D9%85%D9%86-%D9%88-%D8%A2%D9%84%D9%85%D8%
A7%D9%86-%D9%86%D8%A7%D8%B2%DB%8C-%D9%85%DB%8C-%D8%AF%D8%A7%
D9%86%D9%86%D8%AF.

Fadavi, IRGC Gen. Ali. *"Sardar Fadavi: 'Sepah Pasdaran Enghelab Islami' Hich Kalamee Dar Edameh Khod Nadarad Hatta Iran"* [Gen. Fadavi: "The Islamic Revolutionary Guards Corps" Does Not Have Any Words After its Title, Even Iran], Bahar News, (April 22, 2018), https://www.baharnews.ir/news/148310/.

Fallaci, Oriana. *Interview with History.* Boston, MA: Houghton Mifflin Harcourt, 1977.

Falsafi, Ayatollah Mohammad Taghi. *"Khaterat Ayatollah Mohammad Taghi Falsafi"* [Memoirs of Ayatollah Mohammad Taghi Falsafi] Tarikh Shafai Iran, Markaz Asnad Enghelab Islami, https://www.youtube.com/watch?v=GeVYbNqNIIA (posted on You Tube November 11, 2019). This is the link to Part 1. There are over a dozen video recordings of his memoirs.

Farhang, Mansour. *"Malikholiah Sodor Enghelab Va Chalesh 'Gheire Khodiha'"* [Melancholy of the Export of the Revolution and "non-fundamentalists"], (September 12, 2020), http://www.iran-emrooz.net/index.php/politic/more/85845/.

Fatapour, Mehdi. "Interview," IRTV (August 2, 2020), https://www.youtube.com/watch?v=YL Qu46N7rDg&feature.

Fatemi, Hussein. *Khaterat Va Mobarezat Doktor Hussein Fatemi* [Memoirs and Struggles of Dr. Hussein Fatemi], collected by Bahram Afrasiabi, Tehran: Entesharat Sokhan, 1987.

Fatemi, Hussein. *Neveshteh-hay Makhfigah Va Zendan: 28 Mordad 1332 – 19 Aban 1333* [Writings from the Hideout and Prison: 19 August 1953 – 10 November 1954], London: Daftar-hay Azadi, 2004. https://melliun.org/v/wp-content/uploads/2017/06/yaddasht-haye-dr.-Fatemi.pdf.

Fathollahzadeh, Atabak. *Khane Daee Yuusef: Vaghae Tekandahandeh Az Mohajerat Fadaian Aksariyat Beh Shoravi* [Uncle Joseph's House: Shocking Reports from the Emigration of Fadaian-Majority to the Soviet Union]. Tehran: Nashr Ghatreh, 2002. https://melliun.org/v/wp-content/uploads/2020/04/Khaneye-Daei-Yusof.pdf.

Fattahi, Kambiz. *"Kodetay 28 Mordad: Naghsh Kashani Beh Ravayat Asnad America"* [The August 19, 1953 Coup: The Role of Kashani According to the American Documents], BBC Persian, (July 22, 2017), https://www.bbc.com/persian/iran-features-40662792.

Fattahi, Kambiz. *"Payam Makhfiyaneh Abolghassem Kashani Beh Eisenhower"* [Secret Message from Abolghassem Kashani to Eisenhower], BBC Persian, (February 14, 2018), https://www.bbc.com/persian/iran-features-43053577.

Fattahi, Kambiz. *"Kodetay 28 Mordad: 'Sorat Hesab Majera'"* [The August 19, 1953 Coup: "The Bill for the Event"], BBC Persian, (August 20, 2018), https://www.bbc.com/persian/iran-45253663.

Fattahi, Kambiz. *"Kodetay 28 Mordad: Farziyha Dar Mored Sanad Hazineh-ha"* [The August 19, 1953 Coup: Assumptions on the Document on the Costs], BBC Persian, (August 24, 2018), https://www.bbc.com/persian/iran-45300129.

Financial Tribune, "Brian Drain Continues in Iran," (November 9, 2016), https://financial tribune.com/articles/people/53254/brain-drain-continues.

Floor, Willem. "The Revolutionary Character of Iranian Ulama: Wishful Thinking or Reality?" *International Journal of Middle East Studies*, Vol. 12, No. 1 (December 1980), pp. 501–524.

Forouhar, Parastu. *"Kodeta-y 28 Mordad, Dariush Forouhar Va Meidan Baharestan"* [The August 19, 1953 Coup, Dariush Forouhar and Baharestan Field], Radio Zamaneh, (August 18, 2015), https://www.radiozamaneh.com/233101?fbclid=IwAR1CSYVEgD3U_K5VhNz4s-COeYmlYXkyP-jOw1_vbBuhsFSgRBSR_Q-AjZk. This contains segments of Dariush Forouhar's recollections on the coup.

Fromm, Erich. *Escape from Freedom.* NY: Farrar & Rinehart, 1941.

Gasiorowski, Mark J. *U.S. Foreign Policy and the Shah: Building a Client State in Iran.* Cornell: Cornell University Press, 1991.

Gasiorowski, Mark J., and Malcolm Byrne, eds. *Mohammad Mosaddeq and the 1953 Coup in Iran.* Syracuse: Syracuse University Press, 2005.

Gasiorowski, Mark J. "U.S. Perceptions of the Communist Threat in Iran during the Mossadegh Era," *Journal of Cold War Studies*, Vol. 21, No. 3 (Summer 2019), pp. 185–221. https://www.mitpressjournals.org/doi/pdf/10.1162/jcws_a_00898.

Ghaemmagham, Kambiz. *"Khaterati Az Daneshjoyan Iran Dar Kharej Az Keshvar"* [Memoirs of the Iranian Students Outside the Country], Rangin-Kaman TV via You Tube, (May 12, 2020), https://www.youtube.com/watch?v=h3GZ8Z4i3sU.

Ghaemmagham, Mohsen. *"Ghassem Soleimani – Dar Khedmat Nezam Estebdad Mazhabi Va Vali Faghih"* [Ghassem Soleimani – In Service of the System of Religious Dictatorship and Fundamentalist Regime], Melliun, (January 19, 2020), https://melliun.org/iran/223359.

Ghaemmagham, Mohden. *"Dar Peyman Aghay Reza Pahlavi, Chera Sohbati Az Dictatori Shah Nist?"* [Why There is No Talk of the Shah's Dictatorship in Mr. Reza Pahalvi's New Pact?], Melliun, (September 29, 2020), https://melliun.org/iran/243161.

Ghafari, Mahan. *"Marg O Mir Aban 98: Moamae Chand Hezar Nafari Keh Ezafeand?"* [Deaths of November 2019: The Puzzle of Several Thousand Additional Deaths?], Radio Farda, (May 28, 2021), https://www.radiofarda.com/a/commentary-on-death-toll-report-of-november-2019/31276714.html.

Ghafari, Mahan, Alireza Kadivar, and Aris Katzourakis. "Excess deaths associated with the Iranian COVID-19 epidemic: A province-level analysis," *International Journal of Infectious Diseases*, Vol. 107, (June 2021), pp. 101–115, https://www.sciencedirect.com/science/article/pii/S120197122100326X.

Gharib, Ali. *Istad-e Bar Arman* [Standing on Principles], (2006), https://www.enghelabe-eslami.com/pdf/Gharib-Istade-bar-Arman.pdf?fbclid=IwAR2UjiHFOeHH03iyfTbTH6G81gZ8xdnfy6GcJnAHNXEm10wUZ-Iv2knFhAU.

Ghoghnoos, Bijan. *"Aya 'Jomhuri Velayat Faghih' Regimi Fashisti Ast?"* [Is the "Rule of Shia Cleric Republic" a Fascist Regime?], Iran Emrooz, (January 31, 2021), http://www.iran-emrooz.net/index.php/politic/more/87667/.

Glass, Andrew. "Carter lauds shah of Iran, Dec. 31, 1977," Politico, (December 30, 2018), https://www.politico.com/story/2018/12/30/this-day-in-politics-december-31-1077103.

Golshiri, Ghazal. "L'incroyable succès d'Hannah Arendt en Iran," *Le Monde*, (August 6, 2021), https://www.lemonde.fr/series-d-ete/article/2021/08/06/l-incroyable-succes-d-hannah-arendt-en-iran_6090745_3451060.html

Graham, Robert. *Iran: The Illusion of Power.* New York: St. Martin's Press, 1979.

Granada Television, "End of Empire, Chapter 7, Iran," (1985), You Tube, (2014), https://www.
   youtube.com/watch?v=xhCgJElpQEQ.
Griffin, Roger. editor, *Fascism*. Oxford: Oxford University Press, 1995.
Haj Seyyed Javadi, Ali Asghar. *"Seday Paye Fashism"* [Sounds of Fascism's Steps],
   (February 5, 1981) republished at Radio Zamaneh, (July 1, 2018), https://www.radio
   zamaneh.com/401640.
Haj Seyyed Javadi, Ali Asghar. *"Ghool-e Fashism Dar Hal-e Tasalot Bar Iran Ast"* [The Fascist
   Monster is gaining Control Over Iran], (February 1981), republished in Mihan,
   (January 29, 2018), http://mihan.net/1396/11/09/1330/.
Haj Seyyed Javadi, Ali Asghar. "Interview," Harvard University, Iranian Oral History Project,
   Paris, (March 1, 1984), https://curiosity.lib.harvard.edu/iranian-oral-history-project/cata
   log/32-hajiseyd-djavadi__ali-asghar01, audio available at https://www.youtube.com/
   watch?v=s6QOwXndITs&list=PL-PRP1hqq8eLy_nfU112IsfaUlkwZfYd-.
Haj Seyyed Javadi, Ali Asghar. *"Beh Dalil Sansoor, Mardom Va Roshanfekran Ma Az Tarh
   Ayatollah Khomeni Baray Ijad Velayat Faghgih Agahi Nadashtand"* [Because of
   Censorship, Our People and Intellectuals Did Not Know About Ayatollah Khomeini's Plan
   for Rule of the Clerics], Radio France International, (September 19, 2017), https://www.
   rfi.fr/fa/%D8%B9%D9%85%D9%88%D9%85%DB%8C/20170916-%D8%B9%D9%84%DB
   %8C-%D8%A7%D8%B5%D8%BA%D8%B1-%D8%AD%D8%A7%D8%AC-%D8%B3%DB%
   8C%D8%AF%E2%80%8C%D8%AC%D9%88%D8%A7%D8%AF%DB%8C-%D8%A8%D9%
   87-%D8%AF%D9%84%DB%8C%D9%84-%D8%B3%D8%A7%D9%86%D8%B3%D9%88%
   D8%B1%D8%8C-%D9%85%D8%B1%D8%AF%D9%85-%D9%88-%D8%B1%D9%88%D8%
   B4%D9%86%D9%81%DA%A9%D8%B1%D8%A7%D9%86-%D9%85%D8%A7-%D8%A7%
   D8%B2-%D8%B7%D8%B1%D8%AD-%D8%A2%DB%8C%D8%AA%E2%80%8C%D8%A7%
   D9%84%D9%84%D9%87-%D8%AE%D9%85%DB%8C%D9%86%DB%8C-%D8%A8%D8%
   B1%D8%A7%DB%8C-%D8%A7%DB%8C%D8%AC%D8%A7%D8%AF-%D9%88%D9%84%
   D8%A7%DB%8C%D8%AA-%D9%81%D9%82%DB%8C%D9%87-%D8%A2%DA%AF%D8%
   A7%D9%87%DB%8C-%D9%86%D8%AF%D8%A7%D8%B4.
Hakakian, Roya. "Abbas Amir-Entezam: Iranian Politician who went from deputy prime
   minister to longest-suffering political prisoner," *Independent*, (July 17, 2018), https://
   www.independent.co.uk/news/obituaries/abbas-amir-entezam-dead-cause-age-iran-jail-
   political-prisoner-spy-deputy-prime-minister-a8451066.html.
Halliday, Fred. "The Iranian Revolution and Its Implications," *New Left Review*, No. 166
   (November/December 1987), pp. 29–37.
Heiss, Mary Ann. "The United States, Great Britain, and the Creation of the Iranian Oil
   Consortium, 1953–1954," *The International History Review*, Vol. 16, No. 3 (August 1994),
   pp. 511–535.
Hejazi, Masoud. *Roydadha Va Davari, 1329–1339: Khaterat Masoud Hejazi* [Movements and
   Judgment, 1950–1960: Memoirs of Masoud Hejazi]. Tehran: Niloufar, 1997.
Helms, Richard, and William Hood, *A Look Over My Shoulder: A Life in the Central Intelligence
   Agency*. New York: Random House, 2003.
Henderson, Loy. "Telegram From the Embassy in Iran to the Department of State,"
   (August 18, 1953, 10 p.m.), https://history.state.gov/historicaldocuments/frus1951-
   54Iran/d280.

Homayoun, Dariush. "Interview," Harvard University, Iranian Oral History Project, Washington, D.C., (1983), audio available at https://www.youtube.com/watch?v=CDsAu4tGVwA; and https://www.youtube.com/watch?v=pJZMu9nnDwo.

Homayoun, Dariush. *"Mohammad Reza Pahlavi: Sargashteh Miyan Mazhab Va Farangi-Maabi"* [Mohammad Reza Pahlavi: Confused between Religion and Westernization], BBC Persian, (July 27, 2010), https://www.bbc.com/persian/iran/2010/07/100727_shah_an nive30_homayoun_religion.shtml.

Husseini, Keyvan. *"Sarnevesht Naft Iran Baad Az Kodetay 28 Mordad Cheh Shod?"* [What Happened to the Iranian Oil After the 1953 Coup?], Radio Farda, (August 12, 2014), https://www.radiofarda.com/a/fk_downfall_e41/25429849.html.

ILNA, *"Ehsan Soltani Dar Goftogo Ba ILNA: Tavarom Vaghe-e Balay 60 Darsad Ast"* [Interview with Ehsan Soltani: Real Inflation is Over 60 Percent], (September 20, 2020), www.ilna. news/fa/tiny/news-970141.

ILNA, *"Rais Otagh Bazargani Iran Va Chin Dar Goftego Ba ILNA"* [Interview with the Chairman of the Iran-China Chamber of Commerce], (October 4, 2020), https://www.ilna.news/fa/tiny/news-977917.

Iran Human Rights Documentation Center, *No Safe Haven: Iran Global Assassination Campaign* (February 3, 2011), https://iranhrdc.org/no-safe-haven-irans-global-assassi nation-campaign/.

Iran Human Rights Documentation Center, *Deadly Fatwa: Iran's 1988 Prison Massacre* (February 5, 2011), https://iranhrdc.org/deadly-fatwa-irans-1988-prison-massacre/.

Iran International, "Report on the Suppression of Gonabadi Darwishes," (March 5, 2021), https://www.youtube.com/watch?v=v-607PvwpGs.

Iran International, "Report on the Suppression of Gonabadi Darwishes," (March 5, 2021), https://www.youtube.com/watch?v=sWoyOiJZkjU.

Iran International, *"Nezam Parastari Tehran: Mahaneh 500 Parastar Be Dalil Hoghogh Paeen Az Iran Mohajerat Mikonand"* [Tehran Nurses Organization: Every Month 500 Nurses Emigrate From Iran Due to Low Wages], (April 11, 2021), https://iranintl.com/%D8%AA% D8%A7%D8%B2%D9%87-%DA%86%D9%87-%D8%AE%D8%A8%D8%B1/%D9%86% D8%B8%D8%A7%D9%85-%D9%BE%D8%B1%D8%B3%D8%AA%D8%A7%D8%B1%DB% 8C-%D8%AA%D9%87%D8%B1%D8%A7%D9%86-%D9%85%D8%A7%D9%87%D8%A7% D9%86%D9%87-%DB%B5%DB%B0%DB%B0-%D9%BE%D8%B1%D8%B3%D8%AA%D8% A7%D8%B1-%D8%A8%D9%87-%D8%AF%D9%84%DB%8C%D9%84-%D8%AD%D9% 82%D9%88%D9%82-%D9%BE%D8%A7%DB%8C%DB%8C%D9%86-%D8%A7%D8%B2- %D8%A7%DB%8C%D8%B1%D8%A7%D9%86-%D9%85%D9%87%D8%A7%D8%AC% D8%B1%D8%AA-%D9%85%DB%8C%E2%80%8C%DA%A9%D9%86%D9%86%D8%AF. Also available at https://melliun.org/iran/257437.

Iran International, *"Vakonesh Magham Dowlati Beh Koshtar Aban Mah"* [Reaction of the Government Official to the Massacre of November 2019], (April 24, 2021), https://www.youtube.com/watch?v=FiNvX16SF1M.

Iran International, *"Emrooz"* [Today], (July 28, 2021), https://www.youtube.com/watch?v=eVj_ajlNSW4.

Iran Liberal Organization, *"Maram-Nameh Ma"* [Our Charter], (May 2020), https://iranliberal.com/%d8%af%d8%b1-%d8%a8%d8%a7%d8%b1%d9%87-%d9%85%d8%a7/.

Iran National Front, Organizations Abroad. "Iranian Democrats Ask Pro-Democracy Forces Around the World for Solidarity," (February 18, 2018), https://iranazad.info/jebhehkhar ej/jkh18/02/18%20az%20azadikhahan%20jahan%20english.htm.

Iran National Front, Organizations Abroad. "*Sarkoob Darawish Keshvar Va Aparthied Mazhabi Jomhuri Islami Ra Mahkoom Mikonim*" [We Condemn the Suppression of the Country's Darwishes and the Religious Apartheid of the Islamic Republic], (February 26, 2018), https://iranazad.info/jebhehkharej/jkh18/02/26%20daravish.htm.

Iran Party, "*Zendegi-nameh Siasi Ahmad Zirakzadeh*" [Political Biography of Ahmad Zirakzadeh], (no date), https://hezbeiran.com/?p=111.

Iran Party, "*Zendegi-nameh Siasi Allahyar Saleh*" [Political Biography of Allahyar Saleh], (no date), https://hezbeiran.com/?p=120.

Iran Party, "*Zendegi-nameh Siasi Nezamaldin Movahed*" [Political Biography of Nezamoldin Movahed], (no date), https://hezbeiran.com/?p=125.

Iran Party, "*Marasem 77 Salgard Taasis Hezb Iran Beh Sorat Majazi Bargozar Shod*" [The Commemoration of the 77th Anniversary of the Founding of the Iran Party Was Conducted Online], (May 20, 2021), https://hezbeiran.com/?p=441.

Irfani, Suroosh. *Iran's Islamic Revolution: Popular Liberation or Religious Dictatorship?* London: Zed Press, 1983.

IRGC, "*Razmandegan Bedon-e Marz Ra Behtar Beshnasid: Niroyeh Qods Sepah Chegoneh Shekl Gereft?*" [Get to Know Better the Fighters Without Borders: How Was the Qods Force Formed?], Fars News (January 25, 2020), https://www.farsnews.ir/news/ 13981105000470/;

IRGC, "'*Razmandegan Bedon-e Marz' Dar Meydan Razm: Niroyeh Qods Dar Kodam Jang-ha Hozoor Yaft?*" ["Fighters Without Borders" on the Battlefield: Qods Force Was Present in Which Wars?], Fars News (January 26, 2020), https://www.farsnews.ir/news/ 13981106000522/.

ISNA, "*Sarnevesht Daneshjooyan Eshghalkonandeh Sefarat America*" [What Became of the Students Occupying the American Embassy], (November 3, 2016), https://www.isna.ir/ news/95081309267.

ISNA, "*Monadi: 900 Ostad Dar Sal 98 Az Iran Kharej Shodand*" [Mondai: 900 Professors Left Iran in the Year 2019–2020], (March 6, 2021), https://www.isna.ir/news/99121612250.

Jebhe Melli Iran. "*Bayanieh Jebhe Melli Iran Dar Bareh Enqelab Sefid Va Hameh-Porsi Enqelab Sefid 6 Bahman 1341*" [Statement of the Iran National Front on the White Revolution and the Referendum on January 26, 1963], (January 23, 1963), https:// melliun.org/iran/195488.

Jebhe Melli Iran. "*Bayanieh Jebhe Melli Iran Dar Bareh Enqelab Sefid Va Hameh-Porsi Enqelab Sefid 6 Bahman 1341*" [Statement of the Iran National Front on the White Revolution and the Referendum on January 26, 1963], (January 26, 1963), https:// melliun.org/iran/195488.

Jebhe Melli Iran, "*Nazar Jebhe Melli Iran dar bareh Shoraha va Majles Khobregan: Majles Khobregan bayad dar tasmimat khod betore asasi tajdid nazar konad*" [The Perspective of the Iran National Front on the Councils and the Assembly of Experts: The Assembly of Experts Has to Make Fundamental Changes in its Decisions] (Aban 1358) [October 1979].

Jebhe Melli Iran. *Asasnameh Jebhe Melli Iran* [The Charter of the Iran National Front], (2015), http://jebhemeliiran.org/wp-content/uploads/2015/11/JMI-Statute.pdf.

Jebhe Melli Iran, *"Jahat Sabt Dar Tarikh"* [For Documenting History], (August 30, 2016), http://jebhemeliiran.org/?p=1129.

Jebhe Melli Iran. *"Sokhani Dar Bab Melligaraee (Nationalism) Va Mihanparastee Efrati (Chauvinism)"* [Some Words Regarding Nationalism and Chauvinism], *Payam Jebhe Melli Iran*, (December 22, 2017), p. 3, http://jebhemeliiran.org/wp-content/uploads/2017/12/PAYAME-JMI-191-PAGE3.pdf.

Jebhe Melli Iran. *"Dowlat Jomhuri Islami Mojavez Baray Bargozarae Gerdehamaee Beh Jebhe Melli Iran Nadad"* [The Government of the Islamic Republic Did Not Provide Permission for the Holding of a Rally by the Iran National Front], (February 28, 2018), http://jebhe meliiran.org/?p=1374.

Jebhe Melli Iran. *"Pishnehadat Jebhe Melli Iran Beh Hayat Hakemeh Jomhuri Islami"* [Proposals of the Iran National Front to the Ruling Regime of the Islamic Republic], (July 27, 2018), http://jebhemeliiran.org/?p=1374.

Jebhe Melli Iran. *"Bayanieh Tarikhi Jebhe Melli Iran Dar Bareh Enqelab Sefid Va Hameh-Porsi Enqelab Sefid 6 Bahman 1341"* [The Historical Statement of the Iran National Front on the White Revolution and the Referendum on January 26, 1963], (January 26, 2019), https://melliun.org/iran/195488.

Jebhe Melli Iran. *Asghar Parsa Farzand Delavar Nehzat Melli Iran; Be Hamrah Khaterat Montasher Nashodeh Va Yadnameh Asghar Parsa* [Asghar Parsa the Brave Child of the National Movement of Iran; Along with the Unpublished Memoirs and Remembrances of Asghar Parsa], (October 23, 2019), https://melliun.org/v/wp-content/uploads/2020/06/ketab-asghar-parsa.pdf. This official INF publication includes the unpublished memoirs of Asghar Parsa from 1979 onward along with interviews with several INF members about him.

Jebhe Melli Iran, *"Haftad Saal"* [Seventy Years], *Payam Jebhe Melli Iran*, No. 199 (December 5, 2019), https://melliun.org/v/wp-content/uploads/2019/12/payam-jebhe-melli-iran-199.pdf.

Jebhe Melli Iran, *"Melli-Garay-e Jebhe Melli Iran Chegoneh Ast?"* [What is the Nationalism of the Iran National Front?], *Payam Jebhe Melli Iran*, No. 199 (December 5, 2019), https://melliun.org/v/wp-content/uploads/2019/12/payam-jebhe-melli-iran-199.pdf.

Jebhe Melli Iran, *"Sharhi Bar Osol-e Eateghadi Hasht-ganeh Jebhe Melli Iran"* [An Elaboration on the Eight Articles of the Charter of the Iran National Front], *Payam Jebhe Melli Iran*, No. 199 (December 5, 2019), https://melliun.org/v/wp-content/uploads/2019/12/payam-jebhe-melli-iran-199.pdf.

Jebhe Melli Iran, *"Gharardadi Ra Keh Hagh Hakemiyat Melli Iran Ra Makhdoosh Konad Mahkoom Mikonim"* [We Condemn Any Agreement that Undermines Iran's National Sovereignty], (July 13, 2020), http://jebhemeliiran.org/?p=2083.

Jebhe Melli Iran, *"Seyyed Reza Zanjani, Mojtahed Melli-gara"* [Seyyed Reza Zanjani, Nationalist Cleric], (January 2021), http://jebhemeliiran.org/?p=2516.

Jebhe Melli Iran, *"Mellat Iran Az Entekhab Bein Bad Va Badtar Oboor Kardeh Ast"* [The Iranian Nation Has Moved On From Choosing Between Bad and Worse], (April 7, 2021), https://melliun.org/iran/257087.

Jebhe Melli Iran, *"Gharardad Hokumat Jomhuri Islami Ba Chin Ba Manafe Melli Iran Dar Tazad Ast"* [The Agreement Between the Islamic Republic Regime and China Is Against the National Interests of Iran], *Payam Jebhe Melli Iran*, (April 23, 2021), http://jebheme liiran.org/?p=2670.

Jebhe Melli Iran, "*Farakhan Jebhe Melli Iran, Cheh Bayad Kard?*" [Iran National Front's Call, What Should Be Done?], *Payam Jebhe Melli*, (June 2, 2021), http://jebhemeliiran.org/wp-content/uploads/2021/06/PayamJMI209.pdf.

Jebhe Melli Iran, "*Ettehad Melli Baray Tahaghogh Hakemiyat Melli*" [National Unity for the Realization of Popular Sovereignty], *Payam Jebhe Melli Iran*, (August 12, 2021), http://jebhemeliiran.org/wp-content/uploads/2021/08/PAYAM-JMI211.pdf.

Kamran, Ramin. "*Bohrani Ke Dar Raah Ast*," [The Upcoming Crisis], www.iranliberal.com/Maghaleh-ha/Ramin_Kamran/051123_Ahmadi_W_2_RaminK.htm.

Karrubi, Mehdi. "Speech," "*Avalin Sokhanrani Karrubi Pas Az 11 Sal*" [The First Speech by Karrubi After 11 Years], Ensafnews, (October 5, 2021), http://www.ensafnews.com/312263/.

Katouzian, Homa. *Musaddiq and the Struggle for Power in Iran*. London: I.B. Tauris, 1990.

Katouzian, Homa. "Mosaddeq's Government in Iranian History: Arbitrary Rule, Democracy, and the 1953 Coup," in Gasiorowski, Mark J., and Malcolm Byrne, eds. *Mohammad Mosaddeq and the 1953 Coup in Iran*. Syracuse: Syracuse University Press, 2005, pp. 1–26.

Katouzian, Homa. *The Persians: Ancient, Mediaeval and Modern Iran*. New Haven: Yale University Press, 2009.

Katouzian, Homa. *Khalil Maleki: The Human Face of Iranian Socialism*. London: Oneworld Academic, 2018.

Kayhan. "*Ma'muriyat-e niru-ye qods towse'eh-ye enghelab-e eslami dar jahan ast*" [The Quds Force's Mission is to Expand the Islamic Revolution Throughout the World], (October 2, 2014), http://kayhan.ir/fa/news/24370.

Kazemi, Farhad. "The *Fada'iyan-e Islam*: Fanaticism, Politics and Terror," in Said Amir Arjomand, ed., *From Nationalism to Revolutionary Islam*. Albany: State University of New York Press, 1984, pp. 158–176.

Kazemian, Morteza. "*Chera Jomhuri Islami Darawish Gonabadi Ra Khatari Aleh Khod Modanad?*" [Why Does the Islamic Republic Considers the Gonabadi Darwishes a Threat Against Itself?], Iran International, (March 5, 2021), https://www.youtube.com/watch?v=MOpDfhr-VKo.

Kazemzadeh, Masoud. "Teaching the Politics of Islamic Fundamentalism," *PS: Political Science and Politics*, Vol. 31, No. 1 (1998), pp. 52–59.

Kazemzadeh, Masoud. *Islamic Fundamentalism, Feminism, and Gender Inequality in Iran Under Khomeini*. Lanham, Maryland: University Press of America, 2002.

Kazemzadeh, Masoud. "The CIA Coup in Iran," *Middle East Policy*, Vol. 11, No. 4 (2004), pp. 122–129.

Kazemzadeh, Masoud. "Burning Candle: Honoring Abbas Amir-Entezam on the 25th Anniversary of His Arrest," Iranian.com (December 21, 2004), https://iranian.com/BTW/2004/December/Entezam/index.html?site=archive.

Kazemzadeh, Masoud. "The Perils and Costs of a Grand Bargain with the Islamic Republic of Iran," *American Foreign Policy Interests*, Vol. 29, No. 5 (2007), pp. 301–327.

Kazemzadeh, Masoud. "Opposition Groups," in Mehran Kamrava and Manochehr Dorraj, eds., *Iran Today: An Encyclopedia of Life in the Islamic Republic*, Vol. II. Westport, Connecticut: Greenwood Press, 2008, pp. 363–367.

Kazemzadeh, Masoud. "Ayatollah Khamenei's Foreign Policy Orientation," *Comparative Strategy*, Vol. 32, No. 5 (2013), pp. 443–458.

Kazemzadeh, Masoud. "Post-Khamenei Iran and American National Interests," *The Hill* (July 11, 2016), http://thehill.com/blogs/pundits-blog/foreign-policy/287175-post-khamenei-iran-and-american-national-interests.

Kazemzadeh, Masoud. "Ayatollah Rafsanjani's Death and Trump Policy on Iran," *Small Wars Journal*, (January 18, 2017), https://smallwarsjournal.com/jrnl/art/ayatollah-rafsanjani%E2%80%99s-death-and-trump-policy-on-iran.

Kazemzadeh, Masoud. "Protests in Iran: Characteristics, Causes, and Policy Ramifications," *Small Wars Journal*, (January 3, 2018), http://smallwarsjournal.com/jrnl/art/protests-iran-characteristics-causes-and-policy-ramifications.

Kazemzadeh, Masoud. "Five Possible Outcomes Following the Mass Protests in Iran," Radio Farda, (February 6, 2018), https://en.radiofarda.com/a/iran-unrest-scenarios-war-revolution-uprising/29023446.html.

Kazemzadeh, Masoud. *Iran's Foreign Policy: Elite Factionalism, Ideology, the Nuclear Weapons Program, and the United States.* London and New York: Routledge, 2020.

Kazemzadeh, Masoud. *The Grand Strategy of the Islamic Republic of Iran.* Forthcoming.

Kazemzadeh, Masoud. *U.S.-Iran Confrontation: Alternative Scenarios and Consequences.* Forthcoming.

Keddie, Nikki R. *Roots of Revolution: An Interpretive History of Modern Iran.* New Haven: Yale University Press, 1981.

Keshavarz, Fereydoon. *Man Moteham Mikonam Kommiteh Markazi Hezb Tudeh Iran Ra* [I Accuse the Central Committee of the Tudeh Party of Iran], Tehran, 1979, https://www.iran-archive.com/node/17392.

Keshavarz, Fereydoon. "Interview," Harvard University, Iranian Oral History Project, Arlington, Virginia, U.S., (December 4, 1982), https://curiosity.lib.harvard.edu/iranian-oral-history-project/catalog/32-kechavarz__fereydoun01.

Keshavarz Sadr, Houshang, and Hamid Akbari. Eds., *Mossadegh and the Future of Iran.* Bethesda, Maryland: IBEX Publishers, 2005.

Khalkhali, Ayatollah Sadegh. "All the People Who Are Opposed to Our Revolution Must Die," Interview, *MERIP Reports*, No. 104 (March-April 1982), pp. 30–31.

Khamenei, Ayatollah Ali. "Speech," (January 17, 2020), http://english.khamenei.ir/news/7318/Our-Islamic-power-will-overcome-the-superficial-grandeur-of-material.

Khamenei, Imam Ali "*Bayanat Dar Didar Mehmanan Konferance Vahdat Islami Va Jamee Az Masoulan Nezam*" [Speech at the Islamic Unity Conference and a Group of Regime Officials], (October 24, 2021), https://farsi.khamenei.ir/speech-content?id=48891. Brief excerpts of Khamenei's speech in English is available at his site https://english.khamenei.ir/news/8739/Muslims-unity-necessary-for-realization-of-new-Islamic-Civilization. The title "Imam" is in original and not my addition.

Khatami, Mohammad. "Speech," You Tube, (2014), https://www.youtube.com/watch?v=KiygQj96DrQ.

Khavand, Fereydoon. "Interview," Radio Farda, (October 6, 2020), https://www.radiofarda.com/a/30876747.html.

Khavand, Fereydoon. "*Bazaar Arz Iran Taht-e Taasir Entekhabat Amrika*" [Iran's Foreign Exchange Market Under the Impact of the American Elections], Radio Farda, (October 19, 2020), https://www.radiofarda.com/a/30901565.html.

Khazani, Omid. "Just when they're needed most, Iran's doctors are leaving in droves," *The Los Angeles Times*, (May 23, 2021), https://www.latimes.com/world-nation/story/2021-05-23/iran-brain-drain-doctors-exodus-covid-pandemic.

Khomeini, Grand Ayatollah Ruhollah. *Sahifeh Noor*, Vol. 14, (June 14, 1981), https://emam.com/posts/view/2645/.

Khomeini, Grand Ayatollah Ruhollah. "Last Will and Testament," (February 15, 1983), released after his death in June 1989, https://www.al-islam.org/imam-khomeini-s-last-will-and-tes tament.

Khomeini, Grand Ayatollah Ruhollah. "Speech," (1984), the video of the speech available on You Tube, (May 18, 2014), https://www.youtube.com/watch?v=0EmAxl1Ksv0&list=RD0E mAxl1Ksv0&start_radio=1&rv=0EmAxl1Ksv0&t=399.

Khomeini, Grand Ayatollah Ruhollah. "Speech," (no date), posted at You Tube (August 31, 2014), https://www.youtube.com/watch?v=C8nX-IZiWFY.

Khomeini, Grand Ayatollah Ruhollah. "Speech," (1985), You Tube, (May 27, 2015), https://www.youtube.com/watch?v=8uhl1FUeVxA.

Khorsandi, Shappi. "My Family Values," *The Guardian*, (October 23, 2015), interview, https://www.theguardian.com/lifeandstyle/2015/oct/23/shappi-khorsandi-my-family-values.

Kinzer, Stephen. *All the Shah's Men: An American Coup and the Roots of Middle East Terror.* Hoboken, New Jersey: Wiley, 2003.

Kinzer, Stephen. "Abol-hassan Bani Sadr, Former Iranian President Dies at 88," *The New York Times*, (October 9, 2021), https://www.nytimes.com/2021/10/09/obituaries/abolhassan-bani-sadr-dead.html.

Klebnikov, Paul. "Millionaire Mullahs," *Forbes* (July 20, 2003), https://www.forbes.com/glob al/2003/0721/024.html#54378f504108.

Ladjevardi, Habib. "The Origins of U.S. Support for an Autocratic Iran," *International Journal of Middle East Studies*, Vol. 15, No. 2 (May 1983), pp. 225–239.

LaPalombara, Joseph, and Myron Weiner, eds., *Political Parties and Political Development.* Princeton: Princeton University Press, 1966.

Lebaschi, Abolghassem. "Interview," Harvard University, Iranian Oral History Project, Paris, (February 28, 1983), https://curiosity.lib.harvard.edu/iranian-oral-history-project/catalog/32-lebaschi__abolghassem01, audio available at https://www.youtube.com/watch?v=Nn3UeWm8tpY.

Louis, Wm. Roger. "Britain and the Overthrow of the Mosaddeq Government," in Gasiorowski, Mark J., and Malcolm Byrne, eds. *Mohammad Mosaddeq and the 1953 Coup in Iran.* Syracuse: Syracuse University Press, 2005, pp. 126–177.

Maleki, Khalil. *Khaterat Siasi, Ba Moghademe Mohammad Ali Homayoun Katouzian* [Political Memoirs, with introduction by Mohammad Ali Homayoun Katouzian], Hannover, West Germany: 1981.

Marzban, Fariba. "*Chengonegi Koshteshodan Roozname-negar Tarafdar Nehzat Melli, Amir Mokhtar Karimpour Shirazi*" [How Was Amir Mokhtar Karimpour Shirazi, the Pro-Nationalist Journalist, Killed], Melliun, (February 2012), https://melliun.org/iran/80940.

Mehmaneche, Homayoun. "'*Demokrat-hae' Keh Olgoyeshan Dictatorha Hastand*" ['Democrats' Whose Models are Dictators], Melliun, (June 25, 2020), https://melliun.org/iran/235285.

Mehmaneche, Homayoun. "Interview," Kalameh TV, (October 1, 2020), https://melliun.org/iran/243083.

Mirdamadi, Yasser. *"Terrorhay Fadiyan Islam: Az Ahmad Kasravi Ta Hussein Ala"* [The Assassinations of Fadaian Islam: From Ahmad Kasravi to Hussein Ala], BBC Persian, (March 14, 2012), https://www.bbc.com/persian/iran/2012/03/120313_l44_islam_fa daiyan.shtml.

Mirzasen (pseudonym). *"Goftegoy Daneshjo Va Ostad"* [Dialogue Between Student and Professor], Melliun, (May 2010), https://melliun.org/iran/204968.

Moayedzadeh, Mehdi. *"Dar Daheh Shast Cheh Gozasht?"* [What Happened During the Decade of the 1360s], (June 15, 2007), http://www.melliun.org/didgah/d09/09/05moayadz.htm.

Moens, Alexander. "President Carter's Advisers and the Fall of the Shah," *Political Science Quarterly*, Vol. 106, No. 2 (Summer 1991), pp. 211–237.

Moore, Jr., Barrington. *Social Origins of Dictatorship and Democracy: Lord and Peasant in the Making of the Modern World*. Boston: Beacon Press, 1966.

Mosadegh, Sheyda. *"Shahid Rah Azadi, Sargord Seyyed Mahmoud Sakhaee"* [Martyr on the Path of Freedom, Captain Seyyed Mahmoud Sakhaee], (June 29, 2013), http://www.drmo sadegh.blogsky.com/1392/04/08/post-15/.

Mosaiebian, Hamid-Reza. *Dr. Hussein Fatemi*. Kermanshah, Iran: 2015. https://melliun.org/v/ wp-content/uploads/2015/11/Fatemi_Dr-Hosein_940819_96.pdf.

Mosaiebian, Hamid-Reza. *Sarlashkar Mahmoud Afshartus* [General Mahmoud Afshartus], Kermanshah, Iran: 2016. https://melliun.org/v/wp-content/uploads/2016/01/12-Af shartus_Mahmood_950807_146.pdf.

Mosaiebian, Hamid-Reza. *Amir Mokhtar Karimpour Shirazi*. Kermanshah, Iran: 2016. https:// melliun.org/v/wp-content/uploads/2016/12/karimpour-shirazi.pdf.

Mosaiebian, Hamid-Reza. *Sargord Mahmoud Sakhaei* [Captain Mahmoud Sakhaei], Kermanshah, Iran: 2016. https://melliun.org/v/wp-content/uploads/2016/08/sargord-sa khaei.pdf.

Mosaiebian, Hamid-Reza. *Sarhang Jalil Bozorgmehr* [Colonel Jalil Bozorgmehr], Kermanshah, Iran: 2016. https://melliun.org/yaranmos/y06/08/12bozorgmehr.htm.

Mosaiebian, Hamid-Reza. *Mossadeghi-ha* [Supporters of Mossadegh]. Kermanshah, Iran: 2017. https://melliun.org/v/wp-content/uploads/2016/12/did-Mosadeghiha_960231_225. pdf.

Moshir, Seyyed Morteza. *Khaterat Allahyar Saleh* [Memories of Allahyar Saleh], Tehran: Vahid Publishers, 1985. https://hezbeiran.com/wp-content/uploads/2020/09/%D8%AE%D8% A7%D8%B7%D8%B1%D8%A7%D8%AA-%D8%A7%D9%84%D9%87%DB%8C%D8%A7% D8%B1-%D8%B5%D8%A7%D9%84%D8%AD.pdf.

Moussavian, Hussein. *"Dar Rooz 25 Khordad 1360 Bar Jebhe Melli Iran Cheh Gozasht? Gozidehee Az Khaterat Dr. Hussein Moussavian Dar Morede Aan Rooz"* [What Happened to the Iran National front on June 15, 1981? Selections from the Memoirs of Dr. Hussein Moussavian]. (June 11, 2016), http://melliun.org/iran/92885.

Moussavian, Hussein. "Interview with Radio Asr Jadid, Part 1," (October 21, 2018), https://mel liun.org/iran/184415.

Moussavian, Hussein. "Interview with Radio Asr Jadid, Part 4," (November 25, 2018), https:// melliun.org/iran/188055.

Moussavian, Hussein. *"Goftogo-e Doktor Hussein Moussavian, Rais Shora-y Jebhe Melli Iran, Ba BBC"* [Interview with Dr. Hussein Moussavian, Chairman of the Central Committee of the INF, with the BBC], (December 20, 2018), https://melliun.org/iran/191116.

Moussavian, Hussein. "Interview with Radio Asr Jadid, Part 5," (December 29, 2018), https://melliun.org/iran/192128.

Moussavian, Hussein. *"Goftogo Ba Doktor Hussein Moussavian"* [Interview with Dr. Hussein Moussavian], Rangarang TV, (October 2, 2019), https://melliun.org/iran/215417.

Moussavian, Hussein. "Interview" Iran International TV (May 2, 2020), https://melliun.org/iran/231112.

Moussavian, Hussein. *"Goftego Ba Rooznameh Kar Va Kargar"* [Talking With Labor and Laborers Newspaper], *Kar Va Kargar* (August 16, 2020), http://jebhemeliiran.org/?p=2169.

Moussavian, Hussein. "Interview with Radio Asr Jadid," (October 9, 2020), https://melliun.org/iran/243845.

Moussavian, Hussein. "Interview with Dr. Mehmaneche," Channel One TV, (December 10, 2020), https://melliun.org/iran/248202.

Moussavian, Hussein. "Interview with Radio Asr Jadid," (March 12, 2021), https://melliun.org/iran/255058.

Moussavian, Hussein. "Interview," Iran National Front-Organizations Abroad TV, Channel One, (June 20, 2021), https://www.youtube.com/watch?v=XflRlCIejVk.

Moussavian, Hussein. "Interview," Radio Farda, (October 9, 2021), https://www.radiofarda.com/a/31501122.html.

Mozaffari, Mehdi. *Islamism: A New Totalitarianism.* Boulder: CO: Lynne Rienner, 2017.

Mozi, Fatemeh Mozi "Shah Bahram Shahrokh," Institute for Iranian Contemporary History, (no date), http://www.iichs.ir/s/1102.

Musaddiq, Mohammad. *Musaddiq's Memoirs.* trans S. H. Amin and H. Katouzian. London: Jebhe National Movement of Iran, 1988.

Mussolini, Benito. "The Doctrine of Fascism," (1932), https://sjsu.edu/faculty/wooda/2B-HUM/Readings/The-Doctrine-of-Fascism.pdf.

Nahavandi, Houshang. *"Goftogo Ba Houshang Nahavandi,"* BBC Persian, (February 2, 2012), http://www.bbc.com/persian/tvandradio/2012/02/120126_hardtalk_houshang_nahavandi.

Nazih, Hassan. "Interview," Harvard University, Iranian Oral History Project, Paris, (April 3, 1984), https://curiosity.lib.harvard.edu/iranian-oral-history-project/catalog/32-nazih__hassan01, audio available at https://www.youtube.com/watch?v=B6uqIUHeMqs; https://www.youtube.com/watch?v=6chtiCr3Hr0; and https://www.youtube.com/watch?v=9rxR17G7qDE.

Nima, Ramy. *The Wrath of Allah: Islamic Revolution and Reaction in Iran.* London: Pluto Press, 1983.

Obama, Barack. "Remarks by the President at Cairo University," (June 4, 2009), https://obamawhitehouse.archives.gov/the-press-office/remarks-president-cairo-university-6-04-09.

Pahlavi, Reza. *Zaman Entekhab* [Time for Choosing], 2018, https://downloadeketab.files.wordpress.com/2013/11/d8afd8a7d986d984d988d8af-daa9d8aad8a7d8a8-d8b2d985d8a7d986.pdf. Interview with Michel Taubmann.

Pahlavi, Reza. *"Peyman Novin"* [New Pact], (September 28, 2020), https://www.youtube.com/watch?v=pON_QVdAnoU.

Parsa, Misagh. *Social Origins of the Iranian Revolution.* New Brunswick: Rutgers University Press, 1989.

Parsa, Misagh. *Democracy in Iran: Why It Failed and How It Might Succeed*. Cambridge, MA: Harvard University Press, 2016.

Pichdad, Amir. "Interview," Harvard University, Iranian Oral History Project, Le Chesnay, France, (March 3, 1983), https://curiosity.lib.harvard.edu/iranian-oral-history-project/cata log/32-pichdad__amir01, audio available at https://www.youtube.com/watch?v=XbjDOK tUdJk; https://www.youtube.com/watch?v=jAzCjtl5NeQ; and https://www.youtube.com/watch?v=LJF57jSDtGw.

Posch, Walter. "Ideology and Strategy in the Middle East: The Case of Iran." *Survival*, Vol. 59, No. 5 (October-November 2017), pp. 69–98.

Qashqaee, Mohammad Nasser. "Interview," Harvard University, Iranian Oral History Project, Las Vegas, Nevada, U.S., (January 1983), audio available at https://www.youtube.com/watch?v=wuLYQKUGIMO&list=PL-PRP1hqq8eLx_zqkyCtgKws5FpAU84j3.

Radio Farda, "Iranian Currency Roils As Trump Decision Looms," (May 8, 2018), https://en.ra diofarda.com/a/iran-currency-drops-ahead-of-trump-nuclear-announcement/29214907. html.

Radio Farda, "Fresh Wave of Protests Starting From Universities Spread to Several Cities in Iran," (January 12, 2020), https://en.radiofarda.com/a/fresh-wave-of-protests-starting-from-universities-spread-to-several-cities-in-iran/30373141.html.

Radio Farda, "Iran's Rial Hits New Historic Low Against US Dollar, Other Currencies," (July 5, 2020), https://en.radiofarda.com/a/iran-rial-hits-new-historic-low-against-us-dollar-other-currencies/30706985.html.

Radio Farda, "*Bazjui Amir-Entezam: Jasosi Oo Esbat Nashod Va Ghorbani Maarekeh Amrika-Setizi Shod*" [Amir-Entezam's Interrogator: His Espionage was not Proven and Became a Victim of Anti-Americanism], (July 14, 2020), https://www.radiofarda.com/a/motaghi-on-amirentezam/30726246.html.

Radio Farda, "Devaluation of Iran's Currency Accelerates With Dollar Hitting 260,000 Rials," (July 19, 2020), https://en.radiofarda.com/a/devaluation-of-iran-s-currency-accelerates-with-dollar-hitting-260-000-rials/30735734.html.

Radio Farda, "Rouhani Says Sanctions Cost Government 900 Trillian Rials in Revenues," (August 26, 2020), https://en.radiofarda.com/a/rouhani-says-sanctions-cost-government-900-trillion-rials-in-revenues/30803859.html.

Radio Farda, "Iran's Khamenei Says U.A.E. 'Betrayed' Islamic World With Israel Normalization Deal," (September 1, 2020), https://en.radiofarda.com/a/iran-s-khamenei-says-u-a-e-be trayed-islamic-world-with-israel-normalization-deal/30814699.html.

Radio Farda, "Dollar Soars to Near Record Level in Iran," (September 9, 2020), https://en.ra diofarda.com/a/dollar-soars-to-near-record-level-in-iran-/30829462.html.

Radio Farda, "Iran Condemns Bahrain Deal With Israel," (September 12, 2020), https://en.ra diofarda.com/a/iran-condemns-bahrain-deal-with-israel/30834978.html.

Radio Farda, "Iran's Oil Revenue Dropped to Less Than $20 Billion, Rouhani Says," (September 14, 2020), https://en.radiofarda.com/a/30838504.html.

Radio Farda, "IRGC Threatens Bahrain with Tough Revenge," (September 14, 2020), https://en.radiofarda.com/a/30838530.html.

Radio Farda, "*Nerkh Dollar Va Tala Dar Iran Record Dobareh Zad*" [The Price of Dollar and Gold in Iran Hit Another Record], (September 20, 2020), https://www.radiofarda.com/a/30848568.html.

Radio Farda, "*Dollar Beh Kanal 30 Hezar Toman Nazdiktar Shod*" [Dollar Got Closer to 30,000 Toman], (September 26, 2020), https://www.radiofarda.com/a/30859135.html.

Radio Farda, "*Sekkeh Az Marz 15 Million Gozasht; Dollar 30 Hezar Toman Shod*" [Gold Coin Crossed the 15 Million Rial Border; Dollar Became 30,000 Toman], (October 1, 2020), https://www.radiofarda.com/a/30868839.html.

Radio Farda, "Washington Blacklists Iran's Entire Financial Sector," (October 8, 2020), https://en.radiofarda.com/a/washington-blacklists-iran-s-entire-financial-sector/30883130.html

Radio Farda, "*Gheymat Dollar Az 32 Hezar Toman Gozasht*" [The Price of Dollar Crossed 32 Thousand Toman], (October 15, 2020), https://www.radiofarda.com/a/dollar-Iran/30894913.html.

Radio Farda, "*Kahesh Bish-Az 3 Hezar Tomani Gheymat Dollar Dar Bazaar Arz Tehran*" [Reduction of More Than 3,000 Toman of Dollar's Value at Tehran's Foreign Exchange Market], (October 20, 2020), https://www.radiofarda.com/a/30902739.html.

Radio Farda, "Iran's Net Debt, 44% of its GDP, IMF Says," (October 20, 2020), https://en.radiofarda.com/a/iran-s-net-debt-44-of-its-gdp-imf-says/30903332.html.

Radio Farda, "*Navasan-e Gheymat Dollar Dar Ashofteh Bazaar Iran*" [The Fluctuations of the Price of Dollar in Iran's Chaotic Market], (November 9, 2020), https://www.radiofarda.com/a/30938959.html.

Radio Farda, "*Namayandeh Lahestan Dar Parleman Eropa, Zarif Ra Beh Vazir Omor Kharejeh Alman Nazi Tashbih Kard*" [The Representative to the European Parliament from Poland, Considered Zarif to be Similar to the Foreign Minister of Nazi Germany], (December 18, 2020), https://www.radiofarda.com/a/31008036.html.

Radio Farda, "*Rais Kol-e Bank Markazi: Baray Taamin Manabeh Rahi Joz Chaap Eskenas Nadarim*" [Chairman of the Central Bank: We Have No Other Way But to Print Money to Make Payouts], (February 3, 2021), https://www.radiofarda.com/a/31083483.html.

Radio Farda, "*Owjgiri Naghdinegi Va Bedehi Dowlat Iran Beh Bank-ha Dar 9 Mah Aval 99*" [Rise of Liquidity and Iran's Government Debt to the Banks In the First 9 Months of the Year 1399], (February 6, 2021), https://www.radiofarda.com/a/31089592.html.

Radio Farda, "*Payam Panj Darwish Zendani Dar Mored Marg Behnam Mahjoobi*" [The Message of Five Dervishes in Jail on the Death of Behnam Mahjoobi], (February 22, 2021), https://melliun.org/iran/253855.

Radio Farda, "*Enteshar Amar Marg O Mir Dar Aban 98*" [Publication on the Statistics on Deaths During November 2019], (May 27, 2021), https://www.radiofarda.com/a/31276567.html.

Radio Farda, "*Gozaresh Jadid: Jomhuri Islami 'Dast Kam 540 Irani' Ra Dar Kharej Az Keshvar Koshteh Ya Rebodeh Ast*" [New Report: The Islamic Republic Has Murdered or Kidnapped "At Least 540 Iranians" Outside the Country], (July 28, 2021), https://www.radiofarda.com/a/boroumand-foundation-we-has-identified-more-than-540-iranians-whose-murder-or-kidnapping-is-attributed-to-the-islamic-republic-of-iran/31380796.html.

Radio Farda, "*Nerkh Dollar Az 31 Hezar Tooman Obor Kard; Sooghot 25 Darsadi Arzesh Rial Dar 100 Rooz Dowlat Raisi*" [Price of Dollar Crossed the 31 Thousand Tooman; 25 Percent Fall of the Value of Rial During the 100 Days of Raisi's Government], (December 6, 2021), https://www.radiofarda.com/a/iran-dollar-rise-raeisi/31596216.html.

Radio Zamaneh, "*Dollar Az Marz 28 Hezar Tooman Oboor Kard*" [Dollar Crossed the 28,000 Toman Border], (September 23, 2020), https://www.radiozamaneh.com/539959.

Rahnema, Ali. *Behind the 1953 Coup in Iran: Thugs, Turncoats, Soldiers, and Spooks.* Cambridge: Cambridge University Press, 2014.

Rahnema, Ali, and Farhad Nomani, *The Secular Miracle: Religion, Politics & Economic Policy in Iran.* London: Zed Books, 1990.

Raji, Parviz. "BBC Interview," BBC Persian, via You Tube, (February 23, 2010), https://www.youtube.com/watch?v=1GSN8wrXn7U.

Rangin-Kaman TV. *"Jame-e Shenasi Siasi Opposision Iran: Sazeman Cherikhay Fadaian Khalq Iran"* [Political Sociology of the Opposition in Iran: Organization of the People's Fadaian Guerrillas of Iran], (June 11, 2020), https://www.youtube.com/watch?v=aepF_I_ENcc.

Rangin-Kaman TV. *"Jame-e Shenasi Siasi Opposision Iran: Jebhe Melli Iran, Bakhsh 1"* [Political Sociology of the Opposition in Iran: Iran National Front, Part 1], (July 2, 2020), https://www.youtube.com/watch?v=Td4STdpQYTU.

Rangin-Kaman TV. *"Jame-e Shenasi Siasi Opposision Iran: Jebhe Melli Iran, Bakhsh 2"* [Political Sociology of the Opposition in Iran: Iran National Front, Part 2], (July 9, 2020), https://www.youtube.com/watch?v=lLC4ypIeVYw.

Rangin-Kaman TV. *"Jame-e Shenasi Siasi Opposision Iran: Sazeman Aksariyat Va Sazeman Rah-e Kargar, Bakhsh 1"* [Political Sociology of the Opposition in Iran: Fadaian-Majority and Rah-e Kargar, Part 1], (July 17, 2020), https://www.youtube.com/watch?v=6j_b9EL2nr4.

Rangin-Kaman TV. *"Jame-e Shenasi Siasi Opposision Iran: Gerayesh 'Saltanat-Talabi Va Mashrooteh-Khah', Bakhsh 1"* [Political Sociology of the Opposition in Iran: 'Monarchist And Constitutionalist' Tendency, Part 1], (August 28, 2020), https://www.youtube.com/watch?v=jTvIgeQ9_F0.

Rangin-Kaman TV. *"Jame-e Shenasi Siasi Opposision Iran: Gerayesh 'Dr. Shapour Bakhtiar', Bakhsh 1"* [Political Sociology of the Opposition in Iran: The Tendency of 'Dr. Shapour Bakhtiar, Part 1], (September 12, 2020), https://www.youtube.com/watch?v=EK1RodoZcbY.

Rangin-Kaman TV. *"Jame-e Shenasi Siasi Opposision Iran: Gerayesh 'Dr. Shapour Bakhtiar', Bakhsh 2"* [Political Sociology of the Opposition in Iran: The Tendency of 'Dr. Shapour Bakhtiar, Part 2], (September 18, 2020), https://www.youtube.com/watch?v=1GhsIal_nAE.

Rangin-Kaman TV. *"Hamsooe Social Demokrat-hay Secular, Bakhsh 2"* [Cooperation Among Secular Social Democrats], (November 3, 2020), https://www.youtube.com/watch?v=9emWTuJ-s08.

Rasekh-Afshar, Ali, Parviz Davarpanah, Ali Shakeri-Zand, and Mehdi Moghadaszadeh, *"Baray Melliun Hoghogh Shahrvandi Asl Asl Va Azadi Aghideh Az Osol Zirbanaee Va Gheir Ghabel Tagheer Mast"* [For the Nationalists Rights of Citizenship Are Principles And Freedom of Belief Are Our Foundational and Unchanging Principles], (December 4, 2014), https://ehterameazadi.blogspot.com/2014/12/blog-post_4.html.

Razavian, Amir Shahab. *"18 Ask Montasher Nashodeh Az Rahpeymaee Mossadegh Va Hamrahaneshan Beh Kakh Marmar"* [18 Unpublished Photos of the March of Mossadegh and Those Who Were With Him to Marmar Palace], Gooya News (October 21, 2010), https://news.gooya.com/politics/archives/2010/10/112337.php.

Reuters, "Arab League labels Hezbollah terrorist organization," (March 11, 2016), https://www.reuters.com/article/us-mideast-crisis-arabs/arab-league-labels-hezbollah-terrorist-organization-idUSKCN0WD239.

Reuters, "Special Report: Iran's leader ordered crackdown on unrest – 'Do whatever it takes to end it'," (December 23. 2019), https://www.reuters.com/article/us-iran-protests-spe cialreport/special-report-irans-leader-ordered-crackdown-on-unrest-do-whatever-it-takes-to-end-it-idUSKBN1YR0QR.

Reuters, "Israel's outgoing defence minister says Iran starting to withdraw from Syria," (May 18, 2020), https://www.reuters.com/article/us-israel-iran-syria/israels-outgoing-de fence-minister-says-iran-starting-to-withdraw-from-syria-idUSKBN22U2MU.

Reuters, "Rights groups call for prob into Iran's Raisi for crimes against humanity," (June 19, 2021), https://www.reuters.com/world/middle-east/amnesty-calls-investigation-into-irans-raisi-crimes-against-humanity-2021-06-19/.

Risen, James. "Secrets of History: The CIA in Iran," *The New York Times*, (April 16, 2000), https://archive.nytimes.com/www.nytimes.com/library/world/mideast/041600iran-cia-index.html.

Risen, James. "Secrets of History: The C.I.A. In Iran – A Special Report; How a Plot Convulsed Iran in '53 (and in '79)," *The New York Times*, (April 16, 2000), https://www.nytimes.com/2000/04/16/world/secrets-history-cia-iran-special-report-plot-convulsed-iran-53-79.html?

Robertson, Geoffrey. *The Massacre of Political Prisoners in Iran, 1988, Report of An Inquiry.* Abdorrahman Boroumand Foundation, (April 18, 2011), https://www.iranrights.org/li brary/document/1380/the-massacre-of-political-prisoners-in-iran-1988-report-of-an-in quiry.

Sadighi, Gholam-Hussein. "*Mosahebeh Ba Etellaat 27 Dey 1357: Mardom Vatanparast Keshvar Beh Hemayat Az Bakhtiar Barkhizand*" [Interview with Daily *Etellaat* January 17, 1979: Patriotic People of the Country Should Support Bakhtiar], Melliun, (January 19, 2014), https://melliun.org/iran/34996.

Sadighi, Gholam-Hussein. "*Chera Nokhost-vaziri Ra Napaziroftam?*" [Why Did Not Accept Becoming Prime Minister?], *Omid Iran* Weekly, January 28, 1979, http://tarikhirani.ir/fa/news/4926.

Sadighi, Gholam-Hussein. "*Kodeta-e 28 Mordad Beh Ravayat Gholam-Hussein Sadighi*" [The 1953 Coup According to Gholam-Hussein Sadighi], Tarikh Irani, (August 23, 2011), http://tarikhirani.ir/fa/news/1190/.

Safari, Jamal. "*Sarlashkar Mahmoud Afshartus*" [Gen. Mahmoud Afshartus], Enghelab Eslami, (June 25, 2014), https://www.enghelabe-eslami.com/component/content/article/35-didga gha/nevisandegane-ma/9422-20140625-js-1.html.

Sanjabi, Karim. "*Jebhe Melli Iran Ba Mellat Sokhan Migooyad*" [Iran National Front Speaks to the Nation], (November 24, 1980), https://melliun.org/v/wp-content/uploads/2019/09/bayanie-dr.-sanjabi-azar-1359.pdf.

Sanjabi, Karim. *Omid-ha Va Naomidi-ha: Khaterat Siasi Doktor Karim Sanjabi* [Hopes and Disappointments: Political Memoirs of Dr. Karim Sanjabi]. London: Jebhe National Movement of Iran, 1989. http://jebhemeliiran.org/wp-content/uploads/2015/09/Ebook-Sanjabi.pdf.

Sanjabi, Karim. "AP Video of the Arrest of Dr. Sanjabi and Dariush Forouhar at their Press Conference," (November 1978), Dr. Karim Sanjabi Facebook page, (2019), https://www.facebook.com/274402532665234/videos/375129523314074.

Sanjabi, Karim. "Video of Resignation from the Provisional Government," (April 1979), Dr. Karim Sanjabi Facebook page, (2019), https://www.facebook.com/274402532665234/videos/320665275317710.

Sciliano, Elaine. "Interview," PBS, (April 17, 2002), https://www.pbs.org/wgbh/pages/frontline/shows/tehran/interviews/sciolino.html.

Seif, Khosrow. "*Tajdid Khatereh-e Az 28 Mordad Saal 1332*" [Retelling of Memories of August 19, 1953], Melliun, (August 18, 2020), https://melliun.org/iran/239253.

Seif, Khosrow. "*Chegoonegi Tashkil Nehzat Moghavemat Melli Va Nameh 3 Emzae*" [How the National Resistance Movement Was Established and About the Letter Signed by 3], Melliun, (November 2020), https://melliun.org/v/wp-content/uploads/2020/11/chegunegi-tashkil-nehzat-moghavemat-melli.pdf.

Shahi, Afshin. "Iranian nationalism: A theoretical dilemma." e-international relations (January 26, 2009), https://www.e-ir.info/2009/01/26/iranian-nationalism-a-historical-overview/.

Sharif-Imami, Jafaar. "Interview," Harvard University, Iranian Oral History Project, Washington, D.C., (1982–1983), audio available at https://www.youtube.com/watch?v=tY_Zwn2m4YY; https://www.youtube.com/watch?v=r5dOUss8UmY; and https://www.youtube.com/watch?v=v4F_Awza_80.

Siavoshi, Sussan. *Liberal Nationalism in Iran: The Failure of a Movement.* Boulder, CO: Westview Press, 1990.

Sikorski, Radoslaw. "Speech," (December 18, 2020), posted on You Tube https://www.youtube.com/watch?v=YjrnThhS7ZY (December 21, 2020).

Social Democratic and Laic Party of Iran, "*Chera Hezb Ma Beh Jebhe Melli Iran Peyvast?*" [Why Our Party Joined the Iran National Front?], (November 10, 2021), https://melliun.org/iran/287089.

Soleymani, IRGC Gen. Qassem. "Speech," Fars News, (March 29, 2014). The speech was delivered on February 16, 2014, http://www.farsnews.com/newstext.php?nn=13930108000154.

Stecklow, Steve, Babak Dehghanpisheh, and Yeganeh Torbati, "Reuters Investigates: Assets of the Ayatollah," Reuters, (November 11, 2013), https://www.reuters.com/investigates/iran/#article/part1.

Tabari, Azar, and Nahid Yeganeh, *In the Shadow of Islam: The Women's Movement in Iran.* London: Zed Press, 1982.

Tachau, Frank, editor. *Political Parties of the Middle East and North Africa.* Westport, Connecticut: Greenwood Press, 1994.

Tachau, Frank. "Introduction," in Frank Tachau, editor. *Political Parties of the Middle East and North Africa.* Westport, Connecticut: Greenwood Press, 1994, pp. xiii-xxv.

Tajdin, Behrang. "*Eghtesad Iran Beh Ravayat Panj Nemoodar Dar Panjomin Salgard Barjam*" [Iran's Economy According to Five Charts in the Fifth Anniversary of the JCPOA], BBC Persian, (July 13, 2020), https://www.bbc.com/persian/business-53381573.

Taleghani, Ayatollah Mahmoud. "*Sokhanrani Dar Mazar Doktor Mossadegh*" [Speech at Dr. Mossadegh's Grave], (originally March 5, 1979), https://www.youtube.com/watch?v=gJUXNP7yMiE (September 11, 2019), a longer version of the speech is available at https://www.shia-news.com/000ok3.

Taleghani, Ayatollah Mahmoud. *"Akharin Namaz Jomeh Ayatollah Taleghani"* [The Last Friday Prayer Sermon of Ayatollah Taleghani], (originally September 6, 1979), https://www.you tube.com/watch?v=t25EPR0bOZQ.

Tamimi Arab, Pooyan, and Ammar Maleki. "Iran's secular shift: new survey reveals huge change in religious beliefs," The Conversation, (September 10, 2020), https://the conversation.com/irans-secular-shift-new-survey-reveals-huge-changes-in-religious-be liefs-145253.

Taqvaee, Hamid. "Round Two of The Election Puppet Show in Iran," (June 22, 2005) www.wpir an.org/English/wb183%20round%20two%20of%20election%20show%20in%20Iran% 20HT.htm.

Tarikh Irani, *"Jasad Afshartus Peyda Shod"* [The Body of Afshartus Was Found], (April 26, 1953), http://tarikhirani.ir/fa/calendar/151.

Tasnim News Agency, *"Khatereh Ayatollah Falsafi Az Mossadegh Va Masaleh Oo Ba Islam"* [Memoirs of Ayatollah Falsafi on Mossadegh and His Problem with Islam], (August 19, 2017), https://www.tasnimnews.com/fa/news/1396/05/28/1495651/%D8%AE%D8%A7% D8%B7%D8%B1%D9%87-%D8%A2%DB%8C%D8%AA-%D8%A7%D9%84%D9%84%D9% 87-%D9%81%D9%84%D8%B3%D9%81%DB%8C-%D8%A7%D8%B2-%D9%85%D8%B5% D8%AF%D9%82-%D9%88-%D9%85%D8%B3%D8%A6%D9%84%D9%87-%D8%A7%D9% 88-%D8%A8%D8%A7-%D8%A7%D8%B3%D9%84%D8%A7%D9%85.

Tavasoli, Mohammad. *"Payam Tabrik Dabir Kol Nehzat Azadi Iran Beh Doktor Moussavian, Rais Shora-e Markazi Jebhe Melli Iran"* [Congratulatory Message from the Secretary General of the Iran Liberation Movement to Dr. Moussavian, The Chair of the Central Committee of the Iran National Front], Melliun, (November 24, 2018), https://melliun.org/ iran/187971.

Thorpe, Vanessa. "MI6, the coup in Iran that changed the Middle East, and the cover-up," *The Observer*, (August 2, 2020), https://www.theguardian.com/world/2020/aug/02/mi6-the-coup-in-iran-that-changed-the-middle-east-and-the-cover-up.

Tudeh Party, *"Sokhani Ba Jebhe Melli Iran Be Monesabat Kodeta-e Nangin 28 Mordad 1332: Ma Az 'Etehad Melli Baray Tahaghogh Hakemiyat Melli' Esteghbal Mikonim"* [A Talk with the Iran National Front on the Occasion of the Infamous Coup of August 19, 1953: We Welcome the "National Unity for Realization of National Sovereignty"], (August 16, 2021), https://www.tudehpartyiran.org/2021/08/16/%D8%B3%D8%AE%D9%86%DB%8C-%D8% A8%D8%A7-%D8%AC%D8%A8%D9%87%D9%87%D9%94-%D9%85%D9%84%DB%8C-%D8%A7%DB%8C%D8%B1%D8%A7%D9%86-%D8%A8%D9%87-%D9%85%D9%86% D8%A7%D8%B3%D8%A8%D8%AA-%D8%B3%D8%A7%D9%84%DA%AF%D8%B1/.

U.N. Letter to the Iranian Government. Geneva, Switzerland: September 3, 2020. https:// spcommreports.ohchr.org/TMResultsBase/DownLoadPublicCommunicationFile?gId= 25503.

U.S. Government, CIA, "Court Interference in Government Activity," (August 30, 1950), https:// www.enghelabe-eslami.com/component/content/article/21-didgagha/tarikhi/31232-2018-11-17-14-50-28.html?Itemid=0

U.S. Government, Department of State, "Memorandum of Conversation: British Proposal to Organize a Coup d'etat in Iran," (November 26, 1952), https://nsarchive.gwu.edu/dc. html?doc=3914379-01-State-Department-Memorandum-of-Conversation.

U.S. Government, Department of State, "Memorandum of Conversation: Byroade to Matthews, Proposal to Organize a Coup d'etat in Iran," (December 3, 1952), https://nsarchive.gwu. edu/dc.html?doc=3914380-02-State-Department-Memorandum-of-Conversation.

U.S. Government, Department of State, "Report from U.S. Ambassador in Baghdad to Department of State," (August 17, 1953), https://enghelabe-eslami.com/component/con tent/article/21-didgagha/tarikhi/34507-2019-08-15-17-19-41.html.

U.S. Government, Department of State, Loy Henderson, "Telegram From the Embassy in Iran to the Department of State," (August 18, 1953, 10 p.m.), https://history.state.gov/histor icaldocuments/frus1951-54Iran/d280.

U.S. Government, Department of State, "Memorandum for the Record," (August 1953), https://history.state.gov/historicaldocuments/frus1951-54Iran/d281. This is a report from the U.S. State Department to the British Foreign Office. It is a polished summary of Henderson's telegram of August 18, 1953.

U.S. Government, CIA Clandestine Service History, "Overthrow of Premier Mossadeq of Iran, November 1952-August 1953," March 1954, by Dr. Donald Wilber. https://nsarchive2.gwu. edu/NSAEBB/NSAEBB28/. This document is also available at the following with commentary https://www.webcitation.org/5hOKk6ByB?url=http://web.payk.net/politics/ cia-docs/published/one-main/main.html; and https://nsarchive2.gwu.edu/NSAEBB/ NSAEBB28/#documents.

U.S. Government, Department of State, Letter From the Ambassador to Iran (Henderson) to the Director of the Office of Greek, Turkish, and Iranian Affairs, Bureau of Near Eastern, South Asian, and African Affairs (Richards), Tehran, (October 20, 1953), https://history. state.gov/historicaldocuments/frus1951-54Iran/d335.

U.S. Government, Department of State, Office of the Historian, *Foreign Relations of the United States, 1952–1954, Iran, 1951–1954*. Washington, DC: U.S. Government, 2017. https://his tory.state.gov/historicaldocuments/frus1951-54Iran.

U.S. Government, Department of State, *Outlaw Regime: A Chronicle of Iran's Destructive Activities*, (Washington, DC: 2018), https://www.state.gov/wp-content/uploads/2018/12/ Iran-Report.pdf.

U.S. Government, Kermit Roosevelt, (October 2, 1953), https://enghelabe-eslami.com/compo nent/content/article/21-didgagha/tarikhi/39146-2020-08-15-17-17-06.html. The information on to whom the telegram was sent to is redacted after declassification. It was probably sent to the CIA, the National Security Council, or the White House.

VOA, "US Publishes Report on Its Role in 1953 Iran Coup," (June 29, 2017), https://www.voa news.com/middle-east/us-publishes-report-its-role-1953-iran-coup.

VOA, "*Ayatollah Taleghani Va Ghatelan Oo Ra Behtar Beshenasim*" [To Know Better Ayatollah Taleghani and His Murderers], (December 27, 2019), https://www.youtube.com/watch?v= 8d_G8vgbJBw.

VOA, "*Soleimani Ghatel-e Rahbaresh Ham Ghatel-e*" [Soleimani is a Murder, His Leader is a Murderer], You Tube (January 11, 2020), https://www.youtube.com/watch?v=1bl6I TEoStQ&app=desktop.

VOA, "*Moatarezan Dar Tehran Bilbord Qassem Soleimani Ra Atesh Zadand*" [Protesters in Tehran Set Ablaze Qassem Soleimani's Billboards], (January 12, 2020), https://ir.voa news.com/episode/mtrdan-dr-thran-bylbwrd-qasm-slymany-ra-atsh-zdnd-235040.

VOA, *"Pareh Kardan Bannerhay Tablighati Qassem Soleimani Tavasot Mardom Dar Tehran"* [Tearing Down of Propaganda Banners for Qassem Soleimani by the People, of Tehran], (January 12, 2020), https://ir.voanews.com/episode/iran-235050.

VOA, *"Basiji Sepahi, Daesh Ma Shomae"* [Basij and IRGC You are Our ISIS], (January 13, 2020), https://ir.voanews.com/episode/bsyjy-spahy-dash-ma-shmayy-shar-mrdm-mtrd-dr-mshhd-235013.

VOA, *"Koshteh Nadadim Keh Sazesh Konim, Rahbar Ghatel Ro Setayesh Konim"* [We Did Not Have Deaths in order to Compromise, And Praise the Murderer Supreme Leader], (January 13, 2020), https://ir.voanews.com/episode/kshth-ndadym-kh-sazsh-knym-rhbr-qatl-rw-staysh-knym-shar-hzaran-mtrd-nfr-dr-thran-235018.

VOA, *"Marg Bar Setamgar Cheh Shah Basheh Cheh Rahbar"* [Death to the Oppressor, Whether Shah or Supreme Leader], (January 13, 2020), https://ir.voanews.com/episode/iran-protest-sunday-235014.

VOA, *"Paslarzehay Binatijeh Mandan Mozakerat Vean, Arzesh Rial Iran Beh 'Paentarin Had Dar Tarikh' Resid"* [The Aftershocks of Failure of the Vienna Talks, The Value of the Iranian Rial Reached "Its Lowest Point in History"], (December 5, 2021), https://ir.voa news.com/a/iran-rials-jcpoa-talks/6340254.html.

Volkov, Denis V. "The USSR and the Tudeh Party after the Islamic Revolution of 1979: Ideological Cohesion and Operative Controversies," paper presentation at Tudeh Party of Iran at 80 Conference, (April 1, 2021), http://www.mihan.org.uk/TudehAt80/, video available at https://www.youtube.com/watch?v=aqrgkjaMXdE.

Waldman, Peter. "Clergy Capitalism: Mullahs Keep Control of Iran's Economy with an Iron Hand," *The Wall Street Journal*, (May 8, 1992), pp. 1, 16.

Woodhouse, C. M. *Something Ventured*. London: Granada, 1982.

World Bank, "National Accounts Data, GDP Per Capita," (2019), https://data.worldbank.org/in dicator/NY.GDP.PCAP.CD.

Yazdani, Mina. "Towards a History of Iran's Baha'i Community During the Reign of Mohammad Reza Shah, 1941–1979," *Iran Namag*, Vol. 2, No. 1 (Spring 2017), pp. 60–93, https://encompass.eku.edu/cgi/viewcontent.cgi?article=1076&context=fs_re search.

Yousofi-Eshkevari, Hassan. *"Akharin Shah Shii Jahan Aya Mazhabi Bood?"* [Was the Last Shia King in the World Religious?], BBC Persian, (July 27, 2010), https://www.bbc.com/per sian/iran/2010/07/100727_shah_anniv30_eshkevari_religion.shtml.

You Tube. "Jebhe Melli Iran," (July 16, 2009), https://www.youtube.com/watch?v=JkEcUjqUTlo.

Vahabzadeh, Peyman. *A Rebel's Journey: Mostafa Sho'aiyan and Revolutionary Theory in Iran.* London: Oneworld Academic, 2020.

Zabih, Sepehr. *The Communist Movement in Iran*. Berkeley and Los Angeles: University of California Press, 1966.

Zeitoon, *"Abaad Jadidi Az Koshtar Aban 98"* [New Dimensions of the Massacre of November 2019], (May 27, 2021), https://www.zeitoons.com/87839.

Zibakalam, Sadegh. "If a referendum is held today, over 70% would say no to an Islamic Republic," Deutsche Welle, (January 5, 2018), https://www.youtube.com/watch?v=GuX yEtMgAOl.

Zirakzadeh, Ahmad. "Interview," Harvard University, Iranian Oral History Project, Arlington, Virginia, U.S., (May 1986), https://curiosity.lib.harvard.edu/iranian-oral-history-project/

catalog/32-zirakzadeh__ahmad01, audio available at https://www.youtube.com/watch?v=T_uZhbPEX28; and https://www.youtube.com/watch?v=6vkJhWC7GlU.

Index

https://doi.org/10.1515/9783110782158-019

www.ingramcontent.com/pod-product-compliance
Lightning Source LLC
Chambersburg PA
CBHW020532270326
41927CB00006B/548